ECONOMIC IMPLICATIONS OF CHRONIC ILLNESS AND DISABILITY IN EASTERN EUROPE AND THE FORMER SOVIET UNION

ECONOMIC IMPLICATIONS OF CHRONIC ILLNESS AND DISABILITY IN EASTERN EUROPE AND THE FORMER SOVIET UNION

Edited by Cem Mete

THE WORLD BANK

2008 The International Bank for Reconstruction and Development / The World Bank
1818 H Street NW
Washington DC 20433
Telephone: 202-473-1000
Internet: www.worldbank.org

1 2 3 4 11 10 09 08
This volume is a product of the staff of the International Bank for Reconstruction and Development / The World Bank. The findings, interpretations, and conclusions expressed in this paper do not necessarily reflect the views of the Executive Directors of The World Bank or the governments they represent.

The World Bank does not guarantee the accuracy of the data included in this work. The boundaries, colors, denominations, and other information shown on any map in this work do not imply any judgement on the part of The World Bank concerning the legal status of any territory or the endorsement or acceptance of such boundaries.

ISBN-10: 0-8213-7337-4
ISBN-13: 978-0-8213-7337-8
e-ISBN-10: 0-8213-7338-2
e-ISBN-13: 978-0-8213-7338-5
DOI: 10.1596/978-0-8213-7337-8

Library of Congress Cataloging-in-Publication data has been requested.

Contents

Box

Chapter 1

Figures

Chapter 1

Tables

The Report Team and Acknowledgments

This report was prepared by a team led by Cem Mete and comprising Kinnon Scott (coauthor of chapters 2 and 3), Huan Ni (coauthor of chapter 3), T. Paul Schultz (author of chapter 4), and Shirley Liu (coauthor of chapter 5). Jeanine Braithwaite provided valuable input into the overview chapter on the distribution of disability pension beneficiaries, and secured funds to support the piloting of a disability survey instrument that provided important insights into our understanding of the challenges involved in defining and measuring disabilities. Pia Helene Schneider also contributed to the overview chapter, focusing on the main causes of disability in the Eastern Europe and Central Asian countries, and policy implications of the observed trends. Lucian Pop provided useful advice on the nature of social protection programs and data sets in the region, building on his experience in analyzing the (pro-poor) targeting performance of various social assistance schemes. Stefania Rodica Cnobloch provided assistance with the analysis of all data sets that were used in the overview chapter, covering a wide range from household budget surveys, to living standard measurement surveys, to integrated household surveys, to time-use surveys. Daniel Mont provided constructive suggestions throughout the project, based on his in-depth knowledge of the disability literature in industrialized countries. He also worked closely with Kinnon Scott on the design of the piloted disability survey questionnaire.

The team benefited from detailed comments from Martin Raiser, Philip O'Keefe, Akiko Maeda, Jane Falkingham, Marianne Fay, Arup Banerji, Vedat Rmljak, Anthony Ody, Sally M. Zeijlon, Mamta Murthi, and Eluned Roberts-Schweitzer. At the beginning of the project, a critical issue that the team sought guidance on was how to sharpen the focus of the proposed work, since very few (quantitative) papers have been written on the broader topic of the economics of disability using data from Eastern European and Central Asian countries. Thus, one can legitimately argue that there is a need to investigate each and every subtopic in an in-depth manner. Priorities had to be established, not only considering the importance of the issues and the comparative advantage of the World Bank, but also taking into account time, resource, and data constraints. In addition to the guidance from Chief Economist Pradeep Mitra's office, a disability conference hosted by the World Bank in late 2004 entitled "Disability and Development: Setting a Research Agenda," turned out to be particularly relevant for this purpose. This conference brought together an esteemed group of researchers and policy makers to discuss possible contributions that the World Bank can make in this area. When it comes to the prioritization of work, the advice that emerged from these meetings was that the World Bank should focus on two key issues in the short term: the relationship between poverty and disability—because of the World Bank's mission and also considering how little we know about this two-way relationship—and the broadly defined topic of "service delivery"—because a large share of Bank projects deal with service delivery of one type or another. This particular report focuses exclusively on the poverty-disability relationship and various extensions of it, including the linkages among disability and employment, school enrollments, and time-use patterns of adults. The work was carried under the general direction of Pradeep Mitra (chief economist, Europe and Central Asia Region) and Arup Banerji (manager, Human Development Economics, Europe and Central Asia Region).

Key Findings and Future Research Directions

A concise summary of the findings of this research, along with a list of priority areas that may be tackled by future studies, are presented below.

Different Definitions of Disability

Alternative definitions of disability—such as a country's official disability classification, self-reported disability status, functional disability assessment, Activities of Daily Living Index, Instrumental Activities of Daily Living Index, self-reported chronic illness, and self-reported health status—are highly correlated with one another. Also, the cross-country evidence confirms the sharp age gradient in reporting of health ailments, especially for the reporting of chronic illnesses. But different definitions lead to significantly different estimates of the prevalence of disability. It is important to understand the pros and cons of each proxy for disability to make the most use of available information to guide policy makers.

In the Eastern European and Central Asian context, where most countries are well advanced in terms of fertility transition, the most common type of disability is restriction of movement, and a large share of the disability burden is due to noncommunicable diseases and injuries. The composition of the disabled population has economic implications, because individuals with movement restrictions are the most disadvantaged group in terms of employment prospects, along with those with congenital disabilities. The aging transition countries may be able to contain one type of financial burden by being restrictive in granting disability benefits to the elderly. But the functional limitations increase steeply by age with implications for employment and productivity, as discussed next.

Linkages with Employment, Earnings, and Poverty

The linkages between disability and economic and social outcomes of interest tend to be stronger in transition countries when compared with industrialized countries. Despite having experienced respectable economic growth rates starting from the late 1990s, poor population health status and rising health inequalities emerge as main obstacles for equitable and sustainable economic growth and poverty reduction in the region.

Disabled adults are much less likely to work when compared with nondisabled adults in all transition countries considered here. This ranges from a high of 60 percentage points less likely to work in Moldova, to a low of 20 percentage points in Bosnia and Herzegovina. The disabled and chronically ill also earn substantially less than others: the earnings gap is larger for those who categorize themselves as "disabled" compared to those who report having chronic illnesses only. Furthermore, this analysis shows that simple associations tend to downplay the linkage between poor-health/disability and employment because instrumental-variable estimates that attempt to single out causal effects produce larger estimates.

Heterogeneity within the disabled deserves attention as well. For example this report shows that other things being equal, adults with congenital disabilities are less likely to be employed. This may be because those with congenital disabilities are exposed to the disadvantages of being disabled (in terms of intrahousehold resource allocation, access to quality education etc) for a longer duration of time.

Even though the disabled who are employed work less than others, the difference is less than five hours a week in Moldova and Bosnia and Herzegovina. However, it is sizable in Poland, at about nine hours per week.

In contrast to the trends observed in some industrialized countries, in at least one transition economy (Bosnia and Herzegovina), the negative impact of disability on employment accumulates over time after the start of disability, which has implications for the design of social protection programs. Also, in contrast to what is observed in Organisation for Economic Co-operation and Development (OECD) countries, the employment rates of disabled and nondisabled individuals are not correlated in transition economies. Thus general-purpose pro-employment policies may not necessarily improve the employment rates of the disabled in the transition economy context. This divergence in employment trends is driven by the presence of a large informal sector in transition countries, as discussed in more detail by the overview chapter.

The poor are more likely to be disabled. This finding is robust across countries, and is visible both when poverty is measured via a household consumption aggregate and a household assets index. Having said that, the variation in the disability rate based on poverty status is not very large in some countries.

There is evidence that employment protects the disabled from being poor. Of the countries with relevant data, Romania is the only exception to this rule, and in that country, being a wage employee does not remove the poverty disadvantage that affects disabled individuals.

Disability Benefits and the Poor

In most OECD and Europe and Central Asia (ECA) countries, disability benefits as a percentage of GDP have increased since 1990. However, there is wide variation in the share of individuals qualifying for disability benefits in transition countries, with Croatia, Poland, Hungary, and Estonia reporting about twice as many beneficiaries than the European Union (EU) average, and poorer transition countries (Kyrgyzstan, Tajikistan, Uzbekistan, and Romania) reporting less than half of the EU average.

Disability pensions are well targeted to the poor in most countries of the region. Two low-income Commonwealth of Independent States

(CIS) countries, Tajikistan and Georgia, are exceptions to the rule, with almost uniform distribution of disability pension beneficiaries regardless of household consumption. Thus there is room for improvement in the coverage of disability benefits and the pro-poor targeting performance of benefits in *poor* transition countries, where the official disability rates tend to be particularly small.

The sizable discrepancy between the official disability rate and other definitions of disability can make different demographic groups more vulnerable if their poor health status is not recognized as a disability that triggers support in the form of social assistance. In particular, there is evidence that the elderly and females are less likely to receive official disability status, after taking into account other individual characteristics, including levels of functional limitations.

This research shows that households are unable to cope with major deteriorations in the health of the head of the household (as measured by the individual moving from nondisabled to disabled status over time). But household consumption is not sensitive to the gradual deteriorations in activities of daily living, or to the onset of a new chronic disease. At the individual level, considering the evidence that the employment consequences of being disabled worsen over time, there is a need to examine both the duration of disability compensation, as well as the capacity (in terms of skills) and incentives for the individual to reenter the labor force.

Nonmonetary Costs of Disability and Chronic Illness

There are significant nonmonetary costs of disability as well. Nondisabled individuals who live in a household that has at least one disabled individual spend two to five times (in Hungary and Estonia, respectively) as much time assisting adult family members, compared to nondisabled individuals who live in a household without anyone who is disabled. Females, as well as those without tertiary education, spend more time assisting adult household members.

Among households that report provision of adult care, time spent for this purpose is much higher in Romania (at more than 80 minutes per day on average) than in Estonia, Hungary, and the United Kingdom (all below 55 minutes per day on average). Thus, it could be that in poor countries, the nonmonetary costs of disability are higher, although it is not possible to make sweeping conclusions on this topic because comparable time-use surveys have not been implemented in other Eastern European and Central Asian countries. In urban Romania, Hungary and Estonia, time-use patterns are closer to those observed in Netherlands and the United Kingdom, and thus continued urbanization may lead to a convergence across countries in time spent on home care.

Finally, disabled children are significantly less likely to enroll in school. Neither Millennium Development Goals (MDGs) nor the Education for All Initiative can succeed in the absence of a renewed commitment to disabled children's schooling outcomes. Children's human capital accumulation is also sensitive to the deterioration of the health status of their parents: There is some empirical evidence that children are more likely to drop out of school if their parents experience health shocks.

Future Research

The policy implications of certain findings require further consideration. One example is the finding that poor households are not able to fully absorb the income loss caused by major health shocks to the head of the household. Even though universal catastrophic health insurance schemes can be considered in such cases, it is not clear if such universal insurance programs can be implemented successfully in poor countries where a large segment of the population is employed in the informal sector (making it difficult to collect insurance premiums from them).

Another example is the finding that in Bosnia and Herzegovina, after the onset of the disability, the decline in the number of hours worked and earnings becomes more severe over time (the opposite trend is observed in the U.S.). This research revealed that—as opposed to what is observed in OECD countries—the employment rates of disabled and the nondisabled individuals are not correlated in transition economies. The implication is that without institutional and legislative reforms (that also consider the informal sector) the markets are unlikely to fix this particular development challenge. The solution will have to rely on a set of factors including overall improvements in the economy (which, at the very least, would serve to increase the resources available for public service delivery and social protection programs), changes in the duration of disability benefits, implementation of training programs to facilitate the transition from one type of job to another, ensuring the existence of incentives for disabled individuals to go back to work, addressing workplace discrimination, etc.

In some cases there may be tradeoffs between efficiency and equity, and the way such tradeoffs are tackled may be especially important for developing countries with limited resources. This research demonstrates the significant enrollment disadvantage of disabled children, although the solution to this challenge (which might include training for teachers to enhance the benefits of an integrated teaching environment, or in some cases might require specialized education arrangements) will probably need to be formulated separately for rural and urban areas, taking into account the numbers of disabled children involved. More generally, the service delivery arrangements for disabled children require further research in the developing-country context.

Another useful avenue for policy-relevant research would be to calculate the costs and benefits of alternative preventive interventions in a way that can be compared to some of the statistics on the direct costs (such as loss of income) and the indirect costs (such as the value of time devoted for the care of the disabled) of disability that are presented in this report. It also would be beneficial to compare the payoffs from preventive interventions in developing countries to those in industrialized countries.

The researchers' ability to further this line of work will depend on the availability of relevant data sets. As discussed later in this report, there has been some progress in the way disabilities, chronic illnesses, and restrictions on "activities of daily living" are captured in surveys. The early efforts have primarily focused on ensuring the presence of "correct" disability questions in the census data. This approach would improve the estimates of the prevalence of disability in developing countries, but the limited scope of a typical census questionnaire would be of little use to enhance our understanding of key relationships of interest. Thus, one should not underestimate the potential of improving the design of household surveys to inform policy makers. This work shows that increasing the sample size of a survey from 12,387 to 32,337 produced remarkably similar estimates of the prevalence of disabilities and thus the inclusion of "correct" set of questions in standard LSMS-type household surveys can produce valuable information despite relatively small sample sizes.

Finally, it is useful to point out the topics that would benefit from elaborate analysis but are outside the scope of this particular research project. These include the social integration of disabled individuals, the status and shortcomings of institutionalized care in the region, alternative home care and community care models, transport and infrastructure, detailed sectoral perspectives, and discrimination.

PART I

A REGIONAL OVERVIEW

CHAPTER 1

Introduction

Cem Mete with Jeanine Braithwaite and
Pia Helene Schneider*

Disability is an important issue for the countries of Eastern Europe and the former Soviet Union, in large part because a significant portion of the population is either in poor health or disabled, which has implications for labor force participation rates and productivity. Especially in aging transition countries, the sustainability of social protection programs is also a concern due to the projected increases in the share of disabled populations.

During the first phase of the transition from socialism to market economy, poor health status, disability, and premature mortality of individuals received attention primarily as indicators of reduced living standards in the region. The inequality implications of the transition process were also highlighted, in particular through the analysis of the abrupt and significant decline of the life expectancy of Russian males during the early 1990s (Bobadilla, Costello, and Mitchell 1997; Cornia and Paniccia 2000).

In this context, the economic costs of poor health status and disabilities did not receive much attention because in a high-unemployment environment with an abundant supply of skilled labor, the bottlenecks in the labor markets were (and are) considered to be in the domain of labor demand, not labor supply (World Bank 2005). Yet this situation is rapidly changing because many transition countries have experienced respectable economic growth rates starting from the late 1990s, and the labor markets are starting to tighten in many cases. For example, in 8 of 20 transition countries studied by the World Bank (2005), the unemployment rate was at or below the EU-15 aver-

* Cem Mete is a senior economist at the Europe and Central Asia region of the World Bank. Jeanine Braithwaite is a senior social protection economist at the Human Development Network of the World Bank. Pia Helene Schneider is a senior health economist at the Europe and Central Asia region of the World Bank.

age of 9 percent in 2003, even though employment levels in many transition countries remain below the EU-15 average of 65 percent.[1]

Failing to deal with disability issues or dealing with them in an inefficient manner can be very costly—especially for the rapidly aging transition countries that aim to reach the Millenium Development Goals (MDGs). Poverty reduction and universal primary school enrollment MDGs seem particularly at stake, yet at this stage the empirical knowledge base in this area is extremely weak. In particular, there is a remarkable absence of quantitative information on the key linkages among disability and employment, earnings, poverty, and children's school outcomes.[2]

This report argues that it is timely to bring the economic costs of disability to the forefront of development policy because of the large impact poor health status and disabilities have on employment, poverty, children's schooling, and time spent in caring for disabled individuals, especially by adult females (which in turn inhibits higher female labor force participation prospects). In fact, the evidence provided here suggests that the linkages between disability and economic and social outcomes of interest are stronger in transition countries when compared with industrialized countries. As a result, poor health status and disability emerge as major obstacles to equitable and sustainable economic growth in the region.

In recent years, there has been some recognition of the need to discuss disability issues in strategy documents such as Poverty Reduction Strategy Papers (PRSPs) and country assistance strategies (CASs). But in the absence of basic empirical evidence on the living conditions and behavior of disabled individuals, it is a challenge to formulate concrete steps to tackle this particular economic development problem. In fact, it is a challenge to define the magnitude and characteristics of the problem. Not surprisingly then, there is some dissatisfaction in the way disabled populations are covered in the existing strategy documents. One criticism is the way the disabled are only mentioned in the broad discussion of "vulnerable groups." Another is the way in which redistributive policies are emphasized instead of "unlocking the economic potential of the disabled individuals" (ILO 2002).

This report aims to fill in the knowledge gap in this field by analyzing cross-country data on basic indicators, and by carrying out more detailed empirical analysis on causal relationships of interest, including the impact of disability on employment, wages, poverty, and children's school enrollments—focusing on four transition countries with household survey data sets that allow more elaborate econometric analyses. This is a tightly focused effort, leaving out a number of important topics that researchers may want to tackle in the future. The excluded topics include the social integration of disabled individuals, the status and shortcomings of institutionalized care in the region, alternative home care and community care models, transport and infrastructure, detailed sectoral perspectives,[3] discrimination,[4] and cost-benefit analysis of prevention against certain types of disability.[5]

Regional Context

Under the Soviet/Yugoslav system, disabled individuals were both protected and isolated from the general population. Disability was one of the very few acceptable reasons for an adult not to work, but disability was viewed in a narrow, medical way, and its study was (and is) termed *defektlogia* in Russian—the study of defects. Parents were encouraged to place children in residential institutions, as it was thought that institutions could do a better job of raising disabled children than could parents. Noninstitutionalized children with disabilities were typically segregated in special schools and disability was highly stigmatized. However, adults with disabilities were encouraged to join collectives of persons with the same medically defined disability, such as associations for the blind and deaf. Mental disability was even more highly stigmatized.

The impact of transition on disability was pronounced. In many Eastern European and former Soviet Union countries, the number of (officially recognized) disabled individuals increased significantly between 1991 and 1997, reflecting several factors, including the preference of employers to avoid paying severance pay to fired workers—instead placing them on disability rolls—and the sharp deterioration in health indicators (particularly for adult men) and disruptions in the health system. At the same time, financing for residential institutions was devolved to localities, without specific revenue sources, thus resulting in chronic underfinancing for such institutions—which, *ceteris paribus*, may have reduced the number of institutionalized individuals through demand- and supply-side effects. With the freeing of civil society, disabled persons' organizations began to form, in some cases out of the old Soviet collectives, in other cases from exposure to international nongovernmental organizations (NGOs), and in some cases from the grass roots, including from parent-teacher organizations.

Other facts that characterize most Eastern European and former Soviet Union countries are a tradition of universal health care coverage on the positive side, but unsustainable or collapsing health systems and widespread informal consultation fees on the other. They are also well-advanced in terms of demographic transition (and as a result face all the challenges of "aging populations," including the old-age-disability burden), but poor—unlike industrial countries that also face the same demographic situation.[6] They have educated populations, but preventive health behavior is not on par with what is observed in Western societies. There is an increased prevalence of depression and mental health cases—especially, but not exclusively, in post-conflict areas such as Bosnia and Herzegovina and Serbia. There have been significant changes in the labor market environment in a relatively short period of time, with increases in the share of private sector employment and service sector employment,[7] along with the increased prevalence of informal sector employment, which lacks the regulations and social protection benefits that come with formal sector employment. Still, there are some differences among the countries in the region in terms of available resources to tackle the disability-related challenges due to geographical positioning—in particular, some transition countries are either EU members or on the EU membership path, while others will become neighbors of EU members. There are even differences in the extent to which they are exceptions to the facts outlined above (for example, fertility rates are relatively high in Tajikistan, so for that country, aging is not an issue in the medium term).

Different Definitions, Different Prevalence Rates

Capturing the incidence of disability is difficult. The World Health Organization (WHO) estimates that about 10 percent of the world's population experiences some form of physical, mental, or intellectual disability.[8] Industrialized countries with aging populations tend to report higher disability rates, partly because of better data on the disabled, and partly because these countries can afford to (officially) acknowledge and provide disability benefits to a larger share of their populations. The average disability prevalence in OECD countries is 14 percent, of which one-third are severely disabled. Northern European countries and Portugal report the highest disability prevalence.[9]

Alternative definitions of disability provide significantly different estimates of the prevalence of disability.[10] For example, 3.8 percent of the population aged 7 and older in Uzbekistan is officially considered disabled. Yet almost 12 percent of individuals in that age group have at least one serious difficulty or a full limitation in physical functioning (figure 2, discussed in more detail in chapter 2).[11]

The most commonly encountered type of disability is movement restrictions, the least

BOX 1.1

Defining Disability

Disability is an umbrella term that can refer to quite different health ailments, depending on the context. Alternative approaches to measuring disability include diagnosis-based assessments (e.g., "Does anyone in this household have epilepsy?"); Activities of Daily Living (e.g., "Do you have trouble dressing or bathing yourself?"); Instrumental Activities of Daily Living (e.g., "Do you have trouble maintaining the household?"); participation/social-role questions (e.g., "Do you have a mental or physical impairment that limits the amount or type of work you can do?"); or functional questions (e.g.,"Do you have difficulties concentrating, remembering, or making decisions?"). Administrative data, such as those reported by the Transmonee database, are sometimes used for making cross-country comparisons of disability, but the wealthier countries with better administrative recordkeeping capabilities routinely come up as the ones with the highest disability rates.

Depending on the purpose of the study or policy intervention in question, it is natural to work with different definitions of disability. In practice, availability of data also influences the disability definition that is used. One line of research focusing on international comparisons in OECD countries makes extensive use of the Activities of Daily Living (ADL) and Instrumental Activities of Daily Living (IADL) restrictions, distinguishing among "severe disability," meaning individuals with one or more ADL restrictions; "moderate disability," meaning individuals without an ADL restriction but experiencing IADL limitations; and "little or no disability," meaning no ADL or IADL limitations (see Jacobzone, Cambois, and Robine [2001] and the references cited by the authors).

More comprehensive but perhaps less empirically oriented definitions are proposed by the WHO. The 1980 International Classification of Functioning, Disabilities, and Health (ICF) makes the distinction among disorder, impairment, disability, and handicap (WHO 1980). The 2002 ICF revised the definition, with a major difference being the linkages to the environment in which an individual functions—be that the physical, institutional, or cultural environment—and linkages to "involvement in life situations." Despite the additional challenges they pose for measurement and standardization, the more comprehensive definitions of disability seem to have contributed to the formulation of recent strategy documents such as the Community-Based Rehabilitation approach advocated by the ILO-UNESCO-WHO Joint Position Paper (2004). For an in-depth discussion on definitions in the context of social science, see Freedman, Martin, and Schoeni (2004) and OECD (2003).

common ones are hearing and communications, while vision and learning fall somewhere in between.[12] One implication of this finding is that aging populations can expect the prevalence of disability to increase substantially over time. Even if medical advances, positive changes in preventive health behavior, and improvements in health care service delivery slow down this trend, their impact is unlikely to be large enough to undo the aging effect.

Even though different disability proxies lead to significantly different disability prevalence estimates, they are correlated with one another. Furthermore, it is possible to make generalizations about different "groups" of poor health/disability variables and their relation-

FIGURE 1
WHO Definition of Disability

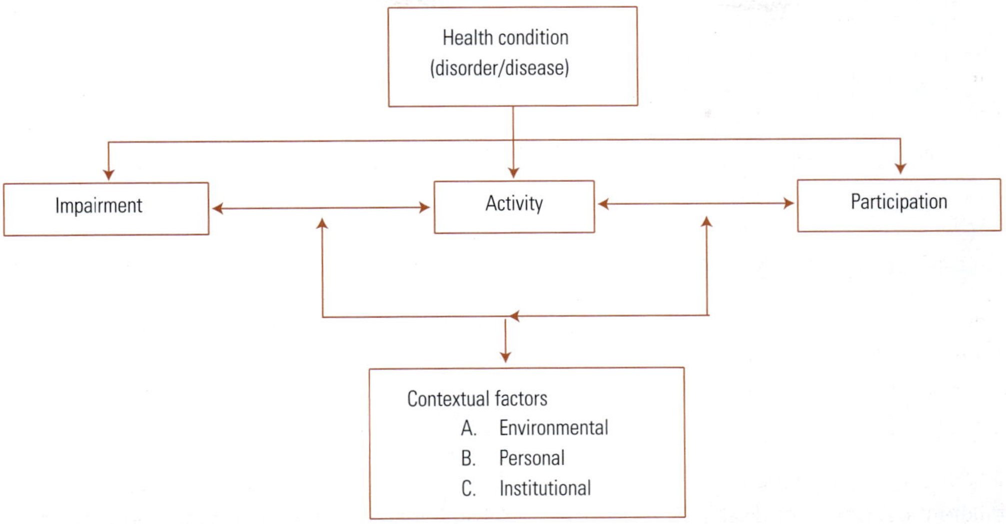

ship with socioeconomic characteristics and poverty. This review of available evidence reveals that it is undesirable to categorically favor one disability indicator over the others. Instead, each disability indicator has strengths and weaknesses, which make some indicators better suited for the analysis of certain issues, but not others. Through an improved under-

FIGURE 2
Various Definitions of Disability Incidence in Uzbekistan

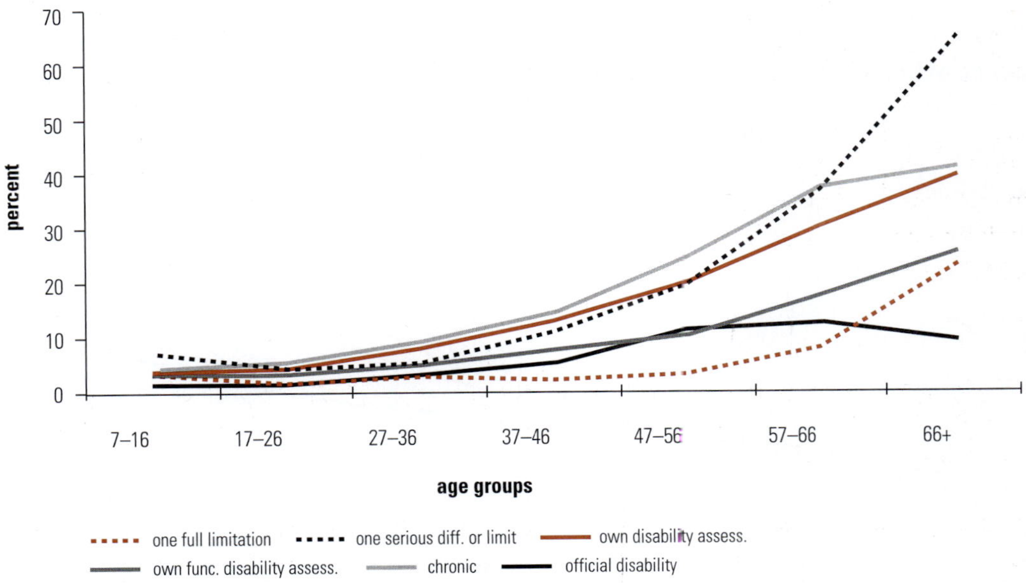

Source: Authors' calculations based on URPS data sets described in chapter 2.

standing of the reasons why various indicators produce the trends that they do, one can improve the way we identify the most vulnerable groups in the population.

The cross-country evidence confirms the sharp age gradient in the reporting of health ailments, especially for the reporting of chronic illnesses (figures 3 and 4). An interesting trend in figure 3 is that disability rates in Poland, the wealthiest transition country with relevant data, display the sharpest age gradient, leading to much higher disability rates among the elderly, as compared to poorer transition countries. This finding may have to do with the fact that in wealthier countries, the disability benefits are highly concentrated among people over age 50

FIGURE 3

Prevalence of Disability by Age Group

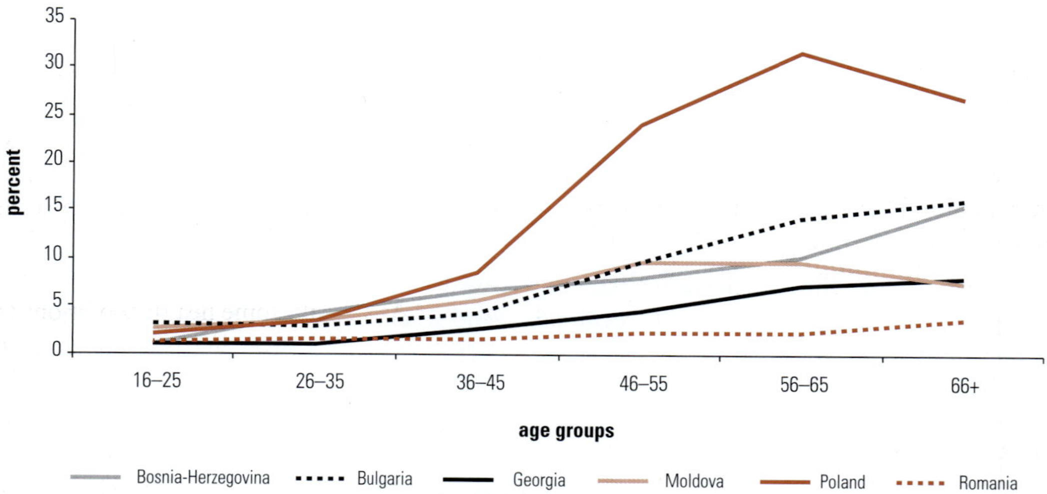

Source: Authors' calculations based on household survey data sets listed in appendix 1.

FIGURE 4

Prevalence of Chronic Illness by Age Group

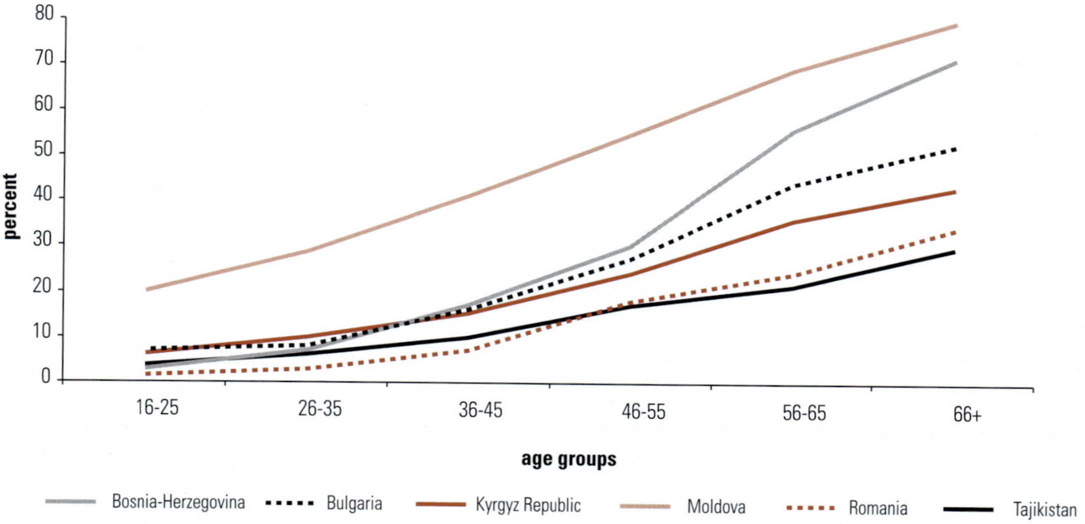

Source: Authors' calculations based on household survey data sets listed in appendix 1.

(OECD 2003), while in poorer developing countries, working-age adults may be favored for the granting of disability benefits (chapter 2), affecting whether the surveyed individuals identify themselves as disabled when approached by interviewers.

Main Causes of Disability in the Region

As countries pass through the health transition, a larger share of the disability burden is due to noncommunicable diseases and injuries. According to the Global Burden of Disease project, the main causes leading to disability among men in Eastern European and Central Asian countries are neuropsychiatric conditions[13] (35 percent of Years Lost to Disability, or YLD), unintentional injuries due to such things as falls and traffic accidents (12.5 percent), sense organ (vision or hearing) diseases (8.3 percent), cardiovascular diseases (8 percent), and musculoskeletal diseases (6.6 percent). The statistics are similar for women.[14] These trends are reflected in percentage-of-deaths-by-cause statistics, where the share of noncommunicable diseases among transition countries is consistently high, at between 75 percent and 85 percent.[15]

For individuals 45 and older, neuropsychiatric diseases, diseases of the sense organs, and cardiovascular and musculoskeletal diseases are the main cause for YLD. Among adults between ages 15 to 44, on the other hand, the cause pattern of disability reveals the importance of mental health. About 30 percent of the ECA total of YLD among men is due to disease and injuries incurred at ages 15–29, and 27 percent in the most productive ages 30–44. At similar disability rates, the main cause for YLD among women aged 15–44 is depressive disorder, injuries, and maternal conditions. For men in this age YLD is mainly due to depressive disorder, alcohol abuse, musculoskeletal conditions, and injuries.

For children aged 0 to 4, YLD is mainly due to iodine deficiency, lead-caused mental retardation, or birth traumas,[16] suggesting that health policy focus on nutritional health and environmental interventions, ensuring access to iodized salt and protection against lead contamination, as well as a focus on reproductive health care. The 2002 Turkey disabilities survey reveals payoffs to early interventions because more than 40 percent of speech and mental disabilities are congenital, and between 20 and 25 percent of orthopedic, sight, and hearing disabilities are congenital.[17]

Employment and Disability

Poor health status/disability is likely to be more detrimental for labor force participation in transition countries as compared to industrialized countries because the health systems in many transition economies are experiencing serious problems with service delivery, quality of care, and even availability of medicines and equipment.[18] As a result, some health conditions that today do not have much of an impact on the daily functioning of individuals in industrialized countries may still be a cause for concern in transition economies.[19] Furthermore, manufacturing and agriculture sector jobs, which tend to be more demanding physically and also more prone to work conditions that may cause disability, still dominate the economic environment in transition countries. But it is also possible that the spread of medical advances across countries, and a shift toward service sector employment over time in transition countries, may counteract these effects. Which set of factors dominates at this point in time?

The only transition country (Poland) that was included in the cross-country analysis of OECD (2003) is also the one where the relative employment rate of disabled over nondisabled people is lowest, at around 0.3. In contrast, the corresponding ratios in Switzerland, Mexico, Korea, France, Norway, Canada, and Sweden are above 0.7. The empirical evidence presented next shows that disabled adults in transition countries are indeed severely handicapped in terms of participation in the labor force.

FIGURE 5
Probability of being an Employee/Wage Employee

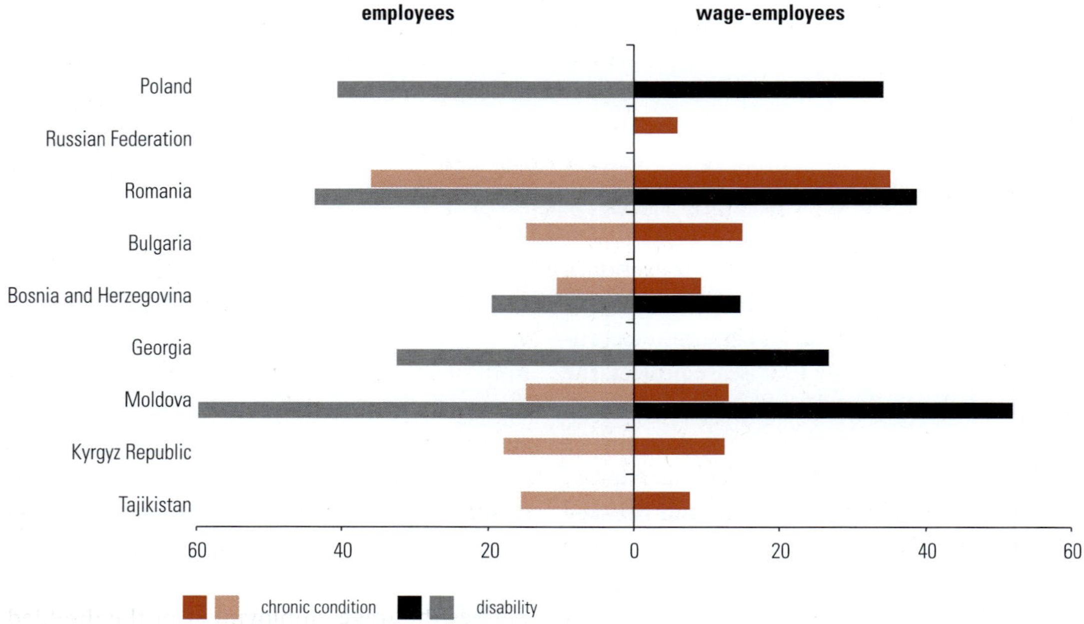

Source: Authors' calculations based on household survey data sets listed in appendix 1.

Note: Urban sample. The employment gap of the disabled individuals is presented as absolute values of percentage points.

Disabled adults are much less likely to work when compared with nondisabled adults in all countries considered here, ranging from a high of 60 percentage points less likely to work in Moldova, to a low of 20 percentage points in Bosnia and Herzegovina (figure 5). Evidence from Uzbekistan, discussed in chapter 2, reveals that while all disability indicators considered are negatively associated with employment, having the official status of being disabled is the indicator linked to the largest decline in the probability of employment (a 52 percentage point reduction), followed by having a full limitation in any one of the six physical functioning domains (a 24 percentage point reduction).

Perhaps the strong correlation between official disability status and employment is to be expected, since those who are officially disabled may risk losing benefits if they work. In the Russian Federation, a one-unit deterioration in health (say, from good to average health) reduces male participation in the labor force by 15 percentage points and female participation by 6 percentage points. This effect is larger if one considers worsening of health as captured by the official disability classification, reducing working by 40 percentage points for men and 22 percentage points for women. Another important finding that emerges from the analysis of Russian data sets is that simple associations tend to downplay the linkage between poor health/disability and employment, since instrumental-variable estimates that attempt to single out causal relationships tend to be substantially larger than the conventional ordinary least squares (OLS) estimates (chapter 4). The analysis of Romanian data sets reported in chapter 5 reveals that the relationship between health ailments and employment is stronger for those who are above 40 years old, reducing the probability of employment by 57 percentage points.

The disabled who are employed work less than others, but the difference is less than five hours a week in Moldova and Bosnia and

Herzegovina, although it is sizable—at about nine hours—in Poland. Further analysis of the data from Bosnia and Herzegovina—which focuses on health shocks that occur between survey waves in an attempt to single out causal relationships, and takes into account main individual and household characteristics—reveal that newly occurring disability leads to an eight-hour decrease in weekly employment, on average. Deteriorating health status, as captured by an ADL index, has a smaller impact, estimated at a five-hour decline in weekly hours of work (see chapter 3). In Russia, the deterioration of health leads to a 9 percentage point decrease in hours worked, both for men and women (chapter 4).

There is no correlation between the employment rates of disabled individuals and nondisabled individuals across transition countries.[20] This finding contradicts the trends observed in the OECD countries, where employment rates of disabled and nondisabled individuals are strongly correlated (OECD 2003). Thus, in the transition economy context, it is difficult to argue that general employment-promoting policies would automatically foster the employment of special groups in the short term. Even during the second phase of transition, with strong economic growth performance across the board in the region, the employment prospects of disabled individuals cannot be entrusted to the markets under the existing institutional frameworks. The challenge, of course, would be to develop a supportive environment for the employment of the disabled without introducing new rigidities to employment legislation, which can slow the speed of economic recovery and poverty reduction in a region that experienced significant declines in living standards during the early to mid-1990s.[21]

Similarly, looking at the trends in three countries with data at two points in time (figure 6), it is possible to see a case where the disabled employment rate declined, even though the overall employment rate rose. This trend is driven by nonwage employment, however. In all three countries considered here, if the wage employment of the nondisabled rises over time, so does the wage employment of the disabled (not reported). The presence of significant informal sector employment in the transition countries may thus explain why transition countries are different from OECD countries in this respect. More generally, how formal and informal labor markets respond to certain policy interventions and the resulting movements to

FIGURE 6

Employment Rates of Disabled and Nondisabled Individuals

1998–2003

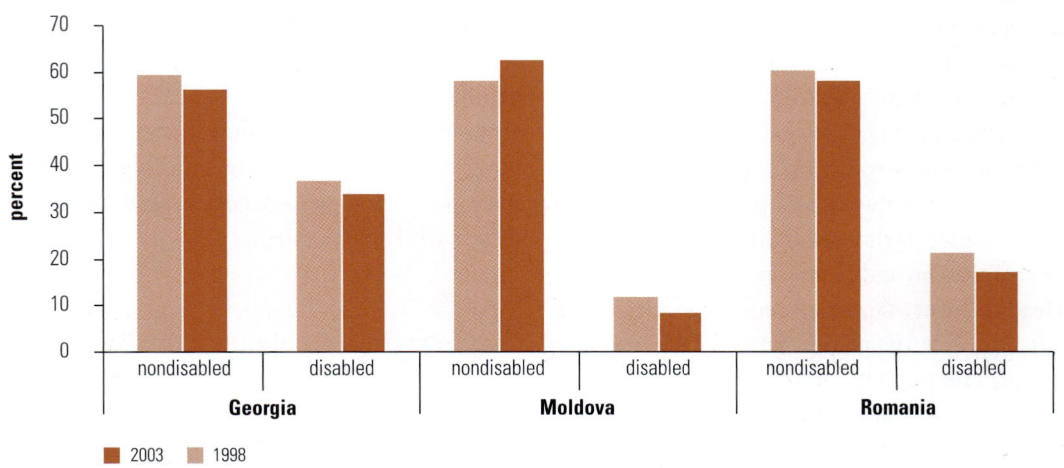

Source: Authors' calculations based on household survey data sets listed in appendix 1.

and from formal and informal employment (in addition to dropping out of the labor force) determine whether the disabled will benefit from an economic boom.[22]

Heterogeneity among the Disabled

It is useful to recognize the heterogeneity among the disabled population in this context, both because the diverging trends in transition countries and OECD countries may be influenced by the composition of the disabled, and because some of the disabled may be more disadvantaged in terms of employment compared to the rest. Few household surveys contain necessary information on different types of disability *and* have sufficient sample sizes to allow for meaningful empirical analyses, but some insights emerge from available data.

In Bosnia and Herzegovina, 26 percent of the disabled report hearing or visual limitations, 38 percent report mobility limitations, and the remaining 36 percent report war-related, learning, or other disabilities. The age group under consideration matters: for example, the war-related, learning, and other category makes up 75 percent of all disabilities among the 24- to 65-year-olds in Bosnia. Those with mobility limitations emerge as the most disadvantaged in terms of employment prospects, with an employment rate of 9.8 percent, followed by war/learning/other (17.5 percent employment rate) and hearing/visually disabled (44.4 percent employment rate).

In Bulgaria, a survey question that inquires about the extent to which disabilities result in reduced ability to work and participate in social functions reveals that disabilities reported by the elderly (aged 66 and older) are much more likely to lead to "over 90 percent reduced ability," with 43.6 percent of respondents choosing this option. The percentage drops dramatically by age, with 24 percent of those aged 24 to 65, and 28 percent of those younger than 24 saying they have "over 90 percent reduced ability." The educated disabled are also less likely to report "over 90 percent reduction in ability to work and participate in social functions" (12 percent among those with tertiary education, 43.4 percent among those with secondary education, and 44.6 percent among those with primary education or less). This might be partly because the types of work that individuals with higher education can undertake tend to be less physically demanding.

The severity of the disability, approximated by the three-category classification used by some transition countries, reveals the expected trends in terms of the likelihood of employment. In Moldova, only 5.8 percent of the most severely disabled are employed, with this percentage increasing to 10.7 percent and 17.9 percent as the severity of disability decreases. Similarly in Poland, the employment rate of those who rank their disability as "considerable" is 8.5 percent, followed by 24.7 percent and 36.8 percent for those who consider themselves as moderately and slightly disabled, respectively.

The timing of the disability deserves attention as well. Other things being equal, those with congenital disabilities will be exposed to the disadvantages of being disabled (in terms of intrahousehold decision making and resource allocation; more limited access to education and health services; and perhaps to limited social interactions) for a longer duration of time, and thus they may be more vulnerable later in life. Indeed, figure 7 shows that adults with congenital disabilities are less likely to be employed. This relationship can be driven in part by this group's educational disadvantage, however, since the same figure shows that adults with congenital disabilities are much less likely to have completed tertiary education compared to others who are disabled.

Earnings Disadvantage of the Disabled Is Larger in Transition Countries

The OECD (2003) reports that there is little difference in work incomes between disabled and

FIGURE 7

Educational Attainment and Employment of Those with Congenital Disability Versus Other Disability

ages 24 to 65

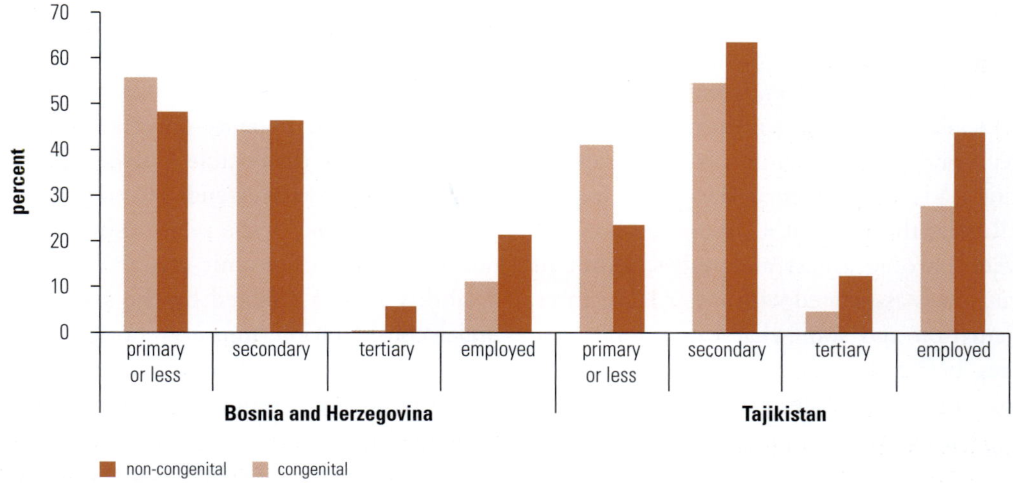

Source: Authors' calculations based on household survey data sets listed in appendix 1.

nondisabled persons in many industrialized countries—exceptions are the United States, Sweden, and Portugal, where the earnings of disabled employees are at or below 70 percent of the earnings of nondisabled employees. The disabled and the chronically ill earn less than others in transition countries, with the reduction in wages being substantially larger for the disabled compared to the chronically ill (figure 8).

The analysis of Russian data that aims to single out the causal relationship between disabilities and wages (reported in chapter 4) finds that the relationship between poor health status/disability and hourly wages is not as strong as the

FIGURE 8

Disabled and Chronically Ill Wage Employees Earn Less

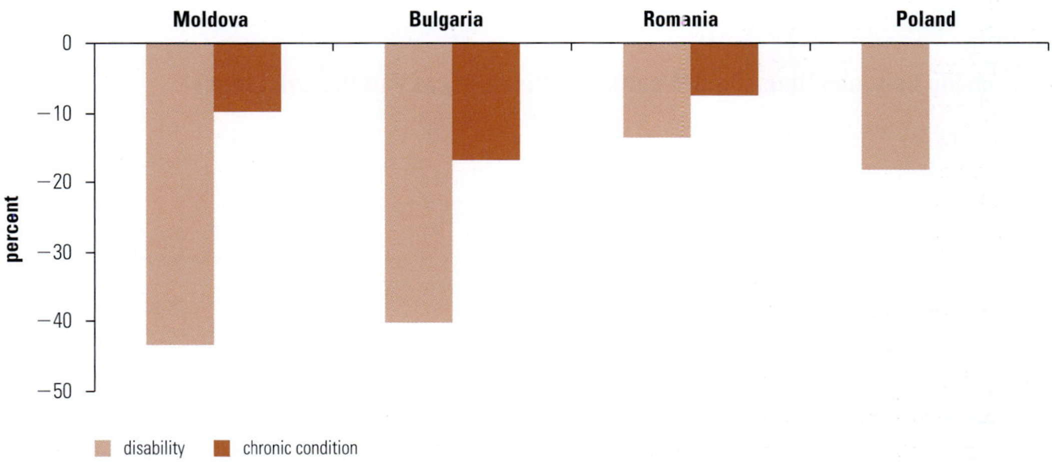

Source: Authors' calculations based on household survey data sets listed in appendix 1.

relationship between disability and employment, although for males, simple OLS estimates suggest that employees who report poor health status earn 13 percent less than others, after taking into account individual, household, and community characteristics that are thought to influence earnings. A one-step worsening in subjective health status ranking (say from very good to good) leads to a 14 percent decrease in wages, while a one-step worsening in the disability ranking leads to a 30 percent decrease in wages. For Russia, there is not a robust relationship between chronic illness and wages, although depression is associated with lower labor force participation and somewhat lower wages for females. In fact, the impact of disability on wages is also larger for females if one considers self-assessed health status or disability status.

Poverty and Disability

Poverty can lead to disability and poor chronic health conditions through a number of mechanisms, including exposure to malnutrition in early life, lack of access to adequate health care, and exposure to unsafe environmental conditions either at work or at home. Disability and poor health conditions can also lead to poverty, not only because of the financial implications of seeking care and securing medication, but also because of the decreased likelihood of employment and the reduced earnings capacity. One difficulty in interpreting the linkages between poverty and disability is that the former is a household-level indicator of living conditions, while disability is an individual-level event (with implications for the broader household). For example, if a significant portion of the disabled move in with their wealthier children or parents, then the observed disability-poverty relationship may not capture the decline in living standards for the disabled or the extended family members.

The discussion of the relationship between household socioeconomic characteristics and disability is also affected by the stage of life under consideration (figure 9). For children, it is easier to argue that the observed correlations between socioeconomic characteristics and poor health/disability are causal, since their earnings potential can be ignored in most cases. On the measurement side, higher mortality rates of disabled children (or shorter lifespans of the disabled elderly, for that matter) can result in smaller disability rates in the population overall. For example, at the time of the 2004 Romania Reproduction Health Survey, the mortality rate among children who were reported by their mothers to have had any disability was 28 percent, as opposed to 1.6 percent for the remaining children. In industrialized countries, the disabled children's survival chances are likely to be better, thus contributing to higher disability rates *ceteris paribus.*

FIGURE 9

Relationship between Household Wealth and Disability at Various Life Stages

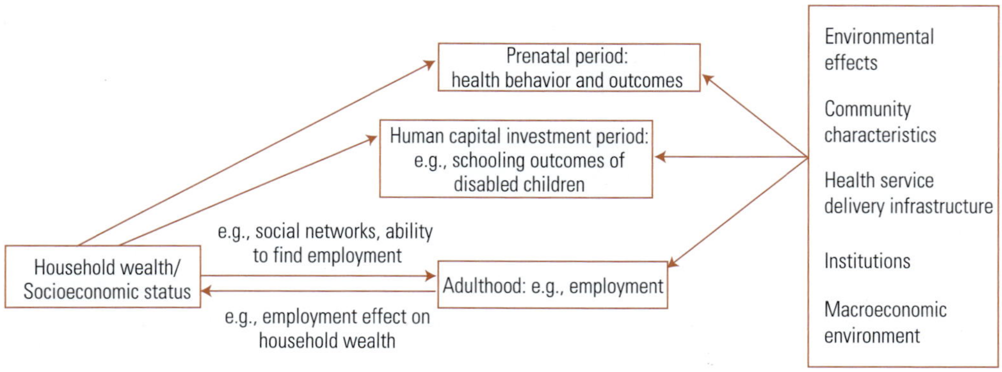

The poor are more likely to be disabled. The disability gradient is quite steep in Bulgaria and Bosnia and Herzegovina, the two countries that also have the highest rates of disability among the countries that are considered here. The poverty-disability linkage is sensitive to at least three sets of factors, one being the way disability is defined. Chapter 2 in this report finds that the disability indicator that is most closely associated with reduced per-capita household consumption in Uzbekistan is having at least one serious difficulty or full limitation in any of the six physical functioning domains (vision, hearing, movement, learning, communication, and self-care)—compared to other indicators of disability, such as reporting of chronic illness, official disability status, and an ADL index.

Similarly, the definition of poverty matters. The standard, consumption-based poverty definition produces a strong correlation with disability in two out of five countries considered, displaying a more subtle relationship for other countries (still in the expected direction). If one uses an asset-based proxy to measure poverty—which may capture longer-term welfare—then the poverty-disability linkage is confirmed, if anything, in a more explicit manner (figures 10 and 11).

Finally, the social stigma associated with being disabled can be more severe for poor households, and thus they may be less likely to consider certain limitations as disability. This would lead to an underestimation of the poverty gradient in the prevalence of disability. Also, as highlighted by Amartya Sen's "capabilities approach" to the study of poverty and inequalities, even if a disabled person and a physically fit person have the same income and physical goods, the disabled person is likely to live a much more restricted or difficult life. Thus, if the objective is to measure the extent to which living standards vary between households with disabled individuals and those without any disabled individuals, then even the lack of a poverty-disability relationship would not mean that the living standards of the two groups are the same, on average. Nevertheless, these findings suggest the need to pay special attention to the identification and economic and social integration of disabled individuals who are poor in the context of developing countries with significant resource constraints.[23]

FIGURE 10

Disability Rates by Consumption-Based Poverty Status

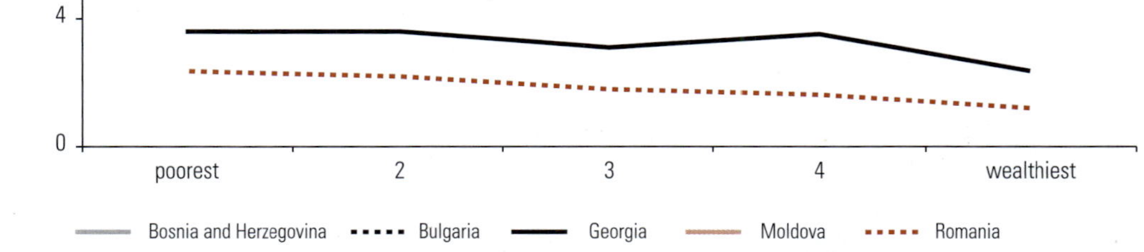

Source: Authors' calculations based on household survey data sets listed in appendix 1.

Note: Survey questions were "Do you have a disability?" in Romania; "Do you get disability allowance?" in Moldova; "Do you have a disabled status 1, 2, or 3?" in Georgia; "Do you have a recognized disability group?" in Bulgaria; and "Do you consider yourself disabled?" in Bosnia and Herzegovina.

FIGURE 11

Disability Rates by Asset-Based Poverty Status

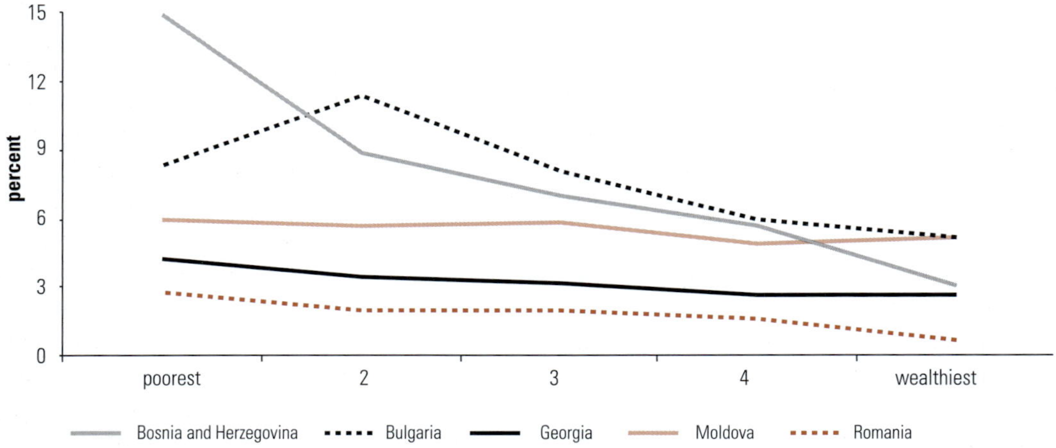

Source: Authors' calculations based on household survey data sets listed in appendix 1.

Does Employment Protect the Disabled from being Poor?

Among employees, the likelihood of being in the poorest quintile of the consumption distribution is about the same for the disabled and the nondisabled (figure 12). Available evidence indeed suggests that employment protects the disabled from being poor. One exception to this rule is Romania, where a significant portion of the disabled wage earners are among the poorest quintile, so being a wage employee does not

FIGURE 12

Percentage of Disabled and Nondisabled Individuals in the Poorest Quintile of the Consumption Distribution

separately for wage earners and self-employed

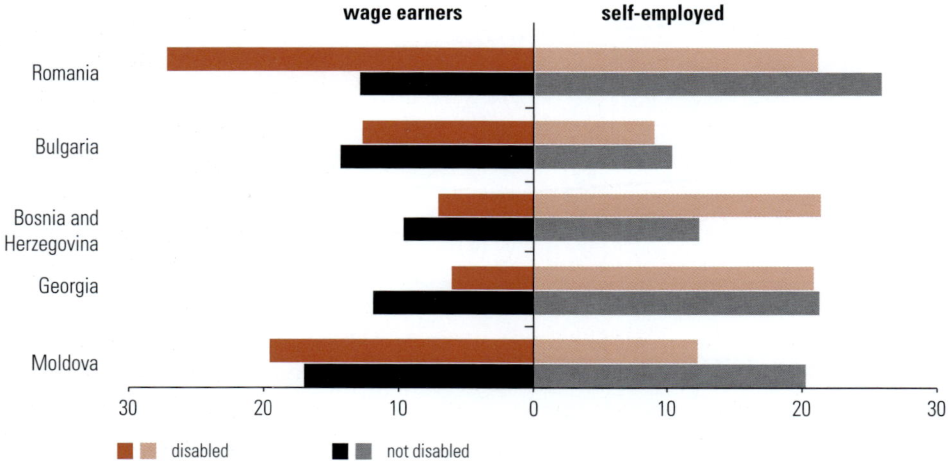

Source: Authors' calculations based on household survey data sets listed in appendix 1.

remove the economic disadvantage of disabled individuals.[24]

Health Shocks, Employment, and Poverty

Households are often unable to cope when there is a major deterioration in the health status of the head of the household. Analysis of longitudinal data from Bosnia and Herzegovina (reported in chapter 3) reveals that per-capita household consumption decreases by 7.8 percentage points, on average, if a household head becomes disabled. Similarly, a worsening of ADL leads to a 4.3 percentage point decrease in per-capita household consumption. But household consumption is not sensitive to the arrival of a new chronic disease.

Furthermore, by making a distinction between health shocks that happened within the last year and health shocks that occurred three or four years ago, one can see that employment protection legislation for the disabled seems effective in preventing an immediate decline in weekly hours of work, although disabilities that began two to three years ago are associated with a startling 17 hours less work per week. This is in contrast to the situation in countries with weaker employment protection legislation but lower unemployment rates, where a sharp initial decline in hours of work is followed by a recovery period. (Presumably after an initial abrupt adjustment, the disabled individuals eventually start working more, though perhaps in a different field.) In the case of Bosnia and Herzegovina, the existing legislation offers temporary relief, but after a one-year period the disabled individuals face an inhospitable labor market environment where formal employment opportunities are scarce and informal employment is often physically demanding. Overall improvements in labor demand would help in easing the longer-term disadvantages of the disabled individuals, and targeted government interventions that provide training and matching for new jobs can be effective in this context.

Social Protection Transfers and the Disabled

As discussed previously, there is room for significant improvement in the labor market environment in transition countries if disabled individuals are to contribute to, and take advantage of, economic growth through gainful employment. One such improvement would be the formalization of informal sector employment, which contributes to the particularly dreadful labor market outcomes for the disabled. The curbing of the informal sector would also boost a government's tax base, in turn generating much-needed resources for the social protection system, which will have to remain as a key policy device to improve the living standards of disabled people who are unable to participate in the labor force. But what are the levels of disability benefits, and to what extent are these benefits targeted to the most vulnerable groups?

The share of individuals that qualify for disability benefits varies significantly across countries, with Croatia, Poland, Hungary, and Estonia reporting about twice as many beneficiaries as the EU average. Mental and physical impairments tend to be covered by sickness benefits paid by health insurance funds before individuals qualify for disability benefits. The SHARE study[25] found that the large differences in disability insurance enrollment across countries is not necessarily due to differences in demographics and health status, but rather to institutional effects that create different enrollment incentives. Such effects include easier enrollment and eligibility rules, and more generous disability benefits in some countries than in others.[26]

One trend that is worth mentioning in the Eastern European and Central Asian region is that while life expectancy at birth is lowest in poor Central Asian countries (and also Russia and Azerbaijan), these are the countries that have the lowest share of persons receiving disability benefits (figure 13). While in theory such a trend can occur if some populations live

FIGURE 13
Persons Receiving Disability Benefits per 100,000, in 2003

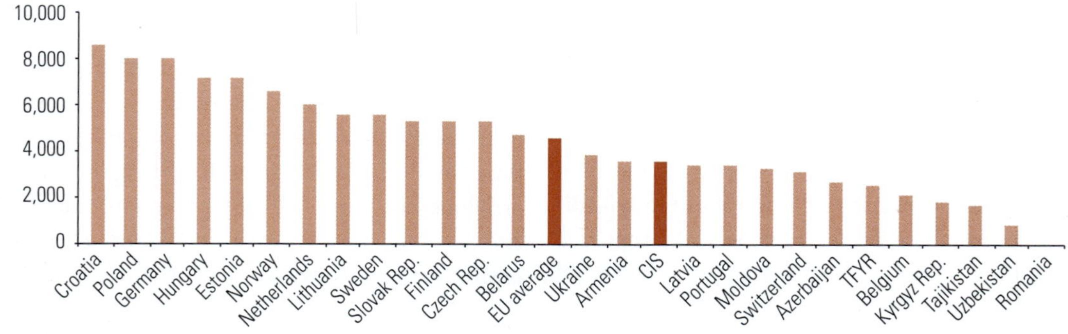

Source: WHO: Health for All database. http://www.euro.who.int/hfadb.

shorter but healthier lives (in the sense of spending few years with disability or chronic illness), in practice this trend is likely to be driven by the fact that poor countries cannot afford to grant social assistance benefits to a larger share of their populations.

In most OECD and ECA countries, the cost of disability benefits as a percentage of GDP has increased since 1990. The exceptions are countries where sick-leave benefits and old-age pensions serve as an alternative to disability insurance. In 1999, spending on disability benefits ranged from 0.2 percent of GDP in Korea, to 3.28 percent of GDP in Poland. Spending for all disability-related programs surpassed 4 percent of GDP in Norway, the Netherlands, Sweden, and Poland.[27] In Slovakia, the growing number of disabled has led to an increase in disability expenditures from 1.6 percent of GDP in 1990 to 2.3 percent in 2001,[28] which is comparable to the EU average. ECA countries spend a similar share of GDP on disability benefits as OECD countries. In 2000, Lithuania spent 1.3 percent of GDP for disability benefits, which is considerably more than Mexico or Korea.[29]

Attaining official disability status is what matters for receiving public (though not necessarily private) transfers. Yet the share of the population that is officially considered disabled can be manipulated through the adoption of stringent or flexible eligibility criteria, perhaps to avoid an excessive burden on public finances.[30] The discrepancy between the official disability rate and other definitions of disability can make different demographic groups more vulnerable if their poor health status is not recognized as a disability that triggers support in the form of social assistance. For example, the gap between the official disability rate and physical functioning limitations is particularly severe for the elderly in Uzbekistan: The official disability rate increases modestly by age, remaining at around 10 percent among those who are older than 66 years. In contrast, the share of individuals with at least one full limitation increases from about 5 percent for the 7 to 16 age group, to 65 percent among those who are 66 and over.

Not only do those who are of working age have an advantage in receiving official disability status, but males also are more likely to have official disability status after taking into account physical-functioning limitations and basic individual, household, and community characteristics. Furthermore, individuals who live in different regions (with otherwise comparable characteristics) face significantly different probabilities of receiving official disability status, signaling variations in the way disability status is granted at the local levels. The observed discrepancies deserve attention both because females tend to earn significantly less than males with similar characteristics and female-headed households are more likely to be poor in many countries,[31] and also because the disadvantage for the elderly in being officially recognized as disabled will become difficult to ignore as the share of elderly increases over time.

Disability pensions are well targeted to the poor in most countries of the region (figure 14). Two low-income CIS countries, Tajikistan and Georgia, are exceptions to the rule, with almost uniform distribution of disability benefits, regardless of household consumption. These two countries are among the poorest in the region, with $2.15 per day poverty rates of 74 percent and 52 percent, respectively. In these countries, too, a substantial portion of the disability pensions reach the poor, but not the extreme poor. The disability pensions also make up a significant share of the consumption in lower quintiles of wealth distribution, serving to improve the consumption ranking of some households that receive these transfers (figure 15). However, an alternative way to describe the observed trends would be that in *poor* transition countries, both the coverage of disability benefits and the targeting performance of benefits are in need of significant improvements.

Disabled Children's Limited Opportunities to Build Human Capital

Disabled children's limited access to public services contributes to undesirable employment and wealth outcomes when they become adults. Both demand- and supply-side factors influence the human capital accumulation of children, including the characteristics of the community; social norms, physical access to and affordability of public services; rationing of secondary or higher education opportunities through selection, quantity, and quality of teachers; labor market conditions and (perceived) returns to human capital; access to credit; household characteristics; and the characteristics of the child (Schultz 1961; Becker 1981). Empirical applications of this human capital accumulation model

FIGURE 14

Distribution of Disability Pension Beneficiaries by Household Consumption

before disability pensions

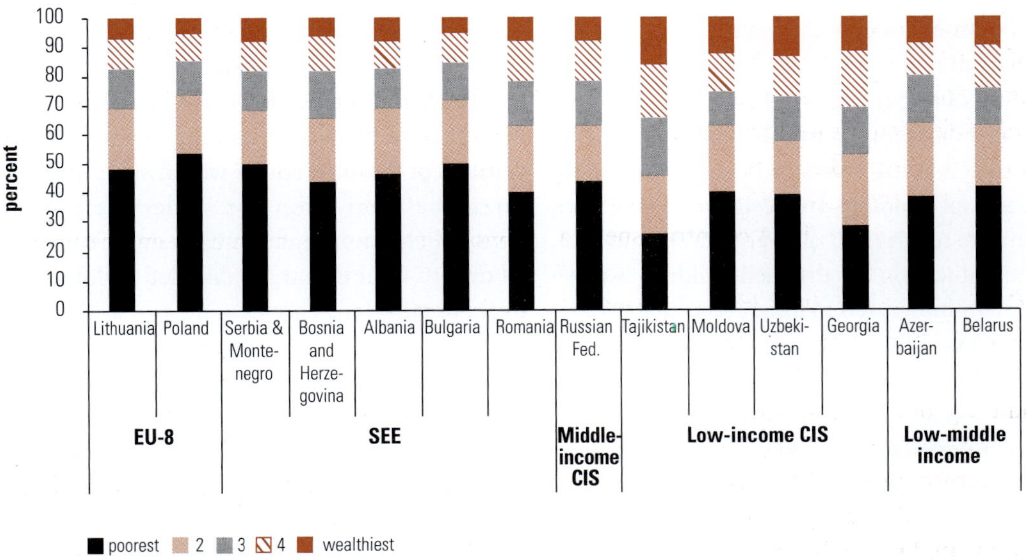

Source: Authors' calculations based on household survey data sets listed in appendix 1.

FIGURE 15

Distribution of Disability Pension Beneficiaries by Household Consumption

after disability pensions

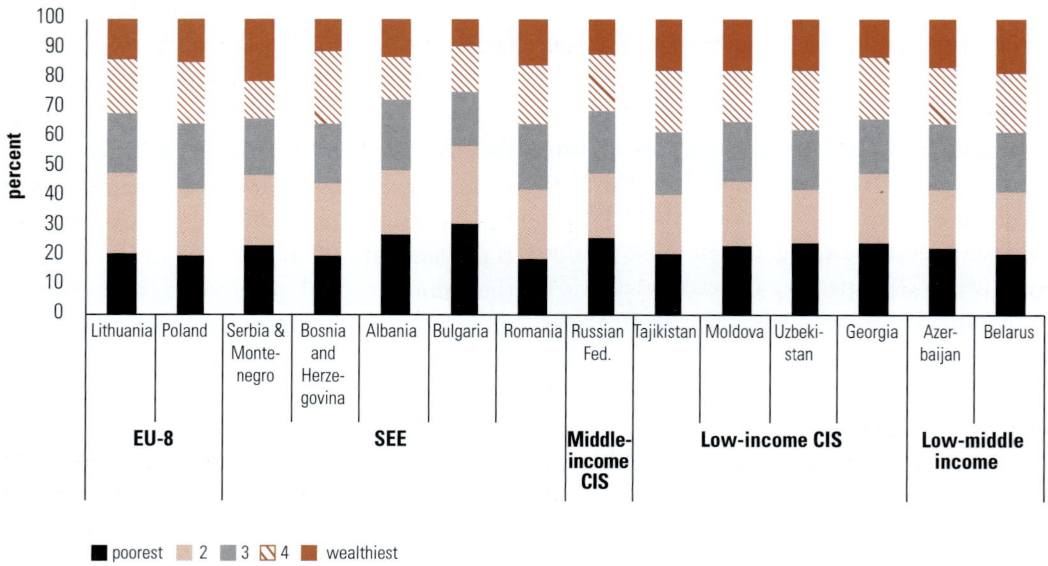

Source: Authors' calculations based on household survey data sets listed in appendix 1.

are often used to explain how the female disadvantage in school enrollments emerges in developing countries and what can be done to reduce the gender gap in school enrollments (Lewis and Lockheed 2006; Lloyd, Mete, and Sathar 2005; Schultz 2001; King and Hill 1993).

The same conceptual framework can be employed to highlight the challenges involved in providing better living conditions for disabled children. For example, in this context, physical access to schooling refers to both the extent to which school buildings are designed to take into account the needs of disabled children, and also whether education for disabled children is provided in an integrated manner: separate educational paths often mean reduced access to schooling for the "vulnerable group," be it the disabled children in transition countries or female children in countries where single-sex education is the norm.

On the household side, a key factor that influences the demand for schooling is how resources are shared among household members with different characteristics and skills. For example, there may be cases where parents invest in nondisabled children's schooling in the belief that total returns for their investments will be higher this way (and perhaps altruistic parents can provide better living conditions for the whole family through redistribution of funds in the future)—a notion that is formalized by Becker (1981). Previous findings that demonstrate the significant employment disadvantage of disabled adults would serve to reinforce the motivation for underinvesting in disabled children's human capital. Having said all this, to what extent are disabled children less likely to enroll in school?

The enrollment gap between disabled and nondisabled children is surprising to few. Neither the MDGs nor the Education for All Initiative can succeed in the absence of a renewed commitment to improve disabled children's schooling outcomes.[32] In countries where primary school enrollments are already high, which is the case for most transition countries, further gains in enrollment cannot be achieved without an emphasis on the schooling of disabled children. For example, as of 2002, enrollment rates of disabled children between the ages of 7 and 15 were 81 percent in Bulgaria, 58 percent in Moldova, and 59 percent in Romania, while the enrollment rates of nondisabled children were 96 percent, 97 percent, and 93 percent, respectively. Similarly, figure 16 confirms the sizable enrollment gap for disabled children between the ages of 16 and 18. These findings do not appear to be sensitive to the definition of disability at early levels of schooling. A multivariate analysis of the determinants of school enrollments in Uzbekistan, reported in chapter 2, finds that most disability proxies have the expected large effect on school enrollments for 7- to 14-year-olds, although for older children, official disability status is the only indicator that has a large impact on enrollments (at over 40 percentage points' drop in the probability of school enrollment).

The observed relationship between disability and poverty, which was documented previously, arises from the interaction of a variety of factors, not only because of limited access to education, but also because of limited access to health care. The ex-socialist countries faced the worst decline in health care utilization during the 1990s, and the poor experienced the worst drops within these countries, with some recovery after 1999 (World Bank 2005). In rural areas of Romania, for example, poor individuals are much less likely to have a hospital or a health center available in their locality (6.9 percent versus 11.3 percent for the wealthiest quintile).[33] Access to health care, in turn, has an influence on the health status of individuals—the Romanian data sets reveal that this effect is especially visible among the elderly.

Similarly, there may be payoffs to distinguishing between urban and rural areas when it comes to the public provision of schooling opportunities for disabled children.[34] In urban areas, the large number of disabled children would make it feasible to invest in school infrastructure and teachers to provide a better learning environment to this group of children. In rural areas such economies of scale do not exist and, at least in some transition countries, the current practice is to provide training through teachers' visits to disabled children's houses. The effectiveness of this approach is yet to be evaluated, although at the very least, oversight and monitoring of such programs may lead to some improvements in learning outcomes.

FIGURE 16
Enrollment Rates of 16- to 18-Year-Olds

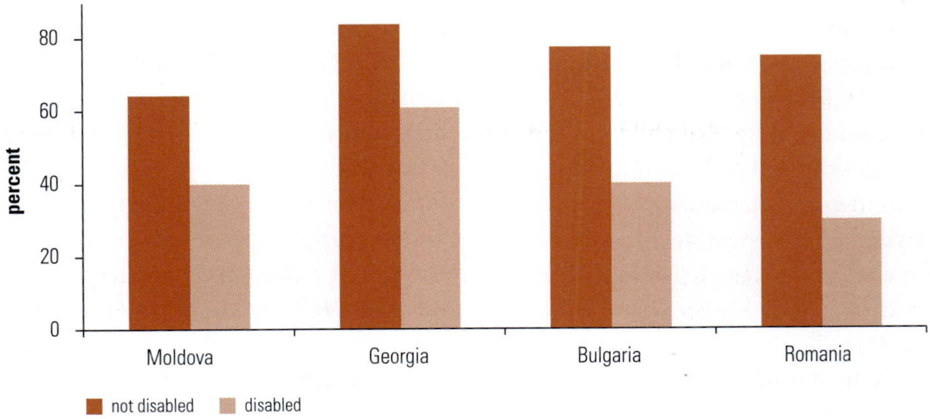

Source: Authors' calculations based on household survey data sets listed in appendix 1.

Note: The sample of disabled children aged 16 to 18 is too small to produce enrollment rate estimates for this group using the Bosnia and Herzegovina data sets.

In addition to ensuring better access to education and health services, in poor developing countries there is room to improve the quality of life and productivity of disabled individuals by relatively straightforward interventions, such as provision of eyeglasses, hearing aids, or wheelchairs to those in need. In Uzbekistan, 55 percent of those with vision problems do not wear glasses or contact lenses. The situation is even more serious for hearing problems, since 96 percent of those who report having such problems do not wear a hearing aid. The poorest two quintiles of the consumption distribution are more likely to fall into these categories, especially when it comes to vision problems, although the differences among various consumption quintiles are not large.[35] Another example to support this point comes from Tajikistan, where the lack of wheelchairs, crutches, and prosthetics appears to be critical. For example, one study assesses that in Dushanbe, the capital city, 200 out of 1,100 registered children with disabilities require a wheelchair but cannot afford one.[36]

Other Nonmonetary Costs of Disability: Caring for the Disabled

The true costs of disability would be underestimated if one focused solely on the implications of disability on the employment status of individuals and on household living conditions, as captured by per-capita household consumption. Indeed, disability prevents children from attending school, and furthermore, when a parent becomes disabled, his or her children's schooling outcomes often suffer.

In particular, male children can be summoned to work and make up lost income due to the disability or poor health condition of the adult (which can be significant, as discussed earlier), while female children may be required to provide more time either directly assisting the disabled household member(s) or helping with other household chores. For example, in Bosnia and Herzegovina, children ages 11 to 15 whose parents experience health shocks are 14 percentage points more likely to drop out of school during the four-year time period between the Wave 1 and Wave 4 surveys (chapter 3). In this case, the effect is visible only for male children though, and it is larger for the children of heads of households who become chronically ill between survey waves, compared to deteriorating ADL (corresponding increases in the likelihood of dropping out of school are 15 percentage points and 9 percentage points, respectively).

The analysis of comparable time-use survey data from three transition countries (Romania, Hungary, and Estonia) and two developed countries (the Netherlands and the United Kingdom) expands on this framework by documenting the prevalence of home care for the disabled, the extent of cross-country variation, and the extent to which certain individuals (for example females) end up playing a more significant role in this aspect of life. The main features of these time-use data sets are presented in appendix 2.

In transition countries, the likelihood of spending time assisting adult household members is not more than it is in the Netherlands and the United Kingdom. But among those who report providing care to adult household members, those who live in the two poorest countries with time-use survey data (Romania and Hungary) spend much more time on this activity (figure 17).[37] One possible explanation for this trend is that because the Netherlands and the United Kingdom are further along in the demographic transition, provision of "some help" to elderly adults is common.[38] Yet the amount of time spent for this purpose does not have to be as much as it is in poorer transition economies because the disabled in wealthier countries are more likely to benefit from state-of-the-art health care and supportive equipment, which would enable them to function more independently.[39]

In urban Romania, Hungary, and Estonia, time-use patterns are closer to those observed in

FIGURE 17

Percentage of Individuals Spending Time Assisting Family Adult, and Time Spent

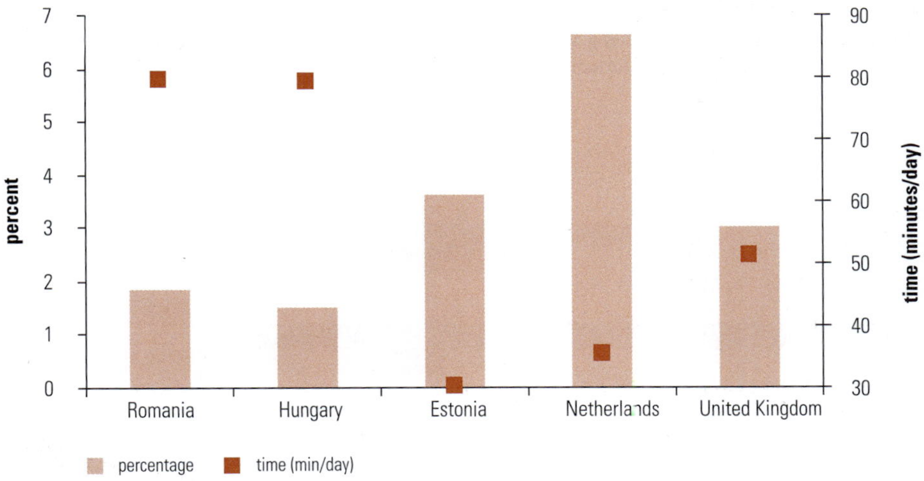

Source: Authors' calculations based on household survey data sets listed in appendix 2.

the Netherlands and the United Kingdom, and thus continued urbanization (and further economic development) may lead to a convergence across countries in time spent on home care. The percentage of individuals who report assisting adult household members is similar in urban and rural areas, but rural residents report spending much more time in caring for adult household members (about 1.4 times more compared to urban residents in all three transition countries considered here).

Females and less-educated household members undertake a disproportionate share of the adult care responsibilities at home. Interestingly, time spent on care does not vary much by household wealth (figure 18). These facts hold true in general, although Estonia's case is unique in that graduates with a basic education are less likely to report taking care of the disabled, although those who do carry out this activity spend almost twice the time on it as compared to graduates with a tertiary education. These findings can be explained by the lower earnings potential of females and less-educated individuals: For example, in Romania and Hungary, females earn about 20 percent less than males who are similarly educated and experienced, and there is a 6 percent return for an additional year of schooling in both countries (Yemtsov, Cnobloch, and Mete 2006). The adult care responsibilities of females may also explain the relatively low employment rates of females in transition countries when compared to OECD countries.

The remaining chapters investigate some of the topics highlighted here in a more detailed manner. Making use of a household survey designed specifically for this purpose, chapter 2 focuses on two basic but extremely important research questions: how can one go about measuring disability; and how are the alternative disability indicators related to one another and to poverty? The remaining three chapters focus on uncovering the causal impact of poor health status and disability on employment, earnings, and poverty. To achieve this goal, chapter 3 makes use of a unique four-wave panel survey that collected information on household characteristics (including household consumption patterns) and individuals' health and disability status. This analysis links emergence of disabilities (and variations in the ADL index) to changes in

FIGURE 18

Who Takes Care of Disabled Household Members?

ratios

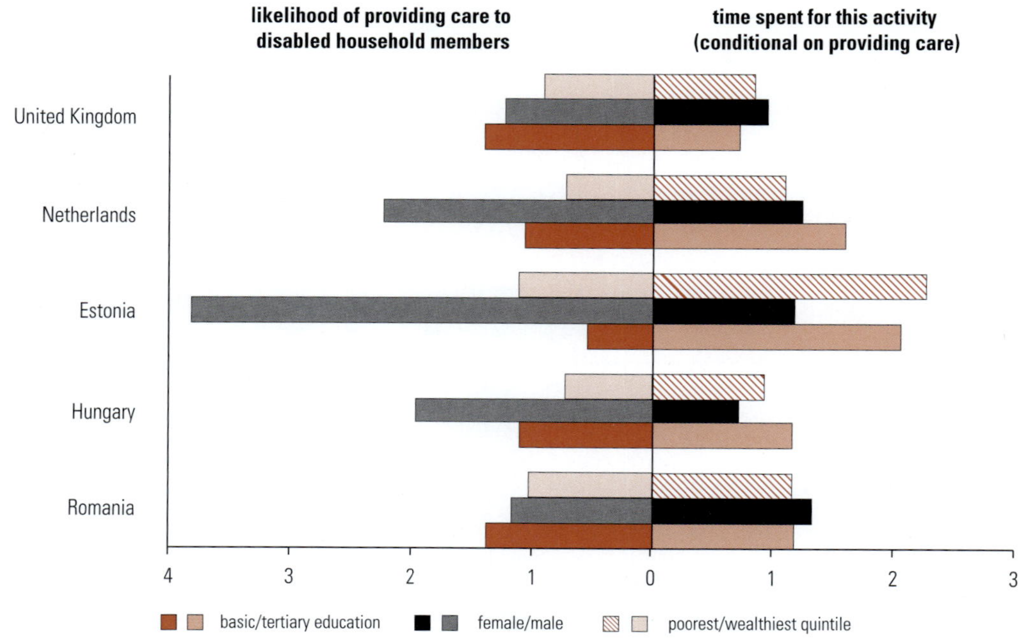

Source: Authors' calculations based on household survey data sets listed in appendix 2.

employment, earnings, and household consumption. The econometric strategy adopted in chapters 4 and 5 relies on the modeling of health status and labor outcomes jointly in an instrumental variables setup to display the impact of health status on labor productivity. Perhaps the most striking finding of this work is the robust and large economic effect of poor health and disability in the region, compared to what is observed in industrialized countries. It would also be useful to compare the trends documented here for transition countries with those that prevail in other developing countries with similar GDP per capita (but with different demographic compositions), although such work does not seem feasible at this time due to data limitations. Appendix 3 lists the alternative definitions of disability used by each chapter of the report, to evaluate the robustness of the key findings.

Appendix I

Disability-Related Questions in Available Household Survey Data

	Albania	Armenia	Armenia	Azerbaijan	Belarus	BiH	Bulgaria		Croatia	Georgia	Hungary	Kazakhstan	Kyrgyz Rep.		Lithuania
Type of survey	LSMS	HBS	DHS	HBS	LSMS	LSMS	HBS	HBS	HBS	HBS	HBS	HBS	LSMS	HBS	HBS
Year of survey	2002	2001–03	2000	2001–02	1998–2002	2001–03	1995 & 2001	2003	1998	1998–2002	1998–2002	2001–03	1998	2000–02	2000
1. Direct question on disability															
1. Do you have a disability?						Y		Y		Y					
2. Do you need any kind of assistance in daily activities?															
3. Type of disability?						Y									
4. Level of disability (I/II/III)?							Y	Y		Y					
5. Since when do you have it?						Y	Y								
6. How much do you spend on it?										Y					
2. Self-evaluated health status															
1. Qualitative question on self-evaluation of health status	Y	Y		Y		Y		Y				Y			
2. Respondent identifies socio-economic status as "disabled"															
3. Chronic illness															
1, Do you have chronic illness/disability?	Y					Y	Y	Y		Y		Y	Y		
2. Type of chronic illness	Y					Y	Y			Y		Y	Y		
3. Does it affect your daily activities?	Y					Y	Y						Y		
4. How long have you had it?												Y	Y		
5. How much do you spend on it?	Y						Y	Y		Y			Y		
6. Days lost due to disability in last month?	Y					Y	Y			Y			Y		
4. ADL?						Y							Y		
5. IADL?															
6. Info on disability transfers															
1. Info on total disability transfers	Y			Y		Y	Y	Y	Y	Y				Y	Y
2. Info on transfers by type of disability						Y	Y								

	Albania	Armenia	Armenia	Azerbaijan	Belarus	BiH	Bulgaria		Croatia	Georgia	Hungary	Kazakhstan	Kyrgyz Rep.		Lithuania
Type of survey	LSMS	HBS	DHS	HBS	LSMS	LSMS	HBS	HBS	HBS	HBS	HBS	HBS	LSMS	HBS	HBS
Year of survey	2002	2001–03	2000	2001–02	1998–2002	2001–03	1995 & 2001	2003	1998	1998–2002	1998–2002	2001–03	1998	2000–02	2000
7. Work-related disability															
1. Work part time because of disability/sickness?															
2. How many hours worked?															
3. Did not work at all because of disability/sickness?	Y			Y	Y	Y	Y	Y		Y		Y	Y		Y
4. When did person stop working?						Y									
8. Wealth Proxy															
1. Consumption aggregate															
1.1 Already constructed	Y				Y		Y	Y		Y	Y	Y	Y	Y	
1.2 Needs to be constructed but data available		Y		Y		Y									Y
9. Panel exists?	N	N		N	Y	Y	N	N		Y	N	Y		Y	

	Moldova	Poland	Romania		Russian Fed.			Serbia	Tajikistan	Turkey		Turkmenistan		Ukraine	Uzbekistan
Type of survey	HBS	HBS	LFS	HBS	HBS	LSMS	NOBUS	LSMS	LSMS	HBS	Disability survey	LSMS	DHS	HBS	HBS
Year of survey	1998–2003	1998–2002		1998–2002	1998–2002	1993–2003	2003	2002–03	1999 & 2003	2002	2002	1998	2000	1999–2003	2001
1. Direct question on disability															
1. Do you have a disability?	Y	Y		Y				Y			Y				
2. Do you need any kind of assistance in daily activities?															
3. Type of disability?				Y				Y	Y		Y				
4. Level of disability (I/II/III)?	Y														
5. Since when do you have it?				Y				Y	Y		Y				
6. How much do you spend on it?															
2. Self-evaluated health status															
1. Qualitative question on self-evaluation of health status	Y					Y			Y						Y
2. Respondent identifies socio-economic status as "disabled"			Y												
3. Chronic illness															
1. Do you have chronic illness/disability?	Y			Y		Y		Y	Y		Y	Y	Y	Y	

	Moldova	Poland	Romania		Russian Fed.			Serbia	Tajikistan	Turkey		Turkmenistan		Ukraine	Uzbekistan
Type of survey	HBS	HBS	LFS	HBS	HBS	LSMS	NOBUS	LSMS	LSMS	HBS	Disability survey	LSMS	DHS	HBS	HBS
Year of survey	1998–2003	1998–2002		1998–2002	1998–2002	1993–2003	2003	2002–03	1999 & 2003	2002	2002	1998	2000	1999–2003	2001
2. Type of chronic illness	Y			Y		Y			Y			Y			
3. Does it affect your daily activities?	Y							Y	Y					Y	
4. How long have you had it?									Y						
5. How much do you spend on it?	Y							Y	Y			Y			
6. Days lost due to disability in last month?	Y											Y			
4. ADL?						Y						Y			
5. IADL?															
6. Info on disability transfers															
1. Info on total disability transfers	Y		Y	Y			Y		Y	Y		Y		Y	Y
2. Info on transfers by type of disability							Y								
7. Work-related disability															
1. Work part time because of disability/sickness?			Y												
2. How many hours worked?			Y												
3. Did not work at all because of disability/sickness?			Y			Y				Y	Y	Y			
4. When did person stop working?			Y												
8. Wealth Proxy															
1. Consumption aggregate															
1.1 Already constructed	Y	Y	Y	Y	Y	Y	Y	Y	Y	Y	Y			Y	
1.2 Needs to be constructed but data available												Y			Y
9. Panel exists?	Y			Y	Y	Y		Y	N	N		N		N	

Appendix II

Basic Information on Time-Use Surveys

Survey period	Estonia April 1999–April 2000	Hungary September 1999–September 2000	Netherlands 2000, weeks 31–45	Romania August–September 2000	United Kingdom June–September 2001
Number of visits	1	4, once every 3 months	3	1	1
Survey instruments					
Household questionnaire	Y	Y		Y	Y
Individual questionnaire	Y	Y	Y	Y	Y
EU individual questionnaire		Y			
Self-completed diaries	Y	Y	Y	Y	Y
Weeklong worksheets	Y			Y	Y
Agricultural diary		Y			
Subjective well-being questionnaire		Y			
Final questionnaire			Y		
Coverage	10+ y.o. individuals	15–84 y.o.	one 12+ ind. per hh	10+ y.o. individuals	8+ y.o.
Sample					
Households	2,581		1,813	7,607	6,414
Individuals	6,234	10,105	1,813	16,949	11,664
Diaries	5,724	43,172		16,285 indiv. * 2 days	19,898
Income variable available					
Incorig (net monthly hh income)	In categories	Prd 2 and 4, categ.	In categories		
Income (total hh income)		Prd 2 and 4, categ.	Y		
Household assets					
PC	Y	Y	Y	Y	Y
Videocamera	Y	Y	Y	Y	
Videorecorder	Y	Y	Y	Y	Y
TV	color	color	all	color and black/white	color
Car	Y	Y	Y	car/light van	car/light van
Motorcycle	Y	Y	Y	Y	Y
Freezer	Y	Y	Y	Y	Y
Dishwasher	Y	Y	Y	n.a.	Y
Microwave	Y	Y	Y	Y	Y
Washing machine	automatic and other	ordinary and automatic	all	automatic and other	Y
CD player		Y		Y	Y
Refrigerator	Y			Y	
Bicycle	Y			Y	

Appendix III

Proxies for Disability and Chronic Conditions Used in the Remaining Chapters

Chapter	Proxies used to capture disability and chronic conditions
Measurement of Disability and Linkages with Welfare, Employment, and Schooling	Official disability classification, self-reported disability status, functional disability assessment, ADL index, IADL index, self-reported chronic illness, self-reported health status
The Impact of Health Shocks on Employment, Earnings, and Household Consumption in Bosnia and Herzegovina	Official disability classification, self-reported disability status, ADL index, self-reported chronic illness, self-reported health status
Health Disabilities and Labor Productivity in the Russian Federation	Official disability classification, self-reported chronic illness, self-reported health status
The Implications of Poor Health Status on Employment in Romania	Self-reported chronic illness, self-reported health status

Notes

1. In 2002, less than 55 percent of working-age adults in Bulgaria, Georgia, Hungary, Moldova, Poland, Romania, Russia, and Tajikistan were involved in wage employment. The only country in the region where wage employment was relatively high (at 70 percent) was Belarus (Yemtsov, Cnobloch, and Mete 2006).
2. Ideally one should go further than simple correlations and aim to single out causal effects, since the design of key policy interventions requires this type of information—examples include productivity loss due to disability (with implications for returns to investments on prevention) and the poverty alleviation impact of disability insurance schemes.
3. For example, the extent to which teachers are trained adequately to teach disabled children in an integrated learning environment.
4. The report documents the earnings gap between disabled and nondisabled individuals, but it does not attempt to distinguish between the lower productivity of disabled individuals versus discrimination against them.
5. The report's findings provide some of the information needed for such work, but they need to be supplemented with costs associated with specific interventions to be useful in a standard cost-benefit framework.
6. The implications of aging for public finances is a major concern for industrialized countries, including questions like whether the health status of the elderly is improving sufficiently compared to life expectancy gains. Jacobzone, Cambois, and Robine (2001) argue that this is the case for OECD countries. The findings may not necessarily apply to ECA countries, however. Many OECD countries increased their public health spending over the last decade and individual health behavior improved for the better during the same period. Neither is necessarily the case for many ECA countries.
7. Occupational structure may have an impact on the prevalence of disabilities: For example Costa (2000) finds that 7 percent of the decline in functional disabilities in the United States from the early 20th century to the early 1990s is due to shifts away from manual labor to white-collar jobs.
8. World Health Organization. "World Report on Disability and Rehabilitation." Concept paper. http://www.who.int/disabilities/publications/dar_world_report_concept_note.pdf (accessed July 24, 2006).
9. OECD: Transforming Disability into Ability. 2003. Paris.
10. One shortcoming of household survey data is the exclusion of the institutionalized population, which can lead to an underestimation of the linkages between being disabled and not participating in the labor force. Even though the numbers of institutionalized disabled are not large enough to have a major influence on the key findings, the analyses focusing on the elderly may be more sensitive to the exclusion of the institutionalized population. For example, in Hungary, 44,000 elderly were institutionalized in 2001—out of roughly 10 million individuals, of which 15 percent are 65 years or older (Daroczi 2005). In Uzbekistan, 34 boarding facilities for the disabled serve around 8,900 individuals: about 1,500 general-disabled adults; 5,600 adults with mental disorders; and 1,800 disabled children (Japan International Cooperation Agency (JICA) and Tahlil 2004). Available evidence suggests the exclusion of institutionalized children in household survey data can be ignored for most purposes: the 2004 Romania Reproductive Health Survey data, for example, inquired about the whereabouts of children who do not live with their mothers and out of 5,275 children, only four were reported to live in special institutions for disabled children (345 children did not reside with their mothers for various reasons).
11. Me and Mbogoni (2001) discuss disability-data availability in developing countries and report a disability prevalence rate of 3 percent. The authors find that generic questions show higher prevalence rates compared to questions based on a checklist, and they argue that social stigma attached to being disabled, as well as interviewer bias, might be contributing to the underreporting of disabilities. Similarly, for 11 developing countries Filmer (2005) reports disability prevalence rates of less than 2 percent and for India, the World Bank (2006) reports a 1.8 percent disability rate based on census data, but argues that the actual figure is likely to be in the neighborhood of 4 to 8 percent. International Labour Organization (ILO) country studies for "Employment of People with Disabilities" cover Ethiopia, Kenya, Mauritius, Sudan, Tanzania, Uganda, Cambodia, Fiji, India, Sri Lanka, and Thailand, listing census question–based disability rates from 0.7 percent in Kenya to 3.36 percent in Mauritius. These studies caution the reader about the likely underestimation of disability rates based on standard census questions.

12. See, for example, Turkey Disability Survey Report (2002) and chapter 2 of this report.
13. Mainly depressive disorders and alcohol abuse.
14. World Health Organization. 2002. "Global Burden of Diseases." http://www.who.int/healthinfo/bodgbd2002revised/en/index.html.
15. U.S. Agency for International Development. 2006. "Non-Communicable Diseases and Injuries in Eastern Europe and Eurasia."
16. World Health Organization. 2002. "Global Burden of Diseases." http://www.who.int/healthinfo/bodgbd2002revised/en/index.html.
17. The 2002 Turkey Disability Survey interviewed 97,433 households. About 2.6 percent of the interviewed individuals were reported to be orthopedically, or mentally disabled, or have disabilities in seeing, hearing, or speaking, and 9.7 percent were reported to have at least one chronic illness. There is a sharp increase in "traditional" disabilities after age 60, with males being more likely to report disability compared to females. On the other hand, the reporting of chronic illnesses is similar to those available for many other countries in the sense that females are more likely to report chronic illness, and the gender gap in reporting chronic illness becomes especially pronounced after age 30. Unfortunately, this survey contains little information on household characteristics and the nondisabled population. As a result, one cannot investigate the linkages between household characteristics (including poverty) and disability using these data.
18. Examples include significant medicine shortages in Romania in 2003; and not being able to afford basic equipment such as wheelchairs, crutches, and prosthetics in Tajikistan (JICA 2002).
19. For example, Kahn (1998) finds that the diabetics significantly increased their labor force participation in the U.S. between 1976 and 1992.
20. The correlation coefficient is -0.03. The countries with relevant data are Bosnia and Herzegovina, Bulgaria, Georgia, Moldova, Poland, and Romania.
21. Disability discrimination laws can have unintended consequences: for example, legislation that requires employers to accommodate disabled workers and outlaw discrimination against the disabled in hiring, firing, and pay in the United States is argued to have a negative influence on the labor force participation and earnings of the disabled individuals (Acemoglu and Angrist 2001; Beegle and Stock 2003) due to accommodation costs and firing and hiring costs arising from the threat of lawsuits. On a related topic, the insider-outsider dilemma is noted for other industrialized countries: A review of employment trends in OECD countries finds that even though legislative approaches to employment promotion differ in many respects (rights based, obligations based, incentives based), all approaches tend to benefit people already in employment much more than those who are out of work and looking for a job (OECD 2003).
22. World Bank (2006) also observes a divergence in the employment rates of the disabled and the nondisabled in India, noting that the employment gap between the disabled and the nondisabled has increased during the last 15 years.
23. Alternative views have been expressed for industrialized countries. For example, one of the proposed reforms for disability programs by OECD (2003) is to recognize the status of disability independent of the work and income situation of individuals.
24. Furthermore, such simple correlations do not rule out the possibility that disabled individuals who are members of nonpoor households to start with are able to find employment.
25. Survey of Health, Aging, and Retirement in Europe (SHARE). April 2005. www.mea.uni-mannheim.de.
26. Where health status requirements are weak for disability benefit eligibility, disability insurance may also serve as an alternative to exit the labor market into early retirement.
27. Organisation for Economic Co-operation and Development. 2003. "Transforming Disability into Ability."
28. International Labour Organization. 2005. "Social Protection Expenditure and Performance Review. Slovak Republic." http://www.ilo.org/public/english/protection/secsoc/downloads/publ/sp_expenditure_slovakie.pdf.
29. United Nations Development Programme. 2001. "Progress for All. Lithuania Country Assessment." http://www.undp.lt/files//ProgressFor%20All.pdf.
30. Alternatively, the generosity of the disability benefits can be reduced while keeping the share of disabled constant.
31. World Bank (2006).
32. Analyzing data from 11 developing countries (with one transition country, Romania), Filmer (2005) also notes that in some countries the school attendance of disabled children is extremely low as compared to the school atten-

dance of nondisabled children, and that when other individual and household characteristics are taken into account, the gap between disabled and nondisabled children widens in most cases.

33. Exposure to humidity and cold weather is also reported more often by the poor, as discussed by chapter 5 in this report.
34. There is a wealth of information on disabled children's special needs, which include perspectives on the training of teachers to maintain high-quality education standards for all. Such sectoral perspectives are beyond the scope of this particular report, however.
35. Data source is the 2005 Uzbekistan Regional Disability Survey.
36. Japan International Cooperation Agency Planning and Evaluation Department. March 2002. "Country Profile on Disability, Republic of Tajikistan."
37. Analyzing the living conditions of the disabled in India, the World Bank (2006) finds that around 45 percent of households with a disabled member report an adult missing work to care for the disabled household member, on average for 2.5 hours. Such a high level of time spent for care is consistent with the trend documented here—namely that the amount of time spent for the care of disabled is disproportionately related to the wealth of a country.
38. In OECD countries, informal care is estimated to account for up to 80 percent of total care (Jacobzone, Cambois, and Robine 2001).
39. Analyzing trends in old-age disability in the United States, Freedman et al. (2004) document consistent declines on the order of 1 to 2.5 percent per year for "difficulty with daily activities" and "help with daily activities." The authors also observe that the proportion of older persons who receive help with bathing has declined at the same time as the proportion who use only equipment (but not personal care) to bathe has increased. The OECD (1998) observes a similar decline in the disability rates of those between the ages of 65 to 80 years, and notes that the economic impact of these trends depends on the institutional arrangements for long-term care and the public costs of formal home care, which differ widely among countries.

PART II

COUNTRY STUDIES

CHAPTER 2

Measurement of Disability and Linkages with Welfare, Employment, and Schooling

The Case of Uzbekistan

Kinnon Scott and Cem Mete*

Introduction

In both developing and developed countries, disability is believed to be a correlate of poverty, with implications for individuals' access to services, educational attainment, labor force participation, and consumption. Indeed, a 1999 review of available evidence describes the poverty-disability linkage as a two-way relationship: disability can lead to greater poverty, but poverty itself makes individuals more at risk of becoming disabled (Elwan 1999). The study also states, however, that there is little systematic research on these issues in developing countries—largely due to the lack of data on populations with disabilities—and that the literature relies heavily on anecdotal evidence and case studies. It is argued that without addressing the disability issue, it will not be possible to reach all of the MDGs; the Education for All initiative[1] will, ultimately, be unsuccessful; and our ability to reduce poverty impeded. However, the limited research available on disability in the context of developing countries prevents a full understanding of the effect of disability on any of these initiatives.

Capturing the incidence of disability is difficult. In part this is due to the heterogeneity of definitions and the concepts that make up disability, ranging from the strictly medical to the broader concepts of functioning (WHO 1980, 2001). And, in part, this is due to the lack of relevant and reliable data on disability. Administrative records are often the only source of data, but these can contain serious biases and do not provide the additional information needed to study the linkages between disability and various aspects of welfare. Traditionally, household sur-

* Kinnon Scott is a senior economist at the Development Research Group of the World Bank. Cem Mete is a senior economist at the Europe and Central Asia region of the World Bank.

veys have not been considered to be good sources of data on disability, not simply because the questions included have been inadequate, but also because disability appeared to be a relatively rare event, not amenable to being captured in the small sample sizes of many household surveys. Data from 35 developing countries in the early 1990s from censuses or surveys that attempted to measure disability show only two developing countries with incidence rates above 5 percent, and the vast majority with rates below 2 percent (United Nations 2005).[2] The WHO, however, estimates that underreporting of disability is high and that the rate of disability in most developing countries is around 10 percent (WHO 1980). Recent efforts to improve the way in which questions on disability are asked have shown that the rates are higher than previously imagined. Uganda substantially revised its 1991 disability question for the 2001 census: The incidence rate went from around 5 percent among the oldest age group to more than 20 percent (Martinho and Banda 2005). A 2005 Nicaraguan survey specifically developed to measure disability gives an incidence rate of 11 percent (INEC 2003), while a comparable survey in Ecuador and the census in Brazil give rates of 12.1 percent and 14.5 percent, respectively (Flores et al. 2005 and Bercovich 2004). Similarly, a 2005 Uzbekistan survey reveals the sizable variations between the official disability rate and survey-based disability indicators, which are described in detail in the next section (figure 1). In particular, figure 1 shows that compared to other disability indicators, the official disability rate does not vary much by age.

While disability itself is difficult to measure, it is even harder to capture the link between welfare and disability. To do so requires not just accurate data on the incidence of disabilities, but also data on a range of key characteristics of individuals and their households. In many developing countries, the only data on disabilities come from administrative records, which can be affected by benefit levels and other program characteristics unrelated to actual disability. And these data do not provide additional information on the characteristics of those individuals and households affected by disability, which is needed to determine the connections that might exist between poverty and disability. Household-level data exist in too few cases.

To shed light on the poverty-disability nexus, as well as the measurement issues, disability questions were added to one round of a panel survey in Uzbekistan that also measures welfare. The data allow us to distinguish among the effects of various measurement issues on the incidence estimates obtained, as well as to link the incidence of disability with monetary measures of welfare, human capital indicators, and participation in the labor force. The paper is organized in the following way. Section I contains discussion of issues surrounding the measurement of disability, the Uzbekistan context, and the data set. Section II presents findings on the relationships among the various disability measures. In Section III, a first assessment of the relationship of disability and a variety of welfare and participation measures is carried out. The paper ends with some conclusions and recommendations for future work on investigating poverty-disability links.

I Measuring Disability

Measurement Issues

In an attempt to address the measurement issues associated with disability, the United Nations formed the Washington Group on Disability Statistics in 1999. The Washington Group has been charged with developing a short set of questions for inclusion in national censuses and an extended set of questions for inclusion in national household surveys that will provide robust and cross-country comparable data on the incidence of disability. For both sets of questions, the Washington Group is focusing on three purposes for the data collection: (i) equalization of opportunities, (ii) monitoring of trends in physical functioning or participation

FIGURE 1

Incidence of Disability Using Various Definitions in Uzbekistan

(by age group)

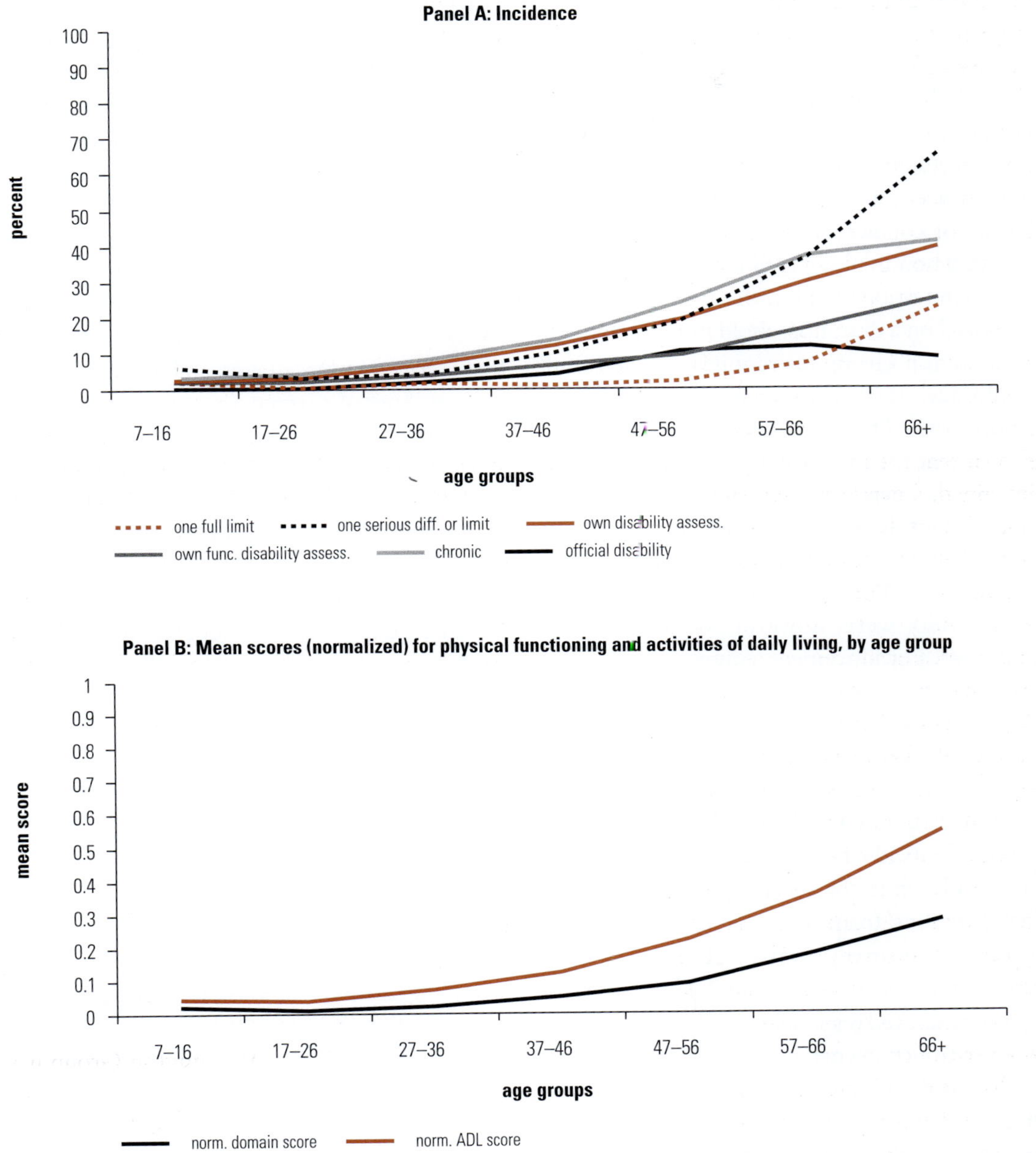

Sources: Uzbekistan Regional Panel Survey, Waves 1, 2, and 3. Authors' calculations.

of the population, and (iii) provision of services (Altman, Cambois, and Robine 2005).[3] For the censuses, a set of six questions has been developed and cognitive testing and field testing is under way in approximately 15 countries. For the household surveys, it is proposed to develop four "extended sets" of questions, one for each of the purposes listed above, and one to address the environmental context. Testing of the extended sets will also be carried out.

Following the lead of the Washington Group, our focus in this work is on functioning, not "disability," per se. What this means in real terms is that it is perfectly possible for two individuals with the exact same physical conditions to have different levels of functioning or "disability." The simplest example of this relates to vision. A person with limited vision could have limited functioning or "disability." Yet if that person was given a pair of appropriate eyeglasses or contact lenses, he or she might have no limitation in physical functioning.[4]

The questions used in the Uzbekistan work are based on a draft household module from the Washington Group for monitoring the trends in physical functioning or participation of the population.[5] The questions refer to six areas of functioning: vision, hearing, movement, learning, communication, and self-care. For hearing, vision, and learning, a filter question was applied, so the incidence is measured with only one question. Persons who indicated some level of disability were, however, asked follow-up questions. For movement, communication, and self-care, filter questions—while asked—were not actually used as filter questions: all individuals were asked two to four questions for each domain. However, for comparability across the six domains, only the filter question is used to determine incidence.

In addition to the specific physical functioning questions from Wave 3, in the previous waves of the survey, individuals were asked if they had "any sign of disability." This very open question allowed respondents to list any physical or cognitive problems they had that were linked to disability. An additional indicator was constructed from this question by using this self-reported health data to assess whether the individual has a limitation of some sort in a domain of physical functioning. Individuals were also asked about chronic ailments and whether they were officially considered disabled. Finally, individuals were asked six questions on Activities of Daily Living (ADL), and a normalized score ranging from 0 to 1 was constructed. The various indicators are listed in table 1; the actual questions are listed in annex 1.

Official Disability Status

Uzbekistan has several laws that cover the definition of disability and the rights of those with disabilities.[6] The laws define three types of official disability categories. Individuals who have lost their ability to work and depend on the care of others fall into category 1, while those who have lost their ability to work but do not depend on others to care for them are classified as category 2. The third category is for those who have partially lost their ability to work. The benefits that accrue vary by category and include disability pensions (of varying amounts), as well as a series of other benefits.

In 2003, 817,000 persons were officially considered disabled in the country, or 3.2 percent of the population. This represented a substantial increase from the 1996 rate of 2.4 percent (State Department of Statistics as cited in Japan International Cooperation Agency [JICA] and Tahlil 2004). A variety of reasons can be posited to

TABLE 1
Indicators of Physical Functioning

Indicator
Specific physical functioning
Seeing (with glasses if uses them)
Hearing (with hearing aid if uses one)
Movement (walking up stairs, walking a kilometer)
Learning (memorizing, focusing attention)
Self-care (dressing, washing, feeding, being alone)
Communicating (understanding, being understood)
Physical functioning index (normalized)
Have official disability status
Self-describe as having some level of disability
Self-describe as having physical functioning limitation
Have chronic illness
Activity of Daily Living
Vigorous activity (lifting heavy objects, running)
Moderate activity (moving a chair, carrying groceries)
Walking uphill
Walking 100 meters
Bending, lifting, or stooping
Self-care (eating, dressing, bathing, using the toilet)
ADL Index (normalized)

explain this dramatic increase, separate from a real rise in impaired physical functioning. First, part of the rise may be attributable to the fact that disease, rather than physical functioning, plays such a large role in the definition of disability in Uzbekistan. Tuberculosis, which is a cause for disability status in Uzbekistan, has been on the rise in recent years as the health system has not been able to maintain itself in the face of declining income and revenues.

Increased numbers of persons who have been granted official disability status may also be linked to incentives to obtain the benefit. It is not clear if this is the case in Uzbekistan. While there is some evidence that disability pensions were better protected than other pensions and social assistance programs in the second half of the 1990s (JICA and Tahlil 2004), from 2001 to 2005, monthly disability pensions as a percentage of average monthly wages decreased from 60 percent to 40 percent (World Bank 2006).

An alternative hypothesis explaining the increase in disability in recent years is that the population (or denominator of the ratio) is not measured with any precision. The last census was conducted prior to independence, and, even in nontransition countries, population projections this far out from the original measurement are very noisy. In a transition economy with post-independence migration flows, there is certainly the likelihood that any proportion that has the national population in the denominator diverges from the true proportion.

In short, various factors affect the official measure of disability—factors that are not always strictly correlated with objective measures of limitations of physical functioning. Household-level data may help to confirm or contradict the official statistics and lead to a greater understanding of the links between disability and other factors.

The Data

The Uzbekistan Regional Panel Survey (URPS) is a Living Standards Measurement Study survey designed to allow measurement of welfare levels and assess the factors that affect welfare. It is carried out in three regions (*oblasts*) of Uzbekistan: Tashkent, Andijan, and Kashkadarya. As a panel survey, the URPS follows individuals over time to look at changes in welfare status, economic activities, and coping mechanisms of the individuals and their households. The first wave of the survey was carried out in March 2005 (pre-planting) and the second in October–November of the same year (post-harvest). A third wave was conducted in December 2005.

The specific purpose of the third wave of the URPS was to shed light on issues of disability measurement in Uzbekistan. The data make it possible to quantify and characterize the levels of disability in the three *oblasts*. The data also provide an opportunity to investigate the linkages between disability and welfare levels, labor force participation, and educational attainment. The sample of the URPS-III was doubled (compared to the first two waves) because, even though the WHO estimates 10 percent of the population is disabled, it was thought that an over-sample would be useful in case disability turned out to be such a rare event that the URPS I and II sample sizes would not be large enough. The over-sample only creates a cross-sectional data set: for anything beyond a very minimal description of the linkages between disability and other welfare characteristics, the panel data is needed.

The panel was constructed by following individuals, not just households. Wave 1 of the URPS was administered to 3,000 households, equally divided among the three *oblasts*. If, at the time of the Wave 2 interview, a person had left the household he or she was in at the time of Wave 1, that person was followed to his or her new residence and interviewed, along with all the other members in this new household. Individuals who emigrated or who moved to remote regions in the northwest of the country could not, however, be followed. The rules were different for Wave 3, given that the data collection was almost immediately after the Wave 2 interviews and the focus was only on collecting disability data. For Wave 3, only those individuals still residing in the same place as in Wave 2 were interviewed for the panel.[7] The number of persons for whom complete data exist for all three rounds (including constructed welfare measures) is 12,387. This represents 80 percent of the potential pool of respondents.

Given the concern that the sample size could be too small for some of the analysis, an additional sample of 3,000 households was created and interviewed. The full Wave 3 sample of 6,170 households and 32,337 individuals is only used here to look at overall incidence rates for the physical functioning variables. It should be noted that while the panel sample is representative of the three included *oblasts*, neither it nor the additional Wave 3 sample is representative of the population of the country: results can only be extrapolated to the three *oblasts* under discussion here.

Table 2 provides summary statistics of the sampled individuals used in the analysis. The first pair of columns shows the data for persons ages 7 and older, while the second pair shows data only for heads of households. The first column of each pair refers to the full sample; the second to the panel sample. As would be expected, there are negligible differences between the two samples.

Measures of Physical Functioning, Disability, and Health

The first key question to be answered by this data is the extent to which different measures of disability lead to different incidence levels. From the Wave 3 data, several variables that are hypothesized to measure physical functioning and disability are constructed and investigated here. First, for each domain of functioning, the respondent was asked to rate the level of difficulty he or she has, on a scale of 1 (no difficulty) to 4 (unable or completely limited). The six filter questions are used here that pertain to each of the domains of functioning: vision, hearing, movement, learning, communication, and self-care. The questions were recoded so that 0 indicates no problem at all, while 3 indicates the person is unable to perform the activity in question. Second, an index or score was also constructed that simply sums the score of the six components. This score is normalized to range from a value of 0, indicating that the person has no difficulty on any component of functioning, to a 1, indicating that the person is completely limited across the six domains of functioning.

A person with a full limitation in any area of physical functioning is someone who cannot do the activity in question. In other words, cannot see (is blind), cannot communicate at all, cannot wash him- or herself. Variables are constructed to identify individuals with a full limitation in any of the six areas. A slightly broader definition of disability is captured by including individuals with severe difficulties, rather than complete limitations. We also look at the number of domains for which a person is fully limited, along with the number for which the person has at least a serious difficulty in performing the activities. Individuals also provided information on whether they had official disability status. Finally, there is the self-reported variable that examines whether a person has an illness or ailment linked to a disability, as well as information on chronic illnesses.

Children under the age of 7 are excluded from the analysis. Clearly, babies would appear quite disabled using the measures included here. Ideally, one would have liked to ask about small children's development with a different set of questions or in relation to "average" or "normal" development. As this could not be done, we have excluded children under the age of 7 from the analysis. The age cutoff is partly driven by the fact that the list of physical activities under the domains of physical functioning should be within the abilities of the average 7 year old. Second, the data seem to indicate this pattern, although it might have suggested a year or two older for the cutoff point. However, because an area of interest for this paper is the

TABLE 2

Characteristics of the Panel and Full Samples

(means and standard deviations)

Variable	Panel		Full Sample	
	All	Hhld Head	All	Hhld Head
Seven and older				
Years of age	31.5	51.0	31.5	50.7
	(18.6)	(14.3)	(18.5)	(14.6)
Female	0.5171	0.2732	0.5183	0.2757
	(0.4997)	(0.4457)	(0.4997)	(0.4469)
In school 2004–05	0.3121	0.0074	—	—
	(0.4634)	(0.0859)	—	—
In school 2005–06	0.2950	0.0051	0.2994	0.0088
	(0.4560)	(0.0714)	(0.4580)	(0.0933)
In school either year	0.3336	0.0074	—	—
	(0.4715)	(0.0859)	—	—
Per Capita Consumption, soum	458,166	560,712	—	—
	(406,004)	(540,525)	—	—
Working age				
Economically active, Wave 1	0.6555	0.8488	—	—
	(0.4752)	(0.3584)	—	—
Economically active, Wave 3	0.6448	0.8154	0.6215	0.7984
	(0.4786)	(0.3881)	(0.4850)	(0.4012)
Economically active either wave	0.7619	0.9059	—	—
	(0.4260)	(0.2920)	—	—
Employed, Wave 1	0.6209	0.8172	—	—
	(0.4852)	(0.3866)	—	—
Employed, Wave 3	0.5610	0.7453	0.5391	0.7400
	(0.4963)	(0.4358)	(0.4985)	(0.4387)
Employed either wave	0.8277	0.9326	—	—
	(0.3777)	(0.2509)	—	—
Unemployed, Wave 1	0.0346	0.0316	—	—
	(0.1829)	(0.1749)	—	—
Unemployed, Wave 3	0.0838	0.0701	0.0824	0.0585
	(0.2771)	(0.2554)	(0.2750)	(0.2347)
Unemployed, either wave	0.1094	0.0925	—	—
	(0.3121)	(0.2898)	—	—

Sources: URPS, Waves 1 and 3; authors' calculations

Note: Includes individuals ages 7 and over. Labor force figures only for persons aged 16–55 (female) and 16–60 (male). Economically active refers to ILO's definition for a person being active, which includes persons working or actively looking for work (unemployed).

link between functioning and schooling, it was considered important to include all children of primary school age in the sample.

II Incidence of Limited Physical Functioning and Health

Incidence rates of limitations in the various domains of physical functioning are presented in table 3. Communication is the domain with the smallest percentage of the population having any type of difficulty (holding a conversation, understanding and making oneself understood), with only 5.5 percent of individuals affected in some way, and less than a half of a percent unable to communicate at all. Hearing difficulties are the second least common type of difficulty, with 7.3 percent of the population reporting some type of hearing problem. Less than one-third of a percent report total deafness. Movement and learning are the most commonly reported areas where problems exist: 18.8 percent of the population reports some restriction in their ability to walk a kilometer, and 16.3 percent report a learning difficulty of some sort. Full limitations in learning affect less than one-third of a percent of the population, however. In contrast, almost 2 percent of the population reports an inability to walk 1 kilometer.

With the exception of communication, men have a lower incidence of physical functioning limitations. Women are slightly more likely to have full limitations than men, but the differences are very small in most areas. The contrast between the lowest and highest consumption quintiles is more complex. For three indicators—vision, movement, and learning—the richest quintile reports substantially more problems (22.8 percent of the top quintile suffers from vision problems of some degree, while only 8.7 percent of those in the lowest quintile report any problems). Yet, the lowest quintile reports more individuals with full limitations in two of these three areas. They also report more full limitations in two of the other three areas—hearing, communication, and self-care. We will return to this apparent contradiction below. In terms of demonstrating a link between poverty and disability, the simple tabulations provide, at best, only weak evidence of such a link.[8] One must also keep in mind that the overall inci-

TABLE 3

Incidence of No and Full Limitations by Domain of Physical Functioning

Variable	All	Female	Male	Quintile 1	Quintile 5
No problems with:					
Vision	0.8556	0.8351	0.8774	0.9137	0.7718
	(0.3516)	(0.3712)	(0.3280)	(0.2809)	(0.4198)
Hearing	0.9265	0.9176	0.9359	0.9358	0.9038
	(0.2610)	(0.2750)	(0.2449)	(0.2452)	(0.2949)
Movement (walk)	0.8122	0.7743	0.8525	0.8673	07593
	(0.3906)	(0.4181)	(0.3547)	(0.3393)	(0.4276)
Learning	0.8366	0.8085	0.8666	0.8741	0.7895
	(0.3697)	(0.3936)	(0.3400)	(0.3318)	(0.4078)
Communication	0.9449	0.9448	0.9450	0.9475	0.9514
	(0.2282)	(0.2283)	(0.2281)	(0.2230)	(0.2150)
Self-care (washing)	0.9174	0.9032	0.9326	0.9129	0.9229
	(0.2752)	(0.2957)	(0.2508)	(0.2820)	(0.2668)
Full limitations with:					
Vision	0.0030	0.0033	0.0028	0.0028	0.0012
	(0.0551)	(0.0572)	(0.0528)	(0.0530)	(0.0343)
Hearing	0.0030	0.0030	0.0031	0.0034	0.0049
	(0.0549)	(0.0547)	(0.0552)	(0.0530)	(0.0702)
Movement (walk)	0.0194	0.0256	0.0129	0.0172	0.0243
	(0.1379)	(0.1578)	(0.1127)	(0.1301)	(0.1539)
Learning	0.0042	0.0040	0.0043	0.0057	0.0034
	(0.0644)	(0.0632)	(0.0658)	(0.0751)	(0.0583)
Communication	0.0045	0.0055	0.0033	0.0064	0.0016
	(0.0666)	(0.0739)	(0.0577)	(0.0796)	(0.0402)
Self-care (washing)	0.0145	0.0175	0.0112	0.0175	0.0065
	(0.1194)	(0.1311)	(0.1054)	(0.1311)	(0.0804)

Sources: URPS Waves 1 and 3; authors' calculations.

Note: Movement refers to the ability to walk 1 kilometer, learning is the ability to memorize and focus attention, communication entails understanding and carrying on a conversation and making oneself understood. Includes persons 7 years of age and older. Standard deviations in parentheses.

dence of full limitations is low, and some caution is needed in interpreting these results.

The measures of functioning by domain are all positively correlated with one another (table 4). *A priori*, there is no need to expect high levels of correlation: an illness that leads to the inability to see might have no effect on the person's ability to walk a kilometer, and an accident that might limit a person's ability to walk could well have no impact on his or her ability to communicate. On the other hand, indicators of various functioning limitations can be highly correlated if the incidences of these limitations are driven by common factors such as aging, poverty, poor health care infrastructure, or unfavorable environmental conditions.

The data provide some support for this explanation: in fact, age alone is a strong driver of the observed correlation. If all persons over age 54 (the retirement age for women) are omitted from the sample, the correlation of age with the domains of functioning drops substantially—actually becoming insignificantly correlated to communication and, somewhat surprisingly, negatively correlated with limitations in the ability to wash oneself.[9] However, per-capita consumption is only negatively correlated with two of the six domains of functioning. No information is available on health care infrastructure or environmental factors.

The official statistics (as reported by individuals) on disability are correlated with the various measures of physical functioning, but the relationship is not completely straightforward. Of course, there is no *a priori* cutoff point that exists for the physical functioning variables to determine if a person should be classified as having disabilities. Here we compare official status with several cutoff points or indicators constructed from the data set.

TABLE 4

Correlation of Scores for Domains of Physical Functioning

	Vision	Hearing	Movement	Learning	Communication	Self-Care	Age
Seven and older							
Vision	1.0000						
Hearing	0.4020*	1.0000					
Movement (walk)	0.4985*	0.4388*	1.0000				
Learning	0.4546*	0.4214*	0.5297*	1.0000			
Communication	0.2003*	0.3171*	0.3141*	0.3986*	1.0000		
Self-care (washing)	0.2757*	0.2785*	0.5032*	0.3914*	0.4111*	1.0000	
Age	0.4788*	0.3829*	0.5522*	0.4130*	0.1429*	0.2238*	1.0000
Consumption, pc	0.0912*	0.0428*	0.0670*	0.0625*	−0.0111	−0.0239	0.1127*
Age (7–55)	0.3147*	0.1405*	0.3035*	0.2175*	0.0017	−0.0810*	1.0000
Heads of Household							
Vision	1.0000						
Hearing	0.3842*	1.0000					
Movement (walk)	0.4781*	0.4263*	1.0000				
Learning	0.4857*	0.4377*	0.5224*	1.0000			
Communication	0.2925*	0.3556*	0.3360*	0.3530*	1.0000		
Self-care (washing)	0.3326*	0.3677*	0.5716*	0.4068*	0.4080*	1.0000	
Age	0.4284*	0.4181*	0.5541*	0.4205*	0.2374*	0.4328*	1.0000
Consumption, pc	0.0426	0.0245	0.0185	0.0380	−0.0344	−0.0498	−0.0568*
Age (7–55)	0.2382*	0.1053*	0.2635*	0.1450*	0.0744*	0.1757*	1.0000

Sources: URPS Waves1 and 3; authors' calculations.

Note: Movement refers to the ability to walk 1 kilometer, learning is the ability to memorize and focus attention, communication entails understanding and carrying on a conversation and making oneself understood. Includes persons 7 years of age and older. Age (7–55) shows the correlation of the age variable to the six domains of functioning if the sample is restricted to persons 7 through 55.

* Significant at the .01 level.

Of the population age 7 and older, 3.8 percent claim to have formal, official disability status (and are eligible to receive or actually receive benefits). This is very close to the official rate of 3.2 in 2003 if the upward trend noted in official statistics continued to 2005. And it is close to the percentage of the panel sample that has at least one full limitation in any of the six areas of functioning: 3.2 percent. However, almost 12 percent of all individuals age 7 and older have at least one serious difficulty or a full limitation. For all individuals over 7 years of age, just under a quarter of all those with official disability status indicate having a full limitation in one or more domains of physical functioning. Clearly other factors affect official disability status. This is investigated more fully below.

There is some disparity between official disability status and physical functioning between males and females. As shown in tables 3 and 5, females are less likely to have no problems at all, and more likely to have full limitations and serious difficulties than men. Yet 4.5 percent of males who are age 7 and older report having official disability status, while only 3.3 percent of women do. This is despite the fact that 3.7 percent of women report having a full limitation, compared to only 2.7 percent of men. It is not clear what this finding reflects. It may be that the limitations that men suffer are more related to their ability to work and, because the ability to work is an important part of the official disability definition, this may result in the greater percentage of men receiving official disability status. On the other hand, the finding may reflect a greater ability of men to obtain disability status or there being a greater benefit to men derived from obtaining disability status.

The differences between those in the bottom and top quintiles of the consumption distribution provide an inconsistent picture of poverty and disability linkages, although welfare status does seem to be linked to official disability status. Of those in the bottom quintile, only 3.2 percent have official disability status, compared to 5.1 percent in the top quintile. Yet the poorer quintile has a similar or slightly higher incidence of full limitations than the top quintile. The population in the top quintile, however, appears to suffer more from partial limitations.

TABLE 5

Disability and Physical Functioning

(means and standard deviations)

Variable	All	Female	Male	Quintile 1	Quintile 5
Official disability	0.0383	0.0326	0.0445	0.0321	0.0507
	(0.1920)	(0.1776)	(0.2061)	(0.1763)	(0.2194)
No full limitations	0.6811	0.6476	0.7167	0.7367	0.5921
	(0.4661)	(0.4778)	(0.4507)	(0.4405)	(0.4916)
One full limitation	0.0323	0.0370	0.0274	0.0348	0.0305
	(0.1769)	(0.1887)	(0.1633)	(0.1834)	(0.1720)
One serious difficulty or	0.1177	0.1381	0.0959	0.1069	0.1294
full limitation	(0.3222)	(0.3450)	(0.2945)	(0.3091)	(0.3358)
Number of full limitations	0.0486	0.0588	0.0376	0.0530	0.0419
	(0.3066)	(0.3461)	(0.2576)	(0.3156)	(0.2659)
Number of serious difficulties	0.2053	0.2399	0.1684	0.1898	0.2235
or full limitations	(0.6858)	(0.7357)	(0.6260)	(0.6644)	(0.7089)
Normalized domain score	0.0526	0.0609	0.0437	0.0433	0.0657
	(0.1095)	(0.1177)	(0.0992)	(0.1048)	(0.1141)

Sources: URPS Waves 1 and 3; authors' calculations.

Note: Normalized domain score ranges from 0 (no difficulty in any domain) to 1 ('unable' in all six domains). Includes persons age 7 and older only.

One factor that could be confounding the analysis is biases found in self-reported health data. There is evidence that individuals' self-ranking of their health status is affected by their own socioeconomic characteristics (Lindeboom and van Doorslaer 2004; Van Doorslaer and Gerdthan 2003; Schultz and Tansel 2002) or may be used to justify inclusion in specific programs or receipt of benefits (Kerkhofs and Lindeboom 1995). What is often found is that the rich report a greater incidence of disease and ill health than poorer groups. Regarding physical functioning questions, it may well be that having a "full limitation"—being blind, being unable to walk a kilometer—is closest to an objective measure of health and is least affected by self-reported health biases, while "partial" or "serious difficulties" are more subjective and thus, more prone to self-reporting biases. If this is the case, the fact that the top quintile suffers more from partial limitations than the poor may be a result of the measurement tool and not a true reflection of disability.

In addition to the six domains of physical functioning, the survey allows the calculation of a series of alternative measures of disability. Table 6 shows incidence rates using these other measures. The other measures—chronic illness, the two self-assessed disability measures, and the ADL measures—all show much higher incidence of disability or physical limitation than the official disability status. Interestingly, these other measures are all higher among the richest group than the poorest one. It may be because these indicators are more subjective than the physical functioning questions.

The various measures of disability are highly correlated, as would be hoped (see table 7). However, having one complete limitation in any of the six physical functioning domains has the lowest correlation with official disability status. In other words, official disability status appears to reflect something other than full limitations in physical functioning. The alternative measure with the highest correlation to official disability status is an individual's own assessment of having a disability. On the surface, this is not surprising as the two should be strongly linked: a person with official disability status would be more likely to respond positively to a question about having signs of a disability. Yet the range of "disabilities" reported by respondents is so broad—from paralysis and blindness to having had a hernia or a hysterectomy to allergies and

TABLE 6

Alternative Measures of Disability and Physical Functioning

(means and standard deviations)

Variable	All	Female	Male	Quintile 1	Quintile 5
Official disability status	0.0383	0.0326	0.0445	0.0321	0.0507
	(0.1920)	(0.1776)	(0.2061)	(0.1763)	(0.2194)
Chronic illness	0.1189	0.1278	0.1093	0.0686	0.2114
	(0.3236)	(0.3339)	(0.3120)	(0.2528)	(0.4094)
Own disability assessment (w2)	0.1031	0.1032	0.1029	0.0715	0.1453
	(0.3040)	(0.3043)	(0.3038)	(0.2577)	(0.3525)
Own functional disability assessment (w2)	0.0577	0.0552	0.0604	0.0495	0.0609
	(0.2332)	(0.2284)	(0.2382)	(0.2169)	(0.2393)
Normalized ADL score, w1	0.1218	0.1436	0.0981	0.1059	0.1539
	(0.2856)	(0.3057)	(0.2600)	(0.2757)	(0.3057)
Normalized ADL score, w2	0.1054	0.1192	0.0905	0.0767	0.1636
	(0.2737)	(0.2874)	(0.2573)	(0.2462)	(0.3210)

Sources: URPS Waves 1, 2, and 3; authors' calculations.

Note: Includes only persons ages 7 and older. W1 and w2 refer to wave 1 and wave 2, respectively.

TABLE 7

Correlations of Alternative Measures of Disability to Official Disability Status

Variable	All	Female	Male	Quintile 1	Quintile 5
No full limitations	−0.2548*	−0.2167*	−0.3007*	−0.2623*	−0.2278*
One full limitation	0.2249*	0.1925*	0.2664*	0.3407*	0.2086*
One serious difficulty or full limitation	0.3364*	0.2709*	0.4211*	0.3741*	0.3157*
Number of limitations	0.2378*	0.2213*	0.2741*	0.3761*	0.1818*
Number of serious difficulties or full limitations	0.3277*	0.2556*	0.4187*	0.4053*	0.3126*
Normalized domain score	0.3306*	0.2665*	0.4169*	0.3602*	0.3167*
Chronic illness	0.3838*	0.3353*	0.4387*	0.4133*	0.3652*
Own disability assessment (w2)	0.4858*	0.4623*	0.5108*	0.4637*	0.5096*
Own functional disability assessment (w2)	0.3684*	0.3394*	0.3951*	0.3940*	0.3125*
Normalized ADL score, w1	0.2781*	0.2037*	0.3759*	0.2883*	0.2869*
Normalized ADL score, w2	0.3048*	0.2605*	0.3605*	0.3299*	0.3060*

Sources: URPS Waves 1, 2, and 3; authors' calculations.

*Significant at the .01 level.

asthma—that it is hard to square it with a single coherent definition of disability.

There are many reasons why official disability status does not match limitations in the six domains of physical functioning. In the first place, as discussed above, the definition of disability in Uzbekistan is not based on physical functioning, per se, but on the actual limitation on the ability to work. Second, the definition includes those with chronic diseases: having a chronic disease is positively correlated with official disability status (.3838, significant at the .01 level), but even including the presence of chronic diseases does not eliminate the lack of overlap between official and survey measures. The third reason for the discrepancy may be that the survey data are self-reported and may well differ from a medical opinion. Finally, there may be incentives built into the benefit program for disability that affect who receives official status.

These descriptive statistics reveal other trends as well: for example, the correlation coefficients for females are always smaller than the correlation coefficients for males.[10] This finding suggests that for females, official disability status is driven not so much by functioning limitations but by other factors. (Perhaps limitations in female decision making regarding their own affairs, including health, may lead to such discrepancies).[11]

To display the determinants of official disability status in a more comprehensive manner, we regress disability status first on the main indicators of physical functioning: the normalized domain score, whether a person has at least one domain where he or she experiences serious difficulty or full limitation, his or her own disability assessment, self-reported chronic illness, and the normalized score of the ADL. We then add in characteristics of the individual that might affect official disability status, primarily those that might also be related to working, as the classification system in the country is highly focused on one's ability to work, along with location variables to take into account differences in the distance to the capital and other administrative characteristics that may affect receipt of disability status and household welfare levels. The best health-related predictors of official disability are: (i) having a serious difficulty in one area of the six physical functioning domains, (ii) one's own assessment of disabling illnesses or injuries, and (iii) the limitations in

TABLE 8

Probability of Having Official Disability Status

(marginal effects and [standard errors])

Variables	Alternative specifications (1)	(2)	(3)
Normalized domain score	−0.001	0.013	0.016
	[0.009]	[0.007]*	[0.006]**
Chronic	0.007	0.005	0.005
	[0.004]*	[0.003]*	[0.003]**
One serious difficulty or full limitation	0.032	0.028	0.025
	[0.010]***	[0.009]***	[0.008]***
Own disability assessment (w2)	0.134	0.106	0.112
	[0.023]***	[0.021]***	[0.022]***
Own functional disability assessment (w2)	−0.002	−0.002	−0.002
	[0.002]	[0.001]	[0.001]**
Normalized score of Activities of Daily Living	0.011	0.009	0.008
	[0.003]***	[0.002]***	[0.002]***
Working age		0.010	0.009
		[0.002]***	[0.001]***
Head of household		0.000	−0.000
		[0.001]	[0.001]
Female		−0.006	−0.005
		[0.002]***	[0.001]***
Resides in Kashkadarya *Oblast*			−0.001
			[0.001]
Resides in Andijan *Oblast*			0.008
			[0.003]***
Per-capita consumption			0.0000017
			[0.0000022]
Observations	11,091	11,091	11,091

Sources: URPS Waves 1, 2, and 3; authors' calculations.

Note: Dependent variable equal to 1 if individual has official disability status. Calculations include only persons 7 years of age or older.
* Significant at 10%; ** significant at 5%; *** significant at 1%, standard errors in brackets.

the ADL. Chronic illness and a score that captures all problems in the six domains of functioning are not good predictors. Additionally, being of working age increases the probability of having official disability status. However, being female lowers that likelihood: Although the effect is small, it is statistically significant. Finally, living in Andijan, rather than Tashkent, increases the probability of having official disability status. This statistically significant regional effect may reflect differences in the implementation of central policies at the local level. Interestingly, the wealth proxy, per-capita consumption, does not have a statistically significant influence on the probability of receiving this status (after taking into account functional and other disability assessments). Thus, our data do not provide support for the hypotheses that the poor are disadvantaged during the process that leads to the granting of official disability status either because the wealthy can afford to "purchase" disability status through informal payments and bribes; or because the poor may have less access to the commissions that carry out the required medical examinations.

The results of this survey have demonstrated that, indeed, different definitions of disability provide different incidence rates and, more important, they identify different people as having a disability. A straight physical functioning definition, whereby a person is considered to have a disability if he or she has serious difficulty in one domain or is unable to carry out the activity included in the domain, indicates almost 12 percent of the population age 7 and above has a disability. If the definition of disability is restricted to individuals who have a full limitation in one of the six domains (blindness, inability to communicate, etc.), the incidence of disability is 3.2 percent. Official disability status, however, is held by 3.8 percent of the population.

It is not just that the different measures give different rates of disability; they also identify different individuals as suffering from disabilities. The question then is whether this shifting definition affects our understanding of the links between disability and human capital formation, labor force participation, and poverty. In the next section we provide some preliminary insights on this issue by looking at the relationships between the different measures of disability and individual characteristics.

III To What Extent are Disabled Individuals Poor, Less Educated, and Out of the Labor Force?

Poverty may expose individuals to greater risks of becoming disabled as the poor may lack adequate health care, be forced to live in unsafe housing and environments, or work in dangerous jobs. On the other hand, disability can lead to lower levels of well being if individuals are unable to participate in society in the same way a person without disabilities can. This is the concept of functional limitations. If an individual cannot attend school, his or her opportunities for future earnings are limited, and without adequate personal and physical devices, an individual might be unable to participate in the labor market. It is not only the person with disabilities who is affected. Other household members may have to restrict their own economic activities to care for or provide personal services to a household member with disabilities. Untangling the causal links between disability and welfare is a complex task, and the data available for Uzbekistan are not adequate for this purpose. However, they can provide insights on the extent to which welfare levels and disability are linked, and the extent to which educational and labor force participation are related to functional limitations, disabilities, and poor health.

Welfare

The first step is to determine whether there is any link between welfare and disability. Welfare here is measured by the log of per-capita household consumption. Household consumption is a measure that incorporates not simply household expenditures, but also the value of home production and the use value of durables and housing. (See Deaton and Zaidi 2002 for the conceptual foundations of this measure.) We regress log per-capita consumption on individual and household characteristics to determine the impact of individual disability on poverty. The results are shown in table 9.

Holding all else constant, having a serious limitation or full limitation has a statistically significant negative effect on consumption, resulting in a 4.8 percent decline after other factors are taken into account. While the estimated coefficients for other disability indicators have the expected sign, none are statistically significant. The lack of a statistically significant official disability status effect on consumption may in part be because disability benefits (from the social security system) help to offset the loss of income or costs associated with having disabilities. Another interpretation, however, may be that older people with limited functioning do not view their condition as "disability," but instead see it as simply part of the aging process. These individuals are thus less likely to seek disability status and, given the definitional link between disability status and employment, might be less likely to obtain it if they did seek it. And the aging process, or having multiple

TABLE 9

Consumption and Disability: Log of per Capita Consumption Is the Dependent Variable, OLS Coefficients, and Standard Errors

(in brackets)

Variables	Alternative Specifications					
	(1)	(2)	(3)	(4)	(5)	(6)
Years of age	0.001*	0.001*	0.001*	0.001**	0.001*	0.001**
	[0.000]	[0.000]	[0.000]	[0.000]	[0.000]	[0.000]
Female	0.004	0.004	0.004	0.005	0.004	0.005
	[0.012]	[0.012]	[0.012]	[0.012]	[0.012]	[0.012]
Household size	−0.049***	−0.049***	−0.049***	−0.049***	−0.049***	−0.049***
	[0.003]	[0.003]	[0.003]	[0.003]	[0.004]	[0.004]
No. of children < 7	−0.002	−0.002	−0.003	−0.003	−0.002	−0.002
	[0.007]	[0.007]	[0.007]	[0.007]	[0.007]	[0.007]
No. children 7–15	−0.076***	−0.076***	−0.076***	−0.076***	−0.076***	−0.076***
	[0.006]	[0.006]	[0.006]	[0.006]	[0.006]	[0.006]
No pens. age adult	0.034***	0.034***	0.034***	0.035***	0.034***	0.035***
	[0.009]	[0.009]	[0.009]	[0.009]	[0.009]	[0.009]
Head's yrs. educ.	0.039***	0.039***	0.039***	0.038***	0.039***	0.039***
	[0.002]	[0.002]	[0.002]	[0.002]	[0.002]	[0.002]
Female head hhld.	0.088***	0.088***	0.088***	0.089***	0.088***	0.089***
	[0.015]	[0.015]	[0.015]	[0.015]	[0.015]	[0.015]
Kashkadarya	−0.530***	−0.529***	−0.530***	−0.530***	−0.530***	−0.529***
	[0.016]	[0.016]	[0.016]	[0.016]	[0.016]	[0.016]
Andijan	−0.634***	−0.634***	−0.634***	−0.636***	−0.635***	−0.635***
	[0.015]	[0.015]	[0.015]	[0.015]	[0.015]	[0.015]
One full limitation		−0.030				
		[0.035]				
Off. disability stat.			−0.032			
			[0.030]			
One serious difficulty or full limitation				−0.048**		
				[0.020]		
Chronic					−0.007	
					[0.019]	
ADLs, norm. score						−0.035
						[0.023]
Constant	13.094***	13.094***	13.095***	13.092***	13.095***	13.092***
	[0.037]	[0.037]	[0.037]	[0.037]	[0.037]	[0.037]
Observations	10,854	10,854	10,854	10,854	10,854	10,854
R-squared	0.44	0.44	0.44	0.44	0.44	0.44

Sources: URPS Waves 1, 2, and 3; authors' calculations.

Note: Calculations include only persons 7 years of age or older.
* Significant at 10%; ** significant at 5%; *** significant at 1%.

limitations in physical activities, is associated with lower monetary welfare.

Education

The investment in education has a high rate of return for individuals. This is true in general for developing countries (Psacharopolous and Tzannatos 1992; Psacharopoulos 1994); for transition countries as they undertake reforms (Yemtsov, Cnobloch, and Mete 2006); and in the specific case of Uzbekistan. The World Bank (2006) finds that higher education is associated with roughly a 60 percent increase in earnings, compared to the attainment of basic education in Uzbekistan. To the extent that disabilities prevent children from attending school, there will be a long-term negative impact on their earnings ability and future welfare.

Enrollment levels in Uzbekistan are fairly high at the basic education level. As shown in Scott (2005), just over 90 percent of all 6- to 14-year-olds were enrolled in school in 2003, and this is consistent across economic regions and urban and rural areas (see table 10). By age 15, however, enrollment levels fall, and by age 18, only two-thirds of children are still in school. The welfare level of the household, the education of the head of household, and the geographic location of the household all affect schooling. Here, in addition to these basic correlates of schooling, we explore the impact that disability has on the probability of children's school enrollment.

Three of the four disability or health variables used here (official disability status, one serious or full limitation, and chronic illness) have statistically significant negative effects on school enrollment for 7- to 14-year-olds (table 11). The coefficient on the fourth (one full limitation) has the expected sign but is not statistically significant. Official disability status has the strongest effect: a 24 percentage point decline in enrollments. This is followed by chronic illness, with an effect ranging from 10 to almost 12 percentage points. Having at least one serious difficulty or full limitation in functioning lowers the probability of enrollment by 6 to 7 percentage points.

If one looks at children between the ages of 15 and 18, other factors, such as the consumption level of the household and the education level of the head of the household, become important in explaining dropout rates.

However, having official disability status is the only one of the four health/disability indicators that is associated with a significant decline in school enrollment. The effect is dramatic: holding all else constant, official disability status is associated with a 42 to 49 percentage point drop in the probability of school enrollment. This may indicate that disability has a much stronger effect on school enrollment at older age levels, perhaps reflecting fewer resources available for such individuals in the school system, or greater costs or fewer benefits associated with enrollment. It may also, however, reflect the incentive structures of official disability status. It may be more

TABLE 10

Gross Enrollment Rates by Economic Region in Uzbekistan, 2002 to 2003

	Ages 6–14		Ages 15–18	
	2002	2003	2002	2003
Urban	88.2	91.4	59.0	69.0
Rural	89.4	91.5	58.3	65.4
Tashkent	89.0	89.3	68.8	68.7
Mirzachul	88.8	92.2	52.8	60.6
Ferghana	86.8	91.4	58.8	68.5
Northern	90.6	91.8	50.3	62.3
Central	89.8	92.3	59.2	67.2
Southern	90.5	92.1	58.1	66.5
National	89.0	91.5	58.5	66.5

Source: World Bank Living Standards Assessment (2007).

Note: Data are from the national Household Budget Survey implemented by the State Statistical Committee, not administrative records.

TABLE 11

Probability of School Enrollment: Children Age 7–14

(marginal effects and [standard errors])

	(1)	(2)	(3)	(4)	(5)	(6)	(7)	(8)	(9)	(10)	(11)	(12)	(13)	(14)	(15)
Age	−0.0004	−0.0007	−0.0001	−0.0003	0.0001	−0.0004	−0.0005	−0.0002	−0.0001	0.00004	−0.0003	−0.0002	−0.0001	−0.0000005	0.000006
	[0.0007]	[0.0004]	[0.0005]	[0.0002]	[0.0003]	[0.0006]	[0.0004]	[0.0004]	[0.0001]	[0.0001]	[0.0004]	[0.0002]	[0.0002]	[0.000001]	[0.00001]
Female	−3E-05	−0.0004	−0.0011	−0.0002	−0.0016	0.0005	−0.0001	−0.0006	0.00003	−0.0005	0.0002	−0.0001	−0.0007	−0.0000005	−0.0002
	[0.0033]	[0.0019]	[0.0023]	[0.0010]	[0.0019]	[0.0026]	[0.0012]	[0.0015]	[0.0002]	[0.0009]	[0.0016]	[0.0005]	[0.0009]	[0.000002]	[0.0003]
Household size						−0.0005	−0.0003	−0.0004	−0.0001	−0.0002	−0.0001	−0.00004	−0.000004	−0.0000002	0.000004
						[0.0007]	[0.0003]	[0.0003]	[0.0001]	[0.0002]	[0.0005]	[0.0002]	[0.0002]	[0.0000007]	[0.00003]
No. of children <7						0.0001	0.0006	0.0006	0.0001	0.0001	0.0002	0.0003	0.0003	0.0000005	0.00002
						[0.0009]	[0.0005]	[0.0006]	[0.0001]	[0.0003]	[0.0006]	[0.0003]	[0.0003]	[0.000001]	[0.00004]
No. of child. 7–15						−0.0019	−0.001	−0.0011	−0.0002	−0.0007	−0.0008	−0.0003	−0.0004	−0.0000006	−0.0001
						[0.0015]	[0.0009]	[0.0008]	[0.0002]	[0.0007]	[0.0007]	[0.0004]	[0.0004]	[0.000002]	[0.0001]
Head's educ., yrs											0.0005	0.0002	0.0003	0.0000003	0.00002
											[0.0004]	[0.0002]	[0.0003]	[0.0000008]	[0.00004]
PC consumption											0.00001*	0.000004	−0.000004	0.00000001	0.0000008
											[0.000006]	[0.000003]	[0.000002]	[0.00000004]	[0.000001]
One full limit.		−0.1017					−0.1062					−0.0673			
		[0.0624]					[0.0670]					[0.0473]			
Official disability status			−0.2278*					−0.2444**					−0.3109**		
			[0.1207]					[0.1224]					[0.1431]		
One serious diffic. or full limit.				−0.0672**					−0.0609**					−0.0123***	
				[0.0317]					[0.0301]					[0.0116]	
Chronic					−0.0992**					−0.1160**					−0.1295**
					[0.0461]					[0.0518]					[0.0566]
Observations	2,383	2,383	2,383	2,383	2,383	2,383	2,383	2,383	2,383	2,383	2,030	2,030	2,030	2,030	2,030

Source: URPS Waves 1 and 3.

* Significant at 10%; ** significant at 5%; *** significant at 1%, standard errors in brackets.

TABLE 12

Probability of School Enrollment, Ages 15–18

(marginal effects and [standard errors])

	(1)	(2)	(3)	(4)	(5)	(6)	(7)	(8)	(9)	(10)	(11)	(12)	(13)	(14)	(15)
Years of age	−0.0929***	−0.0934***	−0.0950***	−0.0940***	−0.0929***	−0.0925***	−0.0932***	−0.0951***	−0.0941***	−0.0929***	−0.0890***	−0.0894***	−0.0911***	−0.0904***	−0.0893***
	[0.0097]	[0.0097]	[0.0097]	[0.0097]	[0.0097]	[0.0103]	[0.0103]	[0.0103]	[0.0104]	[0.0103]	[0.0100]	[0.0100]	[0.0100]	[0.0101]	[0.0100]
Female	0.0024	0.0017	−0.0024	0.0017	0.0033	−0.001	−0.0014	−0.0055	−0.0013	0.0001	−0.0128	−0.0129	−0.0175	−0.0125	−0.0119
	[0.0216]	[0.0214]	[0.0213]	[0.0215]	[0.0216]	[0.0211]	[0.0209]	[0.0209]	[0.0210]	[0.0211]	[0.0191]	[0.0190]	[0.0188]	[0.0191]	[0.0191]
Household size						−0.0092	−0.0094	−0.0097	−0.0091	−0.0098	−0.0033	−0.0033	−0.0038	−0.003	−0.0036
						[0.0070]	[0.0070]	[0.0070]	[0.0070]	[0.0071]	[0.0063]	[0.0063]	[0.0062]	[0.0063]	[0.0063]
No. of child. <7						−0.0139	−0.0113	−0.0113	−0.0129	−0.0128	−0.015	−0.0128	−0.0123	−0.0144	−0.0141
						[0.0155]	[0.0154]	[0.0152]	[0.0154]	[0.0154]	[0.0133]	[0.0130]	[0.0128]	[0.0131]	[0.0132]
No. of child. 7-15						0.0028	0.0023	0.0015	0.001	0.002	0.0115	0.0108	0.0098	0.0097	0.0107
						[0.0121]	[0.0120]	[0.0120]	[0.0121]	[0.0121]	[0.0111]	[0.0110]	[0.0109]	[0.0111]	[0.0111]
Head's educ., yrs.											0.0070**	0.0069**	0.0063**	0.0067**	0.0070**
											[0.0028]	[0.0028]	[0.0028]	[0.0028]	[0.0028]
Female head of hhld.											−0.0421	−0.0357	-0.0429	−0.0385	−0.0387
											[0.0303]	[0.0302]	[0.0301]	[0.0303]	[0.0303]
PC consumption											0.0002***	0.0002***	0.0002***	0.0002***	0.0002***
											[0.0001]	[0.0001]	[0.0001]	[0.0001]	[0.0001]
One full limit.		−0.3513					−0.3138					−0.2722			
		[0.2739]					[0.2590]					[0.2672]			
Official disability status			−0.4261**					−0.4336**					−0.4875***		
			[0.1876]					[0.1800]					[0.1807]		
One serious diff. or full limit.				−0.1811					−0.1737					−0.1595	
				[0.1239]					[0.1213]					[0.1221]	
Chronic					−0.0486					−0.061					−0.0734
					[0.0669]					[0.0680]					[0.0694]
Observations	1,309	1,309	1,309	1,309	1,309	1,309	1,309	1,309	1,309	1,309	1,309	1,309	1,309	1,309	1,309

Source: URPS Waves 1 and 3.

* Significant at 10%; ** significant at 5%; *** significant at 1%, standard errors in brackets.

advantageous for older children to obtain such status, or it may simply be easier once a child reaches a certain age for such status to be obtained. A more detailed understanding of how disability benefits are conferred is needed to clarify this point.

Another way of looking at the link between education and disability would be to assess the effect of disability on the number of years of schooling an individual obtains. To do this properly, information is needed on the individual and his or her household and location during the ages when schooling was (or would normally have been) acquired, as well as information about the onset of any health problems or limitations. Unfortunately, the data set used here does not provide all of this information. In the interest of further exploring the link between disability and education given the strong association shown in terms of enrollment, we regress the number of years of education on age and gender and various indicators of disability. Obviously, the results should be used with extreme caution, but, as can be seen in table 13, there does seem to be further evidence that disability and educational attainment are linked. Having a full limitation or having a serious difficulty is associated with fewer years of schooling. Having a full limitation reduces schooling by almost two and a half years, while having a serious difficulty *or* full limitation lowers it by more than one year. Official disability status has less of an effect (less than half a year in one specification) and chronic illness is not associated with fewer years of schooling, as the previous analysis would suggest.

Labor Force Participation

Household and individual welfare are clearly influenced by an individual's ability to work. Being able to work can be affected by the level of education one obtains, the physical or mental ability required for the job, and the willingness of society to include persons with disabilities in the work force. Here we look at basic individual and household characteristics and the effect they have on whether a person is active in the labor market. The International Labour Organization's (ILO's) definition of being "economically" active is used here, which includes persons working or actively looking for work (unemployed).[12]

The dependent variable takes the value 1 if the person was active in either Wave 1 of the survey (March 2005) or Wave 3 of the survey (December 2005). It may well be that there is seasonality in the labor market: using two points in time should prevent seasonality issues from being confounded with disability or other issues that affect labor force participation.

Table 14 shows that the probability of being economically active is closely linked to the disability and health status of the individuals. All four disability/poor health indicators considered here have statistically significant coefficients at the 1 percent level. Official disability status is associated with a 52 percentage point reduction in the probability of being economically active. Corresponding statistics for having a full limitation, one serious difficulty or full limitation, and having a chronic illness are 37 percentage points; 24 percentage points; and 19 percentage points, respectively. These estimates should be viewed as descriptive associations rather than causal linkages, however. As highlighted by Bound (1991) and discussed in detail by Mete and Schultz (2007),[13] treating disability/poor health indicators as exogenous variables in employment regressions overlooks the (upward) bias that may arise because of self-reporting of heath variables. On the other hand, as shown previously, children who are disabled are much less likely to stay in school after basic education, and so the presence of schooling attainment variables (also treated as exogenous variables here) in the model may lead to an underestimation of the causal effect of disability on labor force participation.

TABLE 13

Years of Schooling Obtained

	(1)	(2)	(3)	(4)	(5)	(6)	(7)	(8)	(9)	(10)
Years of age	−0.044***	−0.036***	−0.044***	−0.031***	−0.046***	−0.049***	−0.041***	−0.048***	−0.035***	−0.047***
	[0.003]	[0.003]	[0.003]	[0.003]	[0.003]	[0.003]	[0.003]	[0.003]	[0.003]	[0.003]
Female	−0.317***	−0.303***	−0.323***	−0.273***	−0.320***	−0.364***	−0.351***	−0.372***	−0.319***	−0.362***
	[0.074]	[0.073]	[0.074]	[0.073]	[0.074]	[0.072]	[0.071]	[0.072]	[0.071]	[0.072]
Andijan						−1.465***	−1.461***	−1.467***	−1.530***	−1.498***
						[0.087]	[0.087]	[0.087]	[0.087]	[0.088]
Kashkadarya						−1.340***	−1.306***	−1.347***	−1.342***	−1.367***
						[0.093]	[0.091]	[0.093]	[0.091]	[0.092]
One full limit.		−2.462***					−2.400***			
		[0.346]					[0.335]			
Official disability status			−0.344					−0.408*		
			[0.227]					[0.223]		
One serious diff. or full limit.				−1.240***					−1.341***	
				[0.165]					[0.160]	
Chronic					0.183					−0.213
					[0.141]					[0.137]
Constant	12.710***	12.468***	12.703***	12.353***	12.735***	13.812***	13.561***	13.807***	13.451***	13.806***
	[0.120]	[0.120]	[0.121]	[0.121]	[0.123]	[0.137]	[0.135]	[0.137]	[0.135]	[0.137]
Observations	7,519	7,519	7,519	7,519	7,519	7,519	7,519	7,519	7,519	7,519
R-squared	0.08	0.10	0.08	0.10	0.08	0.14	0.16	0.14	0.16	0.14

Sources: URPS Waves 1, 2, and 3; authors' calculations.

Note: Includes individuals ages 19 and older.
* Significant at 10%; ** significant at 5%; *** significant at 1%, standard errors in brackets.

TABLE 14

Probability of Being Economically Active

	(1)	(2)	(3)	(4)	(5)	(6)	(7)	(8)	(9)	(10)
Age	0.0039***	0.0041***	0.0057***	0.0052***	0.0050***	0.0036***	0.0038***	0.0054***	0.0049***	0.0046***
	[0.0006]	[0.0007]	[0.0007]	[0.0007]	[0.0007]	[0.0006]	[0.0006]	[0.0007]	[0.0007]	[0.0007]
Female	−0.1814***	−0.1842***	−0.1937***	−0.1817***	−0.1812***	−0.1853***	−0.1877***	−0.1967***	−0.1847***	−0.1856***
	[0.0129]	[0.0129]	[0.0128]	[0.0128]	[0.0128]	[0.0131]	[0.0131]	[0.0129]	[0.0130]	[0.0130]
Education (yrs.)	0.0309***	0.0293***	0.0274***	0.0281***	0.0295***	0.0351***	0.0335***	0.0313***	0.0321***	0.0327***
	[0.0031]	[0.0031]	[0.0031]	[0.0031]	[0.0031]	[0.0031]	[0.0032]	[0.0032]	[0.0032]	[0.0031]
Head of hhld.	0.0661***	0.0673***	0.0698***	0.0651***	0.0712***	0.0621***	0.0638***	0.0664***	0.0619***	0.0644***
	[0.0170]	[0.0171]	[0.0170]	[0.0170]	[0.0167]	[0.0187]	[0.0187]	[0.0187]	[0.0187]	[0.0185]
Hhld. size						−0.0094***	−0.0092**	−0.0088**	−0.0084**	−0.0102***
						[0.0036]	[0.0036]	[0.0036]	[0.0036]	[0.0036]
No. of child. <7						0.0132*	0.0124	0.0090	0.0097	0.0118
						[0.0076]	[0.0076]	[0.0076]	[0.0076]	[0.0077]
No. of child. 7–15						0.0226***	0.0210***	0.0162**	0.0186***	0.0199***
						[0.0067]	[0.0067]	[0.0067]	[0.0067]	[0.0067]
No. of pension-age adults						0.0051	0.0048	0.0049	0.0048	0.0043
						[0.0096]	[0.0096]	[0.0095]	[0.0096]	[0.0096]
Andijan						0.1028***	0.1027***	0.1032***	0.0971***	0.0881***
						[0.0142]	[0.0142]	[0.0140]	[0.0143]	[0.0146]
Kashkadarya						0.0321**	0.0329**	0.0289*	0.0332**	0.0207
						[0.0152]	[0.0152]	[0.0152]	[0.0151]	[0.0155]
One full limit.		−0.3727***					−0.3638***			
		[0.0661]					[0.0672]			
Official disability status			−0.5201***					−0.5201***		
			[0.0379]					[0.0388]		
One serious diff. or full limit.				−0.2431***					−0.2249***	
				[0.0315]					[0.0319]	
Chronic					−0.1901***					−0.1694***
					[0.0257]					[0.0260]
Observations	7,467	7,467	7,467	7,467	7,467	7,467	7,467	7,467	7,467	7,467

Sources: URPS Wave 1, 2, and 3; authors' calculations.

Note: Includes individuals ages 16–55 (female) and 16–60 (male).
* Significant at 10%; ** significant at 5%; *** significant at 1%, standard errors in brackets.

IV Conclusion

The basic finding of this paper is that the rate of disability found in a population will vary substantially, depending on the measure used. More important, our understanding of the linkages among welfare, education, and labor force participation can also be affected by the choice of measure.

We find that almost 12 percent of all individuals ages 7 and older have at least one serious difficulty or a full limitation in physical functioning. If one restricts the definition of disability to individuals who have a full limitation on one of the six domains (blindness or learning, for example), the incidence of disability is 3.2 percent. Official disability status, however, is held by 3.8 percent of the population age 7 and older. While the official disability rate increases by age, it remains at around 10 percent among those who are older than 66. In contrast, the share of individuals with at least one full limitation increases from about 5 percent for the 7-to-16 age group, to 65 percent among those who are 66 and over. This finding suggests that while developing countries with aging populations may be able to contain one type of financial burden by being restrictive in granting disability benefits to the elderly, the functional limitations still increase steeply by age, with implications for employment and productivity.

Even though all disability indicators considered here are correlated with one another, their linkage with official disability status is of particular interest because the officially disabled are entitled to social protection benefits. The best health-related predictors of official disability are: (i) having at least one serious difficulty in one of the six physical functioning domains, (ii) one's own assessment of disabling illnesses or injuries, and (iii) limitations in the ADL. Chronic illness and a score that captures all problems in the six domains of functioning are not good predictors. Additionally, being of working age increases the probability of having official disability status, while being female reduces the likelihood. Living in Andijan, rather than Tashkent, increases the probability of having official disability status. The wealth proxy, per-capita consumption, does not have a statistically significant influence on the probability of receiving official disability status. Thus, two ways that the current system can be improved emerge as: (i) improving females' access to information and to commissions that determine disability levels, and (ii) ensuring consistent implementation of nationally determined criteria for granting disability status across different regions.

As mentioned previously, the extent to which disability is related to welfare, education, and labor force participation is sensitive to the disability measure that is used. For example, official disability status plays the most important role in explaining school enrollment for 15- to 18-year-olds. (Official disability status is associated with more than a 40 percentage point drop in the probability of school enrollment. The effect of other disability indicators ranges from a 6 percentage point to 35 percentage point drop.) Similarly, official disability status is strongly related to probability of being economically active among adults (official disability status is associated with a 52 percentage point reduction in the probability of being economically active, while the effect of other disability indicators ranges from a 19 percentage point reduction to a 37 percentage point reduction). In contrast, having a serious difficulty or full limitation is most closely associated with reductions in household consumption (resulting in a 4.8 percent decline), while the effect of having official disability status remains statistically insignificant, and less than half in magnitude. This last finding is perhaps a natural result of a process in which disability benefits are granted to the officially disabled based on a medical evaluation (as opposed to considerations of functional disabilities as well).

Finally, the original panel sample (which collected information on 12,387 individuals) and the full Wave 3 sample (which collected information on 32,337 individuals) provide remarkably similar estimates of the prevalence of disabilities, regardless of the definition that is used. This finding sheds doubt on the validity of the view that disability is a rare event that can be captured best by the inclusion of appropriate questions in census questionnaires. Such an approach, while useful for estimating prevalence rates according to one or two disability definitions, would be of very limited use for establishing linkages with poverty because census questionnaires do not inquire about household consumption patterns. Furthermore, given the nature of census questionnaires, the implementation of a comprehensive set of questions on disabilities is out of question. Yet the Uzbek data shows that there is no single disability indicator that overshadows other indicators for many questions that might interest policy makers. Instead, various disability indicators, together, provide insights on identifying the most vulnerable populations.

Appendix I

Health, Disability, and Physical Functioning Questions in URPS, Waves 1, 2, and 3

Waves 1 and 2

CHRONIC

- Does [NAME] suffer from a chronic illness, such as asthma, diabetes, palsy, etc.?

  Yes/No

ACTIVITIES OF DAILY LIVING

- Has [NAME]'s health limited his/her ability to perform vigorous activities such as lifting heavy objects, running, and for how long?
  - Yes, for more than three months..........................1
  - Yes, for less than three months............................2
  - No..3
- Has [NAME]'s health limited him/her from doing moderate activities such as moving a table or carrying groceries, and for how long?
  - Yes, for more than three months..........................1
  - Yes, for less than three months............................2
  - No..3
- Has [NAME]'s health limited his/her ability to walk uphill, and for how long?
  - Yes, for more than three months..........................1
  - Yes, for less than three months............................2
  - No..3
- Has [NAME]'s health limited him/her from walking 100 meters?
  - Yes, for more than three months..........................1
  - Yes, for less than three months............................2
  - No..3
- Has [NAME]'s health limited him/her from bending, lifting, or stooping, and for how long?
  - Yes, for more than three months..........................1
  - Yes, for less than three months............................2
  - No..3
- Has [NAME]'s health limited him/her from eating, dressing, bathing, or using the toilet, and for how long?
  - Yes, for more than three months..........................1
  - Yes, for less than three months............................2
  - No..3

Wave 2

DISABILITY-SELF ASSESSED AND OFFICIAL

- Does [NAME] have any signs of disability?

  Bad hearing..1
  Deaf...2
  Bad vision..3
  Blind..4
  Adynamia/aspen9z.......................................5
  Palsy..6
  Absence of hands, legs......................................7
  Mental disease 8
  Consequence of tuberculosis, heart disease 9
  Other, specify ______________________
  None 98

- Is [NAME] officially recognized by medical workers as disabled?

  ■ Yes, and with written confirmation 1
  ■ Yes, BUT written confirmation not given 2
  ■ No...3
  ■ Did not refer to officials 4

Wave 3

PHYSICAL FUNCTIONING

ID CODE	EYESIGHT				
	(1)	(2)	(3)	(4)	(5)
	Does [NAME] use optical glasses or contact lenses?	**Does [NAME] have any problems with [HIS/HER] vision when using [HIS/HER] glasses or lenses? If so, what are these problems?**	**Does [NAME] have any difficulties with vision? If so, what are these difficulties?**	**Does [NAME] have difficulties with vision when trying to recognize a person he/she knows at a distance of 7 meters? If so, what are these difficulties?**	**Does [NAME] have difficulties with vision and recognizing subjects at arm's length?**
	Yes.............1 No..............2>>**3** No need, - is blind...........3>>**6**	No.......................1››**6** Yes, some..............2 ››**4** Yes, many..............3›› **4** Yes, - cannot see......4 ››**6**	No.......................1››**6** Yes, some..............2 Yes, many..............3 Yes, - cannot see......4››**6**	No.........................1 Yes, some...............2 Yes, many...............3 Yes, - cannot see........4	No.........................1 Yes, some...............2 Yes, many...............3 Yes, - cannot see........4
	CODE	CODE	CODE	CODE	CODE
01					

ID CODE	(6)	(7)	(8)	(9)	(10)
	Does [NAME] use hearing device, or any other device helping him/her hear?	**Does [NAME] have any difficulties with hearing even when using a hearing device or other device? If so, what are these difficulties?**	**Does [NAME] have any difficulties with hearing? If so, what are these difficulties?**	**Does [NAME] have difficulties with hearing when somebody is speaking in a normal voice in the other end of the room? If so, what are these difficulties?**	**Does [NAME] have difficulties with hearing when he is talking about with another person at a table in a quiet room? If so, what are these difficulties?**
	Yes……………1 No……………2>> **8** No need, - is deaf……….3>> **11**	No………………………1›› **11** Yes, some……………2›› **9** Yes, many……………3›› **9** Yes, not able to hear…4›› **11**	No…………………1 ››11 Yes, some…………2 Yes, many…………3 Yes, not able hear...4 ››11	No……………………1 Yes, some…………………2 Yes, many…………………3 Yes, not able to hear……..4	No…………………………1 Yes, some…………………2 Yes, many…………………3 Yes, not able to hear…….4
	CODE	CODE	CODE	CODE	CODE
01					

PHYSICAL CONDITION

ID CODE	(11)	(12)	(13)	(14)
	Does [NAME] have any physical difficulties with walking down and up the stairs (on his/her own)?	**Does [NAME] have any problems with walking such a distance as one kilometer? If so, what are these problems? [IN URBAN AREAS - THE DISTANCE BETWEEN TWO BUS STOPS, -- IN RURAL AREAS - THE DISTANCE BETWEEN [LANDMARK 1] AND [LANDMARK 2]**	**Does [NAME] have any physical difficulties with walking outside the house/apartment? If so, what are these difficulties?**	**Does [NAME] have physical difficulties with moving around the house/apartment? If so, what are these difficulties?**
	No………………………1 Yes, some………………2 Yes, many………………3 Not able to do that….4	No…………………………1›› **15** Yes, some………………2 Yes, many………………3 Not able to do that…..4	No…………………………1 **››15** Yes, some………………2 Yes, many………………3 Not able to do that.....4	No…………………………1 Yes, some………………2 Yes, many………………3 Not able to do that……4
	CODE	CODE	CODE	CODE
01				

ID CODE	MEMORY			
	(15)	(16)	(17)	(18)
	Does [NAME] have any difficulties with memorizing, or focusing attention, or when taking a decision? If so, what are these difficulties?	**Does [NAME] have difficulties with focusing attention on something, or on some action during 10 minutes? If so, what are these difficulties?**	**Does [NAME] have difficulties with remembering important things or the need to do important things? If so, what are these difficulties?**	**Does [NAME] have difficulties with studying new things? If so, what are these difficulties?**
	No…………………. 1 **››18** Yes, some……...........2 Yes, many…..………..3 Not able to do that....4 **››18**	No……………....……1 Yes, some……............2 Yes, many…..………..3 Not able to do that….4	No……………….........1 Yes, some…………....2 Yes, many…..……..…3 Not able to do that…..4	No…………………...…1 Yes, some…………......2 Yes, many…..……..…..3 Not able to do that…...4
	CODE	CODE	CODE	CODE
01				

I D C O D E	(19)	(20)	(21)	(22)	(23)	(24)	(25)	(26)
	Does [NAME] have difficulties with washing the whole body on his/her own? What are these difficulties?	**Does [NAME] have difficulties with putting on clothes or footwear on his/her own? What are these difficulties?**	**Does [NAME] have difficulties with feeding himself/herself on his/her own? What are these difficulties?**	**Does [NAME] have any physical or psychic difficulties when being left alone for several days? What are these difficulties?**	**Due to a physical, mental or emotional condition, does [NAME] have difficulties when communicating with other people, - e.g. does he/she understand what other people are telling him/her, and do other people understand what he/she is telling them?**	**Does [NAME] have difficulties with general understanding of what other people are saying? What are these**	**Does [NAME] have difficulties with starting and maintaining a conversation? What are these**	**Do other people have difficulties with understanding what [NAME] is saying?**
	1. No difficulties	1. No difficulties	1. No difficulties	1. No difficulties	1. No difficulties	1. No difficulties	1. No difficulties	1. No difficulties
	2. Yes, some	2. Yes, some	2. Yes, some	2. Yes, some	2. Yes, some	2. Yes, some	2. Yes, some	2. Yes, some
	3. Yes, many	3. Yes, many	3. Yes, many	3. Yes, many	3. Yes, many	3. Yes, many	3. Yes, many	3. Yes, many
	4. Not able to do that	4. Not able to do that	4. Not able to do that	4. Not able to do that	4. Not able to do that	4. Not able to do that	4. Not able to do that	4. Not able to do that
	CODE	CODE	CODE	CODE	CODE	CODE	CODE	CODE
01								

	DISABILITY			
	(27)	(28)	(29)	(30)
	Does [NAME] have any signs of disability?	**What is [NAME's] disability group ?**	**Can we copy [NAME's] diagnosis, which gives him/her the disability status?**	INTERVIEWER! WAS THIS INFORMATION ON THE DIAGNOSIS TAKEN FROM AN OFFICIAL CERTIFICATE OF DISABILITY?
	CARD 27			
I	1. Poor hearing (check Q.6-Q.10)			
D	2. Deaf (check Q.6-Q.10)		WRITE DOWN A FULL DIAGNOSIS FROM THE CASE HISTORY OR FROM THE MEDICAL-AND-LABOR EXAMINATION COMMISSION CERTIFICATE OF DISABILITY	
	3. Poor vision (check Q.1-Q.5)			
C	4. Blind (check Q.1)			
O	5. Impotence (check Q.11-Q.26)			
D	6. Paralysis (check Q.11-Q.26)			1. Yes, from an official
E	7. Missing arm(s), leg(s), etc.(check Q.11-Q.26)	1. Group 1		document
	8. Mental disease (check Q.11-Q.26)	2. Group 2		2. The document wasn't
	9. Consequences of diseases (tuberculosis,	3. Group 3		3. The document hasn't
	heart diseases, etc.) (check Q.11-Q.26)			been received yet
	OTHER (SPECIFY)	4. No disability >>		4. No document available
	98. No, he/she doesn't	**next member**		
	CODE	CODE	DIAGNOSIS	CODE
01	34			

Notes

1. Rough estimates, however unreliable, are that 40 million of the 115 million children not enrolled in school have a disability ("Education for All: Including Children with Disabilities," Education Notes, The World Bank, August 2003).
2. Similarly, analyzing household survey data from 10 developing country household surveys, Filmer (2004) reports less than 2 percent of the population as disabled.
3. This section is based largely on the paper by Altman, Cambois, and Robine, 2005. For more details on the background, tasks, and progress to date of the Washington Group on Disability Statistics, see their web site at http://www.cdc.gov/nchs/citygroup.htm.
4. Differences in community resources (such as wheelchair accessible transport and services) or individuals themselves (such as education) could also affect functioning even if the disability were the same. In this work we are able to control for assistive devices but not for community resources.
5. One shortcoming of household surveys is their inability to take into account disabled individuals who reside in institutions. In Uzbekistan, the Ministry of Labor and Social Protection operates 34 boarding facilities for the disabled, serving around 8,900 individuals (about 1,500 general-disabled adults, 5,600 adults with mental disorders, and 1,800 disabled children). See Japan International Cooperation Agency (JICA)/Tahlil 2004 for more information.
6. Major pieces of legislation relating to disability in Uzbekistan are: the Law on Social Protection for Disabled Persons, 1991 (amendments in 1998, 2001); Law on State Pension Security for Citizens, 1992; Law on Pension Security for Military Service Persons, 1990; Law of Employment of the Population, 1992; Labor Code of the Republic of Uzbekistan (JICA and Tahlil 2004).
7. This could be problematic if persons with disabilities are more prone to migration than others. The data does not, however, allow us to examine this issue.
8. When other factors such as household structure and household head's gender, age, and schooling are controlled for, disability is associated with a decline in per-capita consumption for all indicators that are considered, although the coefficient is significant in only one case. (This is reported in table 9 later in the main text.)
9. This may reflect people's ability to adapt to certain limitations if the condition is static, as it may well be if not age related.
10. The correlation coefficients for the poorest quintile tend to be larger than the ones for the wealthiest quintile (save for one exception).
11. The World Bank (2006) reveals that only 43 percent of adult females have a final say on their own health care and almost 25 percent of adult females are not allowed to go to the health center alone.
12. Open unemployment is relatively low in Uzbekistan, at less then 5 percent (World Bank 2006).
13. See also Autor and Duggan 2006.

References

Altman, Barbara M., Emmanuelle Cambois, and Jean-Marie Robine. 2005. "Extended Question Sets: Purposes, Characteristics, and Topic Areas." Paper presented at the 5th meeting of the Washington Group on Disability Statistics, Rio de Janeiro, Brazil.

Autor, David H., and Mark G. Duggan. 2006. "The Growth in the Social Security Disability Rolls: A Fiscal Crisis Unfolding." Working Paper Series, No. 12436, National Bureau of Economic Research, Cambridge, Massachusetts.

Bercovich, A. 2004. "People with Disability in Brazil: A Look at 2000 Census Results." Working Paper, *Instituto Brasileiro de Geografia e Estatística*, Rio de Janeiro, Brazil.

Bound, John. 1991. "Self-Reported Versus Objective Measures of Health in Retirement Models." *Journal of Human Resources*, 26 (1): 106–38.

Deaton, Angus, and Salman Zaidi. 2002. "Guidelines for Constructing Consumption Aggregates for Welfare Analysis, Living Standards, Measurement Study," Working Paper No. 135, World Bank, Washington, DC.

Elwan, Ann. 1999. "Poverty and Disability: A Survey of the Literature." Social Protection Discussion Paper Series No. 9932, World Bank, Washington, DC.

Filmer, Deon. 2004. "Disability, Poverty, and Schooling: Results from 10 Household Surveys." Presentation for conference on Disability and Inclusive Development, World Bank, Washington, DC.

Flores, R., D. Yepez, and M. Pramatarova. 2005. *"Ecuador: La discapacidad en cifras." Instituto Nacional de Estadísticas y Censos de Ecuador*, Quito, Ecuador.

Kerkhofs, M., and Maarten Lindeboom. 1995. "Subjective Health Measures and State Dependent Reporting Errors." *Health Economics*, 4: 221–35.

Instituto Nacional de Estadísticas y Censos-Nicaragua. 2003. "Encuestas Nicaragüense para personas con discapacidades, *ENDIS*," Managua Nicaragua.

Japan International Cooperation Agency (JICA) and Tahlil Center for Social Research. 2004. "Review of Situation of Disabled People in the Republic of Uzbekistan." Report prepared for Japan International Cooperation Agency, Tashkent, Uzbekistan.

Lindeboom, M., and Eddy van Doorslaer. 2004. "Cut-Point Shift and Index-Shift in Self-Reported Health." Tinbergen Institute Discussion Paper TI-2003-042/3.

Martinho, Maria, and Jeremiah Banda. 2005. "United Nations Collection of National Disability Statistics from Population and Housing Censuses and Related National Surveys and Administrative Records." Presentation at the 4th meeting of the Washington Group on Disability Statistics, Rio de Janeiro, Brazil.

Mete, Cem, and T. Paul Schultz. 2007. "Health and Labor Force Participation of the Elderly in Taiwan." In *Allocating Public and Private Resources across Generations*, ed. Anne H. Gauthier, C.Y. Chrus, and Shripad Tuljapurkar, 163–200, New York: Springer.

Mont, Daniel. 2005. "Disability in Central America." Presentation at the 4th meeting of the Washington Group on Disability Statistics, Rio de Janeiro, Brazil.

Psacharopoulos, George. 1994. "Returns to Investment in Education: A Global Update." *World Development* 22 (9): 1325–43.

Psacharopolous, George, and Zafiris Tzannatos, eds. 1992. *Women's Employment and Pay in Latin America*, Washington, DC: World Bank.

Scott, Kinnon. 2005. "An Update on Living Standards in Uzbekistan, 2000–2003." Background paper for the Uzbekistan Poverty Assessment, World Bank,Washington, DC.

Schultz, T. Paul, and Aysit Tansel. 1997. "Wage and Labor Supply Effects of Illness in Côte d'Ivoire and Ghana: Instrumental Variable Estimates for Days Disabled." *Journal of Development Economics* 53 (2): 251–86.

United Nations. 2005. "Disability Statistics Data Base." Statistics Division, http://unstats.un.org/unsd/demographic/sconcerns/disability/disab2.asp.

Van Doorslaer, Eddy, and Ulf. G. Gerdtham. 2002. "Does Inequality in Self-Assessed Health Predict Inequality in Survival by Income? Evidence from Swedish Data." *Social Science and Medicine* 57: 1621–29.

World Bank. 2003. "Education for All: Including Children with Disabilities." Education Notes, Washington, DC.

World Bank. 2006. *Uzbekistan Living Standards Update*. Washington, DC: World Bank.

World Health Organization. 2001. *International Classification of Functioning, Disability, and Health*, Geneva, Switzerland: World Health Organization.

———. 1980. *International Classification of Impairments, Disabilities, and Handicaps*, Geneva, Switzerland: World Health Organization.

Yemtsov, Ruslan G., Stefania R. Cnobloch, and Cem Mete. 2006. "Evolution of the Predictors of Earnings during Transition." Manuscript. Washington, DC: World Bank.

CHAPTER 3

The Impact of Health Shocks on Employment, Earnings, and Household Consumption in Bosnia and Herzegovina

Cem Mete, Huan Ni, Kinnon Scott*

Introduction

Ill health, disease, and disability can have significant effects on individual and household welfare in developing countries. Households may be able to smooth the negative impact on household consumption that comes from episodes of relatively minor illness (Townsend 1994; 1995), but they are unlikely to be able to cope with the occurrence of a major illness or disability in the same manner (Gertler and Gruber 2002).[1] If we are to understand the linkages between health shocks and poverty, we need to be able to distinguish among different types of illnesses and disability and their effects on consumption. In addition, there may be payoffs to considering the impact of health shocks on a broader set of household wealth indicators—for example, by taking into account children's school attendance and enrollment patterns—instead of exclusively focusing on earnings and household consumption.[2] Despite the potential significance of this line of research on policy making (through instruments such as catastrophic health insurance), the evidence is scarce. This is especially true in terms of the linkages between disability and poverty: the developing country literature consists primarily of studies based on anecdotal evidence and case studies (as observed by Elwan 1999, and Wagstaff 2005).

The relationship between poor health/disability and poverty may be particularly strong in the transition economies. Common coping mechanisms may not work in these economies, especially those where GDP levels declined by more than half during the first decade of transition (World Bank 2003). Informal social protection arrangements through networks of family

* Cem Mete is a senior economist at the Europe and Central Asia region of the World Bank. Huan Ni is an assistant professor at the economics department of the Kennesaw State University. Kinnon Scott is a senior economist at the Development Research Group of the World Bank.

and friends that can provide relief for small or temporary economic shocks are unlikely to be effective in the face of such widespread and extreme deprivation. Nor is there much room for intrahousehold adjustments to be made to smooth consumption: Many transition countries have had low fertility rates and nuclear household living arrangements for decades (as opposed to high fertility rates and extended family living arrangements observed in poor South Asian countries). Furthermore, during the 1990s, the health care infrastructure crumbled, and thus disabled individuals in many transition countries have not benefited as much from the continuous advances in medical technology that developed country residents enjoy (Kahn 1998; Costa 2000).

The link between poor health/disability and employment outcomes would also be expected to be strong given that the transition economies are characterized by high unemployment and a relative abundance of skilled labor. The disabled and ill are further constrained because the option of taking informal sector jobs (often in the agriculture sector) is limited, both because such work tends to be physically demanding and because informal sector employment, by definition, is not bound by regulations and policies (such as tax incentives) designed to protect the vulnerable populations.

This chapter uses data from a four-wave panel survey of households in Bosnia and Herzegovina to assess the extent to which households are able to smooth the impact of unexpected health shocks on key welfare indicators. The factors that make individuals in transition countries more vulnerable to health shocks clearly apply to the Bosnia and Herzegovina case. The health-welfare linkage may be especially strong given the fact that the country has also experienced massive movements of population due to the war: more than 200,000 people are estimated to have died in the conflict and close to 2 million people (half the prewar population) was internally displaced or became refugees.

A key contribution of this work is that we tackle the question of the presence or absence of a relationship between health shocks and household consumption by focusing on several indicators of poor health/disability: an "Activities of Daily Living" Index (ADL); self-reported chronic disease; and self-reported disability status information. By doing this, we seek to determine which disability/poor health indicators are more closely related to household consumption. This analysis builds on Gertler and Gruber's proposition that the measures of health that are used may make a difference in the analysis of health shock impacts, particularly the difference between unexpected major illness versus minor illness. We also investigate whether the timing of the onset of disability or disease has an impact on the observed trends in employment, earnings, and household consumption. The motivation for this extension to the basic empirical framework is the implications for the design of social protection programs: more specifically, is it possible to obtain insights into the optimal starting time and duration of such programs if the sole objective were to smooth household consumption? Finally, to better understand what is behind the observed variations in household consumption, we investigate the impact of newly acquired disability or disease on employment and earnings.

Bosnia and Herzegovina Context

Prior to the breakup of the former Yugoslavia into six separate countries, the population of Bosnia and Herzegovina enjoyed a well-coordinated health system that had health indicators similar to those in OECD countries (World Bank 2005) and a reasonably high level of living. The 1992–95 war had two immediate effects in the postwar period: per-capita income fell from US$2,429 (in 1990) to US$456 by 1995, and the health care system, like many government structures and services, became highly fragmented. As a result of the Dayton Peace

Accords, Bosnia and Herzegovina is a country made up of two entities—the Federation of Bosnia and Herzegovina (FBiH); and the Republika Srpska (RS)—and a central Bosnia and Herzegovina government of fairly limited (but increasingly expanding) authority. An additional administrative unit, the District of Brcko, has also existed since 2000.

The fragmentation of the political sphere translated into the fragmentation of the provision of the health care system. Serious problems affected the health care system in the postwar period, weakening individuals' protection from health shocks. It was estimated that 30 to 40 percent of the country's hospitals were destroyed or seriously damaged during the war, and that up to 30 percent of the prewar health care staff had emigrated or died in the conflict (World Bank 2005). The disjointed system that resulted from the war led to low levels of risk pooling for health insurance funds (particularly in the smaller cantons in the FBiH), unequal access to health care, lack of portability of health insurance, a large share of the population no longer being covered by health insurance, and a high rate of expenditures devoted to health care—12 percent of GDP, with one-third of this being out-of-pocket expenditures (World Bank 2000, 2003). Even though individuals in Bosnia and Herzegovina are covered by a mandatory health insurance scheme, during the period under investigation, the health system did not provide adequate coverage, and out-of-pocket expenditures remained high due to a disconnect between the legislated entitlements and the governments' ability to collect taxes (European Observatory on Health Care Systems 2002).

There are four types of disability support systems in Bosnia and Herzegovina (see IOS 2003 for a more detailed description of the social protection system). The social assistance system targets the poorest individuals who are disabled and unable to work. The social insurance system offers protection to the disabled who contributed to the pension and invalid fund. The veterans system provides assistance to disabled veterans, as well as to their dependents and the dependents of soldiers killed in action. Finally, civilian victims of war are entitled to separate disability benefits. Each program provides significantly different benefits. In particular, a disabled individual who is eligible for veterans' benefits can be expected to receive much more support than others who are similarly disabled. The following figures provide a sense of the coverage and level of benefits associated with each scheme. Almost 100,000 individuals received benefits under contributory invalid pensions in 2001; war veterans and social assistance programs were the next largest in terms of enrollments, with about 85,000 and 36,000 beneficiaries, respectively; followed by assistance to about 6,000 civil victims of war. The ratio of disability benefit to average wage was largest for the veterans' benefits (63 percent), followed by disability pensions (38 percent), civil victims of war (10 percent), and social assistance (6 percent).

A recent study of individuals with disabilities, their families, and others working to assist them, demonstrates the impact of the conflict on the health system (Prism 2006). Problems and issues raised by the focus groups interviewed for the qualitative study relate to the dropoff in service availability, the differential benefits for similar limitations or disabilities, and the cost of health services. The prewar health care system appears to have been able to deliver a broader range of services to individuals with health problems and disabilities.

If an employee becomes sick or disabled at work, employers are required to assist them with rehabilitation and alternative job placements.[3] There are also tax incentives to encourage employers to employ individuals with disabilities, although in an economic environment where the share of informal sector employment is estimated to be 36 percent of total employment, and compliance with tax laws is believed to be low, the tax incentives are unlikely to produce the intended employment outcomes for the disabled.

Data

The data used here are from the Bosnia and Herzegovina Living Standards Measurement Study Survey (LSMS) and the follow-up panel survey called Living in Bosnia and Herzegovina (LBiHS). The LSMS was the first nationally representative household survey capable of measuring welfare carried out in the newly formed Bosnia and Herzegovina.[4] The survey was conducted by the three statistical organizations of the country—the State Agency for Statistics, the Federation Institute for Statistics, and the Republika Srpska Institute for Statistics.[5] The first round of the LSMS was carried out in 2001, with a sample of 5,400 households—3,000 in the Federation of Bosnia and Herzegovina (FBiH) and 2,400 in the Republika Srpska (RS).[6] A total of 16,976 people were interviewed.

The purpose of the LSMS was to provide a money-metric measure of poverty for the country, to assess individuals' and households' access to and use of government services, and to document the population's economic activities and levels of human capital a few years after the war. The LSMS provides household-level data on a wide range of individual and household characteristics that affect welfare.[7]

Three further rounds of data collection were carried out between 2002 and 2004 on a yearly basis under the LBiH Survey. The LBiH formed a panel using a subsample of households interviewed in the full LSMS of 2001. This included all of the rural households from the original sample and approximately one-third of the urban households for a total of 3,007 households. [8] The focus of the LBiH was on a narrower set of issues—primarily labor and social protection—than the LSMS. Given the change in focus of the survey, not all of the same variables, concepts, and indicators exist in the four rounds of data collection. Nor, even when they are present, are the same definitions used. This complicates the analysis of health shocks undertaken here. However, care has been taken to ensure that only comparable variables are included in the analysis. A more detailed discussion of the variables used is found in the following sections.

Empirical Framework

The Model

The model we use is as outlined by Gertler and Gruber (2002), where the change in labor supply for individual i in community j is explained by community fixed effects, α_j, changes in health status, Δh_{ij}, individual and household characteristics, X_{ijk}, and a random error term ε_{ij}.

$$\Delta L_{ij} = \alpha_j + \beta \Delta h_{ij} + \sum_k \lambda_k X_{ijk} + \varepsilon_{ij}$$

Taking advantage of the presence of a four-wave household survey (although the health-related questions are only comparable in Waves 1, 3, and 4), we can write the change in health status as

$$\Delta h_{ij} = h_{ij4} - h_{ij3} + h_{ij3} - h_{ij1}.$$

This gives a more flexible specification that provides insights on the extent to which the timing of the health shock matters. Making this distinction seems beneficial, because empirical evidence from the United States suggests that disabled men experience sharp drops in expected annual earnings (caused mainly by a reduction in hours, rather than changes in wages) at around the time of onset of disability, but that earnings recover relatively rapidly by two years after the onset of disability—still, with a long-term earnings loss of at around 12 percent per year (Charles 2003).[9]

$$\Delta L_{ij} = \alpha_j + \beta_4 \Delta_4 h_{ij} + \beta_3 \Delta_3 h_{ij} + \sum_k \lambda_k X_{ijk} + \varepsilon_{ij}$$

We use a similar specification to explain changes in per-capita household consumption ΔC_{ij} over time.

$$\Delta C_{ij} = \alpha_j + \beta_4 \Delta_4 h_{ij} + \beta_3 \Delta_3 h_{ij} + \beta_2 \Delta_2 h_{ij} + \sum_{i} \lambda_k X_{ijk} + \varepsilon_{ij}$$

In an attempt to see if deterioration of the head of the household's health has an impact on the schooling of children, we turn our attention to children who were between ages 11 and 15 *and* who were enrolled in school at the time of the full LSMS (Wave 1). The dependent variable, S_{ij}, takes the value 1 if the child dropped out of school, and takes the value 0 if the child remained enrolled in school.

$$S_{ij} = \alpha_j + \beta_4 \Delta_4 h_{ij} + \beta_3 \Delta_3 h_{ij} + \beta_2 \Delta_2 h_{ij} + \sum_{k} \lambda_k X_{ijk} + \varepsilon_{ij}$$

Many of the studies of the impact of health shocks have been limited to a single indicator that happened to be captured by the data set used. The Bosnia and Herzegovina data set, in contrast, provides several indicators of disability and poor health. We separately explore the linkages of these various indicators with employment, earnings, and household consumption.[10]

Alternative Approaches to Measuring Changes in Health Status

The model is designed to assess the impact of changes in health status on various facets of welfare. However, measuring health status outside of a clinical setting is fraught with difficulties. Subjective assessments of health status (SAHS) have been shown to have predictive power for morbidity and mortality (Mete 2005; van Doorslaer and Gerdtham 2003; Idler and Kasl 1995; McCallum et al. 1994). Yet, it has also been shown that an individual's self-ranking of health status is affected by his or her own demographic and cultural characteristics (Mete and Cnobloch 2006; Lindeboom and van Doorslaer 2004; Van Doorslaer and Gerdthan 2003; Schultz and Tansel 2002). SAHS may also overstate the effect of health on the supply of labor as individuals use health status as a way of justifying labor decisions (Bound 1991; Straus and Thomas 1995) or justifying inclusion in other programs or receipt of benefits (Kerkhofs and Lindeboom 1995).

These studies suggest the need to evaluate the robustness of the findings by considering alternative proxies of poor health and disability. Fortunately, the Bosnia and Herzegovina LSMS offers three quite different health measures, which are comparable across survey waves: presence of chronic illness, disability, and ADL. Six ADL are included in the LSMS survey. However, only three of these were included in the subsequent rounds of the LBiH survey. This is probably because an ADL index constructed by these three variables explains 95 percent of the variation in an ADL index constructed with all six activities. The ADL index is thus constructed from these three variables (whether the person's health limited him or her from: vigorous activities such as lifting heavy objects, running, or participating in strenuous sports; walking uphill; or bending, lifting, or stooping). We use two alternative specifications to capture changes in ADL. One indicator captures the changes in all ADL (an index) between the first and fourth waves, while the other indicator focuses on whether the head of the household acquired a limitation (for the first time) in the same time period.

Both the presence of chronic disease and disability are captured with a simple question on whether the person has a chronic disease (disability). For disability, relying on such a simple question may lead to underestimating the incidence of disabilities. The format of the question is expected to only capture those individuals with severe disabilities or those with access to disability benefits, i.e., have formal disability status. While the WHO estimates that 10 percent of the population in developing countries suffers from disability (WHO 1980), results from census and survey data with questions similar to the ones used in the Bosnia and Herzegovina panel show much lower estimates: data from 35 countries in the early 1990s from censuses or surveys show only two countries with incidence rates greater than 5 percent (United Nations 2005). In all likelihood, different questions would have captured a much larger group as improvements in questionnaire design have a significant impact on reported incidence.[11] Table 1 shows how these different indicators are related to one another.

Results

Analysis of the effects of health shocks on welfare is restricted by the nature of the panel data set. As noted above, some of the definitions and variables varied by survey wave. The most consistent approach is that followed here: looking at changes between the first wave of the LSMS (2001) and the fourth wave (2004). It is also possible to decompose the health condition changes to those that occurred between Waves 1 and 3, and those that occurred between Waves 3 and 4. This allows more insight into the effect of timing of shocks on welfare.

The means of the four health indicators used are included in table 2. The first is the ADL index, which takes on a value of 0 to 1, indicating the share of limitations to ADL suffered by the individual. The second ADL variable is a dummy variable indicating whether the person has a limitation in any of the three measures of ADL. The change shows the percentage of individuals who had a new limitation occur since the first wave of the survey. Chronic illness is also measured using a dummy variable, indicating the presence or absence of chronic illness. The same is true of disability. For both of these last two variables, the change between Waves 1 and 4 indicates the percentage of individuals suffering from a new chronic illness (disability) since the first wave of the survey.

Household Head's Employment and Earnings

Documenting the impact of health shocks on employment prospects is critical both because those who become disabled need at least as much earnings after the onset of a disability as before, and because being employed—independent from the earnings from employment—influences the quality of life for individuals with disabilities. To be consistent with the previous literature, our discussion focuses on the heads of households (although we have explored trends in other adult household members' employment and earnings as well; the results are mentioned in the text as appropriate). Typically, a person is identified as the head of household by other household

TABLE 1

Correlation among Indicators of Health and Disability

	Correlations (of levels) Wave 1			
	Chronic disease	Disability	ADL index	Any limitation to daily activity
Chronic disease	1			
Disability	0.2174	1		
ADL index	0.5744	0.2343	1	
Any limitation to daily activity	0.5469	0.2009	0.8565	1
	Correlations (of changes between Waves 1 and 4)			
	New chronic disease	New disability	Worsening of ADL index	New limitation to daily activity
New chronic disease	1			
New disability	0.0345	1		
ADL index worsened	0.2456	0.1134	1	
New limitation to daily activity	0.2022	0.0543	0.6801	1

Sources: Bosnia and Herzegovina LSMS 2001 and LBiHS (Wave 4, 2004).

TABLE 2

Household Heads: Sample Statistics, Means, and Standard Deviations

Variables	Period 1 (2001)	Period 2 (2004)	Change (2001–2004)
Health status			
ADL index	0.367	0.451	0.108
	(0.402)	(0.435)	(0.418)
Any ADL	0.532	0.586	0.200
	(0.499)	(0.493)	(0.400)
Chronic disease	0.403	0.419	0.141
	(0.491)	(0.493)	(0.348)
Disability status	0.105	0.125	0.069
	(0.306)	(0.331)	(0.254)
Economic status			
Per-capita consumption (nonmedical)	3529.151	4262.487	760.695
	(2220.522)	(2294.596)	(1908.045)
Per-adult equivalent consumption (nonmedical)	3665.542	4393.514	732.495
	(2027.478)	(2118.465)	(1860.79)
Head's monthly earnings	389.541	502.628	98.078
	(361.523)	(431.608)	(389.613)
Head's monthly earnings, per capita	121.700	153.133	26.645
	(157.745)	(136.446)	(155.330)
Head's monthly earnings, per adult equivalent	156.692	202.586	38.898
	(179.318)	(174.069)	(181.480)
Head's hours of work	40.034	37.862	-2.164
	(17.222)	(18.420)	(21.993)
Head not working	0.065	0.074	0.064
	(0.246)	(0.261)	(0.245)
Demographic characteristics			
Head's age	54.140		
	(14.081)		
Head is male	0.753		
	(0.431)		
Head has 0–4 years' education	0.262		
	(0.440)		
Head has 5–8 years' education	0.195		
	(0.396)		
Head has 9–12 years' education	0.435		
	(0.496)		
Head has 13+ years' education	0.108		
	(0.311)		
Head is married	0.694	0.681	
	(0.461)	(0.466)	
Family structure			
Spouse's age conditional on head being married	48.344		
	(13.645)		
Household size	3.151	3.130	-0.077
	(1.574)	(1.608)	(0.872)
Children under age 6	0.248	0.166	-0.099
	(0.562)	(0.454)	(0.456)
Children between age 7 and 15	0.359	0.348	-0.038
	(0.670)	(0.671)	(0.556)
Household members older than 66	0.396	0.437	0.081
	(0.649)	(0.670)	(0.389)
Observations	2997	2416	

Sources: Bosnia and Herzegovina LSMS 2001 and LBiHS (Wave 4, 2004); authors' calculations.

Note: Household consumption excludes medical expenditure.

members because his or her earnings represent the principal source of earned income in the household.[12] Thus, a decline in this person's earnings and overall employment is expected to have a substantial impact on both the person's own *and* the household's welfare.

We examine the impact of health shocks on three labor-related variables. The first specification looks at the change in the number of hours worked per week.[13] The second dependent variable of interest is the probability of working for pay, a slightly restricted labor force participation model. In the third specification, we look at changes in earnings adjusted for annual inflation.

We regress the labor force variables on basic characteristics of the head of household: age, gender, marital status, and education level. Additionally, we control for changes in the size and structure of the household. The results on hours worked are found in table 3. A comparison of the coefficients on each of the four health indicators is found in table 4.

Declines in health are associated with a decline in the number of hours worked: all five health measures show the same tendency,

TABLE 3

The Effect of a Change in Household Head's Health on His or Her Hours Worked

Alternative specifications	(1)	(2)	(3)	(4)	(5)
Head's ADL index worsened[a]	−4.84				
	(2.058)***				
Actual change in ADL index[b]		−5.642			
		(2.301)***			
Newly acquired limitation in daily activity			−1.018		
			(2.230)		
Newly acquired chronic disease				−3.232	
				(2.792)	
Newly acquired disability					−8.292
					(4.540)*
Head's age	−0.213	−0.301	−0.583	−0.242	−0.469
	(0.647)	(0.645)	(0.653)	(0.640)	(0.646)
Head's age squared/100	0.260	0.328	0.608	0.293	0.562
	−0.653	(0.653)	(0.661)	(0.648)	(0.657)
Head is male	1.078	0.835	1.441	0.747	1.249
	(4.114)	(4.112)	(4.255)	(4.052)	(4.042)
Head has 0–4 years' education	−8.731	−8.672	−11.711	−10.004	−11.693
	(3.790)***	(3.789)***	(4.008)***	(3.715)***	(3.829)***
Head has 5–8 years' education	−4.488	−4.709	−3.377	−4.397	−4.543
	(3.041)	(3.041)	(3.219)	(2.982)	(2.991)
Head has 9–12 years' education	−4.964	−4.788	−4.314	−4.739	−4.669
	(2.397)***	(2.396)**	(2.508)*	(2.378)***	(2.386)**
Head is married	−2.311	−1.913	−2.466	−1.757	−1.827
	(3.666)	(3.661)	(3.853)	(3.573)	(3.554)
Change in the number of children younger than 15	2.487	2.497	2.422	2.451	2.201
	(1.461)*	(1.460)*	(1.494)	(1.444)*	(1.462)
Change in the number of adults	1.244	1.349	1.454	1.173	1.444
	(1.206)	(1.205)	(1.262)	(1.193)	(1.210)
Observations	656	656	656	673	653

Sources: Bosnia and Herzegovina LSMS 2001 and LBiHS (Wave 4, 2004); authors' calculations.

Note: a/ This is a dummy variable taking on the value of 1 if the individual's ADL index worsened in any way over the time period, and 0 otherwise.
b/ An increase in the value of this variable indicates a decline in health status.
* Significant at .10 level; ** significant at .05 level; *** significant at .01 level.

TABLE 4

Effect of a Change in Household Head's Health on Labor Supply and Earnings

	Head's ADL ADL index worsened	Actual change in ADL index	Head's newly acquired limitation to daily activity	Head's newly acquired chronic disease	Head's newly becoming disabled
Change in head's working hours	−4.840 (2.058)***	−5.642 (2.301)***	−1.018 (2.230)	−3.232 (2.792)	−8.292 (4.540)*
Observations	656	656	656	673	653
Change in head's labor force participation	0.060 (0.125)	0.113 (0.115)	0.085 (0.131)	0.026 (0.155)	−0.247 (0.273)
Marginal effects	0.004	0.007	0.005	0.002	−0.013
Observations	1850	1850	1850	1880	1807
Change in head's monthly earnings	−56.910 (35.959)	−56.342 (39.877)	−36.802 (34.068)	−3.813 (49.694)	1.019 (79.828)
Observations	517	517	517	530	518
Change in head's per-capita monthly earnings	−38.661 (16.523)***	−48.569 (18.286)***	−32.661 (17.757)*	7.484 (22.885)	12.032 (36.804)
Observations	517	517	517	530	518
Change in head's per adult equivalent monthly earnings	−50.053 (20.275)***	−42.556 (18.305)**	−34.343 (19.107)*	6.949 (25.530)	13.199 (41.044)
Observations	517	517	517	530	518

Sources: Bosnia and Herzegovina LSMS 2001 and LBiHS (Wave 4, 2004); authors' calculations.

* Significant at .10 level; ** significant at .05 level; *** significant at .01 level.

although the results are not statistically significant for two of them. A worsening in the ADL index decreases hours worked by almost five hours per week. However, moving from no limitation to having any limitation in ADL has a smaller effect, at about one hour per week, which is not statistically significant at the 10 percent level. The most substantial decline in hours worked is linked to the onset of disability. For these individuals, the number of hours declined by eight, or 20 percent of the average hours worked. The onset of a chronic illness is associated with a decline in hours worked, although this is not a statistically significant effect. This could be because many chronic ailments may have little impact on the ability to work and may more closely approximate the minor illnesses that Gertler and Gruber (2002) discuss.[14]

The effects of health shocks vary not just by type of shock, but by type of labor force outcome. As shown above, a worsening in ADLs or the onset of a disability lowers the number of hours worked. Yet none of the health shocks examined is closely linked to the probability of employment (table 4). This suggests that the legislation aimed at protecting jobs in the face of illness or disability is binding. Or, more generally, the labor code is such that dismissal of any employee is costly and time-consuming.

Earnings are negatively and substantially affected by a worsening in the ADL index or the onset of a new limitation in ADL. Becoming more seriously limited in ADL decreases the head of household's per-capita monthly earnings by approximately KM 39, from mean earnings of KM 89. A new limitation will decrease per-capita earnings by almost KM 32. The onset of chronic illness does not have a statistically significant impact on earnings, again, perhaps reflecting the heterogeneity of chronic illness and the fact that not all will affect a person's ability to work. Note that while the onset of a disability lowered the hours worked, it does not lower earnings. This finding is consistent with the possibility that disability labor legislation compensates for the negative effects of deteriorating health status, at least in the short term.

Household Consumption

The extent to which negative effects of health shocks on employment are reflected in consumption patterns of households depends on whether the deterioration in the head of household's health triggers a response from other household members in the form of increased work hours and earnings. Other factors that may prevent significant declines in per-capita household consumption include adjustment in the size and composition of households; increases in social protection or assistance benefits; and increases in transfers from friends and relatives.

In the Bosnia and Herzegovina case, the data reveal that other household members do not move between employment states in a manner that can be linked to variations in the head of household's health status (results available from authors upon request; a similar trend is also noted by Gertler and Gruber for Indonesia). Similarly, changes in household size and composition before and after a health shock are negligible. Increased receipt of remittances and other private transfers is a further mechanism for offsetting the impact of health shocks. Unfortunately, the data on private and public transfers are not comparable between Waves 1 and 4 of the surveys, so we cannot estimate the changes in these variables. A simple comparison of the difference in the receipt of public and private transfers between households whose head is disabled or suffering ill health and all other households does show, however, a much higher likelihood of receipt of transfers by the former. Close to 40 percent of all households whose head is disabled receive disability benefits, compared to 11 percent of those without a disabled head of household.[15] Other social assistance (public transfers) does not seem to be targeted toward disability or sickness, but somewhat on worsening levels of ADL. In contrast, private

TABLE 5

Comparison of Household Situations before and after Health Shocks

	ADL Index worsened?		New ADL limitation?		New chronic disease?		New disability?	
	No	Yes	No	Yes	No	Yes	No	Yes
Receive disability benefit	11.8%	17.3%	12.5%	18.1%	13.6%	13.4%	11.2%	37.0%
Value of disability benefit	2,252.03	2,409.50	2,376.05	2,456.77	2,241.59	2,685.52	2,336.50	2,336.43
	(2,156.69)	(2,191.61)	(2,168.98)	(2,383.38)	(2,161.36)	(2,156.56)	(2,197.60)	(2,239.38)
Receive non-disability social assistance benefit	34.1%	51.5%	39.7%	39.4%	38.2%	48.5%	39.4%	39.4%
Value of benefit	2,369.07	2,486.62	2,339.09	2,545.24	2,460.77	2,309.76	2,481.43	1,822.66
	(1,564.34)	(1,722.33)	(1,468.86)	(1,901.73)	(1,725.03)	(1,253.92)	(1,652.32)	(1,416.13)
Receive any social assistance benefit	42.4%	63.7%	48.4%	52.8%	48.0%	57.1%	46.9%	70.9%
Value of benefit	2,517.48	2,657.08	2,521.27	2,739.93	2,581.21	2,594.43	2,631.11	2,203.39
	(1,816.20)	(1,949.41)	(1,733.57)	(2,204.91)	(1,936.62)	(1,604.21)	(1,861.03)	(2,015.39)
Receive private transfers	9.8%	12.7%	16.6%	14.0%	14.3%	22.0%	14.3%	26.8%
Value of private transfers	616.71	702.02	633.07	486.61	550.55	803.20	588.65	692.27
	(714.27)	(973.01)	(716.54)	(436.76)	(556.07)	(978.02)	(643.90)	(863.85)
Household size	−0.06	−0.13	−0.06	−0.16	−0.07	−0.12	−0.07	−0.17
	(0.78)	(0.96)	(0.83)	(0.95)	(0.84)	(0.86)	(0.83)	(0.94)
Observations	1,241	631	1,372	343	1,635	268	1,703	127

Sources: Bosnia and Herzegovina LSMS 2001 and LBiHS (Wave 4, 2004); authors' calculations.

* Significant at .10 level; ** significant at .05 level; *** significant at .01 level.

transfers are targeted to households where the head of the household is disabled or suffers from a chronic ailment.

The Bosnia and Herzegovina data show that such mechanisms fail to fully insure per-capita household consumption against the onset of disability and deteriorating ADL. Per-capita household consumption decreases by 7.8 percentage points, on average, if the head of household becomes disabled. There is no evidence of differential effects for the poorest individuals versus the rest.[16] Similarly, worsening of the ADL index leads to a 4.3 percentage point decrease in per-capita household consumption. Variations in the reporting of chronic illnesses do not influence per-capita household consumption. This finding is consistent with the literature, which argues that households might deal with minor health events but are not able to cope with the economic costs of major illnesses. Note that consumption data used here do not include health expenditures. Previous work on disability in Bosnia and Herzegovina has shown that health expenditures by the disabled are higher than for others (Tsirunyan 2005): this spending may be

TABLE 6

Effect of a Change in Household Head's Health on Per-Capita Household Consumption

	Alternative specifications				
	(1)	(2)	(3)	(4)	(5)
Head's ADL index worsened	−0.043 (0.021)**				
Change in ADL index		0.003 0.024			
Newly acquired limitation to daily activity			−0.022 0.026		
Newly acquired chronic disease				−0.013 0.028	
Newly occurred disability					−0.078 (0.040)**
Head's age	0.003 0.006	0.002 0.006	0.002 0.006	0.001 0.006	−0.0001 0.006
Head's age squared/100	−0.003 0.005	−0.002 0.005	−0.002 0.005	−0.001 0.005	−0.0003 0.005
Head is male	−0.008 0.037	−0.008 0.037	0.018 0.038	−0.011 0.036	−0.0110 0.037
Head: 0–4 years of education	0.013 0.037	0.011 0.037	0.0[illegible]9 0.039	0.001 0.037	0.0010 0.038
Head: 5–8 years of education	−0.051 0.037	−0.053 0.037	−0.028 0.039	−0.066 (0.037)*	−0.052 0.037
Head: 9–12 years of education	−0.038 0.033	−0.039 0.033	−0.026 0.035	−0.050 0.033	−0.046 0.033
Head: married	−0.066 (0.035)*	−0.065 (0.035)*	−0.084 (0.036)***	−0.059 (0.034)*	−0.053 0.035
Change in the number of children younger than 15	−0.182 (0.018)***	−0.182 (0.018)***	−0.19 (0.018)***	−0.178 (0.018)***	−0.175 (0.018)***
Change in the number of adults	−0.141 (0.014)***	−0.140 (0.014)***	−0.144 (0.015)***	−0.141 (0.014)***	−0.140 (0.014)***
Observations	1,843	1,843	1,843	1,873	1,801

Sources: Bosnia and Herzegovina LSMS 2001 and LBiHS (Wave 4, 2004); authors' calculations.

Note: Consumption excludes medical expenditure.
* Significant at .10 level; ** significant at .05 level; *** significant at .01 level.

crowding out consumption expenditures on other goods and services.

Children's Schooling

To investigate the possibility that health shocks influence not only household consumption levels, but other aspects of household living standards and decision making as well, this section presents predictors of school dropout (between Wave 1 and Wave 4) among children ages 11 to 15. Table 7 shows that new chronic disease developed by the head of household is associated with up to a 14 percentage point increase in children's probability of dropping out of school. Boys are consistently about 5 percentage points more likely to drop out of school than girls, although the difference is statistically significant in only one specification. When separate models are estimated for males and females (not reported), we see that a worsening of the household head's ADL index increases the probability of male children dropping out of school by 9 percentage points (the effect is statistically significant at the 5 percent level). Similarly, if a household head reports a new chronic disease between Waves 1 and 4, boys' probability of dropping out of school increases by 15 percentage points (the effect is, however, only statistically significant at the 10 percent level). None of the health shocks considered here has a statistically significant effect on girls' school enrollments.

Does Timing of the Onset of Disability or Poor Health Matter?

By taking into account the time of onset of the health shock, we see that the labor market protections for those with disabilities may be short-

TABLE 7

Marginal Effects of Changes in Household Heads' Health on their Children's Schooling
(Ages 11 to 15)

	Alternative specifications					
	(1)	(2)	(3)	(4)	(5)	(6)
Head's ADL index worsened	0.01					0.01
	(0.03)					(0.03)
Actual change in head's ADL index		0.01				
		(0.03)				
Head's newly acquired limitation to daily activity			0.01			
			(0.03)			
Head's newly acquired chronic disease				0.13**		0.14**
				(0.07)		(0.07)
Head's newly occurred disability					−0.06	−0.06
					(0.03)	(0.03)
Child's age	0.09	0.08	0.04	0.07	0.08	0.06
	(0.38)	(0.37)	(0.38)	(0.35)	(0.37)	(0.36)
Child's age squared/100	0.00	0.02	0.16	0.03	0.02	0.07
	(1.12)	(1.11)	(1.15)	(1.05)	(1.09)	(1.08)
Child is male	0.04	0.04	0.05*	0.04	0.04	0.04
	(0.03)	(0.03)	(0.03)	(0.03)	(0.03)	(0.03)
Change in the number of children younger than 15	0.02	0.02	0.01	0.02	0.02	0.02
	(0.03)	(0.03)	(0.03)	(0.03)	(0.03)	(0.03)
Change in the number of adults	0.02	0.02	0.02	0.02	0.02	0.02
	(0.03)	(0.03)	(0.02)	(0.03)	(0.03)	90.03)
Observations	334	334	334	339	331	322

Sources: Bosnia and Herzegovina LSMS 2001 and LBiHS (Wave 4, 2004); authors' calculations.

* Significant at .10 level; ** significant at .05 level; *** significant at .01 level.

lived and vary from those that exist for other types of health shocks. Disabilities that occur within the previous year do not have a significant, negative effect on hours worked, contrary to what one might expect. The sign of the estimated coefficient is negative, but the impact is not statistically significant. But, if one looks at the impact of a disability that began two to three years earlier, the picture is quite different. Disabilities that began two to three years ago lead to a decline of almost 17 hours of work per week, close to half the average of a 40-hour work week (table 8). This drop in hours may reflect an adjustment made in the workplace to accommodate the person's disabilities and changed work ability, or it may simply reflect the person's inability to work more hours either physically or because jobs are unavailable.

TABLE 8

Effects of Decomposed Changes in Household Head's Health on Change in His or Her Hours Worked

	Alternative specifications				
	(1)	(2)	(3)	(4)	(5)
ADL index worsened:	−8.38**				−8.96**
Wave 1 to 3	(2.80)				(3.05)
ADL index worsened:	9.54**				9.59**
Wave 3 to 4	(3.20)				(3.42)
Newly acquired limitation		−2.89			
to ADL: Wave 1 to 3		(3.26)			
Newly acquired limitation		1.27			
to ADL: Wave 3 to 4		(2.97)			
Newly acquired chronic			−3.34		−1.59
disease: Wave 1 to 3			(2.86)		(3.08)
Newly acquired chronic			−5.59*		−4.94
disease: Wave 3 to 4			(2.92)		(3.11)
Newly occurred disability:				−17.70**	−11.08
Wave 1 to 3				(8.94)	(9.80)
Newly occurred disability:				−5.10	−1.48
Wave 3 to 4				(5.23)	(5.38)
Head's age	−0.28	−0.20	−0.17	−0.44	−0.35
	(0.64)	(0.73)	(0.64)	(0.65)	(0.66)
Head's age squared/100	0.34	0.11	0.24	0.55	0.47
	(0.65)	(0.74)	(0.65)	(0.66)	(0.67)
Head is male	−0.26	5.36	1.17	0.76	0.02
	(4.13)	(4.80)	(4.05)	(4.13)	(4.23)
Head: 0–4 years of education	−9.16**	−13.05**	−9.93**	−12.02**	−11.30**
	(3.78)	(4.35)	(3.71)	(3.93)	(4.03)
Head: 5–8 years of education	−4.63	−4.41	−4.28	−4.68	−5.24*
	(3.03)	(3.61)	(2.38)	(3.04)	(3.10)
Head: 9–12 years of education	−4.58*	−4.09	−4.87**	−4.61*	−4.84**
	(2.39)	(2.78)	(2.38)	(2.40)	(2.43)
Head: married	−1.51	−5.36	−2.06	−1.49	−1.62
	(3.66)	(4.41)	(3.57)	(3.66)	(3.75)
Change in the number of	2.57*	2.41	2.29	2.34	2.15
children under 15	(1.46)	(1.63)	(1.45)	(1.48)	(1.51)
Change in the number of adults	1.33	1.26	1.09	1.71	1.67
	(1.21)	(1.40)	(1.19)	(1.24)	(1.26)

Sources: Bosnia and Herzegovina LSMS 2001, LBiHS (Wave 3, 2003, and Wave 4, 2004); authors calculations.

* Significant at .05 level; ** significant at .01 level.

Surprisingly, for those whose ADL worsened in the past year, the number of hours they worked increased, but the (expected) negative effect on hours of work occurs if ADL worsened two to three years ago. It may be that individuals with a serious health shock, but not one that leads to formal disability status, have to work additional hours to partially make up for lowered productivity. This is in contrast to those who obtain disability status and are thus better protected from the loss of earnings or losing their job in the short run. The data appear to show, however, that this temporary increase in hours is not sustainable in the medium term.

In contrast to disability and worsening ADL, the onset of chronic illness appears to be an event from which the individual is able to recover. The negative effect of chronic disease occurring recently (within one year) is statistically significant, lowering hours worked by just over five and a half. Yet, the effect of having a chronic disease that began two to three years earlier is not statistically significant. Thus, there appears to be an ability to recover and adjust to the effect of chronic disease in the medium term.

Taking into account the timing of health shocks on per-capita household consumption and children's schooling outcomes does not produce statistically significant estimates on any of the variables considered. While one of the two ADL variables is associated with a reduction in earnings if the limitations took place two to three years previously, the other ADL limitation variable (the difference between ADL scores) is linked to a positive change in earnings.[17]

Conclusions

This paper showed that individuals who experience a health shock reduce their hours of work significantly, although the likelihood of stopping employment altogether is small. Thus it is possible to miss a large effect on employment—for example, onset of disability leads to an eight-hour decline in weekly hours of work—if one distinguishes only between being employed or not. Furthermore, by making a distinction between health shocks that happened within the last year and those that occurred three or four years ago, we see that the employment protection legislation for the disabled seems effective in preventing an immediate decline in weekly hours of work, but not for continued protection as disabilities that began two to three years ago are associated with a startling 17 fewer hours of work per week. This is in contrast to the situation in countries with weaker employment protection legislation but lower unemployment rates, where a sharp initial decline in hours of work is followed by a recovery period.[18] In the Bosnia and Herzegovina case, the existing legislation offers temporary relief, but after a one-year period the disabled individuals face an inhospitable labor market environment where formal employment opportunities are scarce and informal employment is often physically demanding. Overall improvements in labor demand would help to ease the longer-term disadvantages of disabled individuals and *targeted* government interventions that provide training and matching for new jobs could be considered in this context, subject to thorough evaluations of such programs on a pilot basis at first.

A natural next step in the analysis of the economic implications of health shocks is to move away from what happens to the household head and instead examine whether households themselves can deal with the deterioration of the head of household's health. In Bosnia and Herzegovina, only major health shocks, as captured by the onset of new disability, and to a lesser extent deterioration in ADL, have an influence on per-capita household consumption, reducing it by 7.8 percentage points and 4.3 percentage points, respectively. The way households (partially) smooth the effects of such health shocks also matters. In Bosnia and Herzegovina, other adult household members do not respond to the head of the household's deteriorating health condition (and reduced number of work hours) by working more. This may be because of lack of employment opportunities in a high-unemployment environment, or because of the need to provide care to the disabled individual at home. Instead, in addition to social protection transfers, transfers from friends and relatives come into play. At this stage, public disability assistance is strongly biased in favor of war veterans, with much more generous benefits to this group. Thus in terms of the allocation of funds, the social protection system is not designed to smooth the negative impact of nonwar-related disabilities (other than the formal employment protection legislation). This research highlights the need to balance the benefits designed for war veterans with those for other disabled individuals, since the short-term (formal) employment protection alone is not sufficient to maintain the wealth levels of the latter group.

A by-product of health shocks to the household head that is often ignored is the implications for the education prospects of children. The Bosnia and Herzegovina data provide weak evidence on this, revealing that if a household head reports a new chronic health condition, his or her children are 14 percentage points more likely to drop out of school compared to others. In addition, male children's school outcomes are influenced by a deterioration in household head's ADL index in the expected direction. However, this part of the analysis raises more questions than it answers, including why male children's school outcomes react to changes in the head of household's health, but female children's do not; and also why we see a statistically significant relationship when the health proxy is reporting chronic illnesses (and ADL in the case of male children), but fail to confirm such a linkage when the health proxy is reporting disability status.

Notes

1. Townsend (1994) finds that the proportion of the year an adult male is sick has no impact on consumption in three villages in India. In contrast, using data from Indonesia, Gertler and Gruber (2002) find that households cannot insure consumption against illness if one measures health shocks as changes in an Activities of Daily Limitations (ADL) index.
2. Chetty and Looney (2005) show that evaluating the value of social safety nets in developing countries by exclusively focusing on variations in household consumption levels may be misleading, if households—especially those that are close to a subsistence level of consumption to start with—avoid a substantial consumption drop as a result of an unexpected shock by, for example, taking children out of school or sending additional household members into the labor force. Thus, the authors argue that in such cases, social insurance could yield large welfare gains. Empirical evidence supporting this finding has started to emerge in a variety of countries, suggesting that girls' schooling prospects may be particularly vulnerable to unexpected household shocks (see Lloyd, Mete, and Grant 2006 using data from Pakistan; Skoufias and Parker [forthcoming] using data from Mexico).
3. The legal protection for disabled employees states: "An employee who has been injured at work or has obtained a disease as a result of work, cannot be dismissed by an employer while he/she is medically unfit for work, regardless or whether the employee has made a contract with the employer for permanent or temporary employment. If the Pensions and Invalids' Insurance fund establishes him/her to have remaining work capacity, the employer is obliged to offer the employee a different position that is suitable to his/her remaining capacity... If an employer is not able to offer an appropriate alternative work position, then the employee has the right to claim benefits from the Pensions and Invalids Insurance." However, there are questions about the extent to which the employment protection for the disabled is implemented in practice.
4. A Multiple Indicator Cluster survey was the first nationally representative household survey carried out in the newly formed Bosnia and Herzegovina. This was done by UNICEF in 2000, but focused largely on maternal and child health.
5. The first round of the LSMS received financial and technical support from the World Bank, DfID, UNDP, the EU, and Sida. The subsequent waves forming a panel of a subset of the LSMS households was supported by DfID and was called the Living in Bosnia and Herzegovina survey.
6. The sample excluded the Brcko district.

7. For more details, see State Agency for Statistics et al. 2003.
8. The actual number of households interviewed varied by year as the panel followed individuals, not households, and new household formation increased the sample, while deaths and emigration decreased it. See "Field Work and Technical Reports," (Birks and Sinclair, and the Independent Bureau for Humanitarian Issues) for further information on each wave of Living in Bosnia and Herzegovina survey.
9. Charles (2003) does not consider the extent to which households compensate for the initial drop in earnings.
10. The most commonly available question on health is whether a person was sick or injured in a specific reference period. But, as Gertler and Gruber (2002) demonstrate, not being able to distinguish between minor and major illnesses is a drawback—one that can be partially overcome with an ADL index. Another indicator that may be considered in this context is nutritional status—for example, Wagstaff (2005) uses a body mass index (BMI) as a proxy for health shocks. But, in this context, a nutritional measure is problematic. It is not a measure of disability: many of the individuals who are suffering from malnutrition may be functioning at reasonable levels and their BMI may hit normal levels if and when they find employment (this is clearly not the case for most disabled individuals). Also, the reverse causality issue, namely the possibility that reduced consumption itself leads to lower BMI rather than the other way around, is a more serious concern when BMI is used to capture changes in health status.
11. The revision of the Uganda census disability question from the 1991 to the 2001 census changed the estimate of disability among the oldest group from around 5 percent to more than 20 percent (Martinho and Banda 2005) and a survey in Nicaragua in 2005 designed specifically to measure disability gives an incidence rate of 11 percent (INEC 2003).
12. This was not, however, an official criterion of being the head of the household: households were free to identify one member based on whatever criteria they felt to be appropriate.
13. The reference period for hours worked per week in each round of the survey is the week prior to the administration of the interview, not a fixed reference period for all households.
14. Gertler and Gruber (2002) document even larger effects using Indonesia data, where moving from completely healthy in the ADL index to completely sick lowers hours of work by almost 31 hours per week.
15. Another member of the household, not the head, is disabled.
16. Jalan and Ravallion (1999), for example, show that in the poorest wealth decile, 40 percent of the income shock is passed onto current consumption, while the richest third of households are protected from almost 90 percent of an income shock in rural China. The estimates for different consumption quintiles are not reported here; results available from the authors upon request.
17. The estimates from these specifications are available from the authors upon request.
18. Presumably after an initial abrupt adjustment, the disabled individuals eventually start working more, perhaps through moving to a different field or sector.

References

Beegle, Kathleen, and Wendy A. Stock. 2003. "The Labor Market Effects of Disability Discrimination Laws." *Journal of Human Resources* 38 (4): 807–59.

Birks and Sinclair. 2005. "Field Work and Technical Report, Household Survey Panel Series Wave 4." Independent Bureau for Humanitarian Issues Consultant Report for U.K. Department for International Development Project on Labor and Social Policy in Bosnia and Herzegovina: The Development of Policies and Measures for Social Mitigation.

———. 2003. "Field Work and Technical Report, Household Survey Panel Series Wave 2." Consultant Report for U.K. Department for International Development Project on Labor and Social Policy in Bosnia and Herzegovina: The Development of Policies and Measures for Social Mitigation.

Bound, John. 1991. "Self-Reported versus Objective Measures of Health in Retirement Models." *Journal of Human Resources* 26 (1):106–38.

Charles, Kerwin Kofi. 2003. "The Longitudinal Structure of Earnings Losses among Work-Limited Disabled Workers." *Journal of Human Resources* 38 (3): 619–46.

Chetty, Raj, and Adam Looney. 2005. "Consumption Smoothing and the Welfare Consequences of Social Insurance in Developing Countries." Working Paper No. 11709, National Bureau of Economic Research, Cambridge, MA.

Costa, Dora L. 2000. "Long-Term Declines in Disability among Older Men: Medical Care, Public Health, and Occupational Change." Working Paper No. 7605, National Bureau of Economic Research, Cambridge, MA.

Crossley, Thomas F., and Steven Kennedy. 2002. "The Reliability of Self-Assessed Health Status." *Journal of Health Economics* 21:643–58.

Elwan, Ann. 1999. "Poverty and Disability: A Survey of the Literature." Social Protection Discussion Paper No. 9932, World Bank, Washington, DC.

European Observatory on Health Care Systems. 2002. *Health Care Systems in Transition: Bosnia and Herzegovina*. Copenhagen, Denmark: European Observatory on Health Care Systems.

Gertler, Paul, and Jonathan Gruber. 2002. "Insuring Consumption against Illness." *American Economic Review* 92 (1):51–70.

Gertler, Paul, David I. Levine, and Enrico Moretti. 2002. "Do Microfinance Programs Help Families Insure Consumption against Illness?" Unpublished Manuscript.

Instituto Nacional de Estadísticas y Censos-Nicaragua. 2003. "Encuestas Nicaragüense para personas con discapacidades, ENDIS." Managua Nicaragua.

IOS Partners. 2003. "Policies for Persons with Disabilities." Report prepared for PIU_PELRP, FBiH Development and Employment Foundation of Republika Srpska.

Jalan, Jyotsna, and Martin Ravallion. 1999. "Are the Poor Less Well Insured? Evidence on Vulnerability to Income Risk in Rural China." *Journal of Development Economics* 58: 61–81.

Kahn, Matthew E. 1998. "Health and Labor Market Performance: The Case of Diabetes." *Journal of Labor Economics* 16 (4): 878–99.

Kerkhofs, Marcel, and Maarten Lindeboom. 1995. "Subjective Health Measures and State Dependent Reporting Errors." *Health Economics* 4: 221–35.

Lindeboom, Maarten, and Eddy van Doorslaer. 2004. "Cut-Point Shift and Index-Shift in Self-Reported Health." Discussion Paper TI-2003-042/3, Tinbergen Institute.

Lloyd, Cynthia B., Cem Mete, and Monica Grant. 2006. "The Implications of Changing Educational and Family Circumstances for Children's Grade Progression in Rural Pakistan: 1997–2004." Working Paper No. 209, Population Council Policy Research Division, New York, New York.

Martinho, Maria, and Jeremiah Banda. 2005. "United Nations Collection of National Disability Statistics from Population and Housing Censuses and Related National Surveys and Administrative Records." Presentation at the 4th meeting of the Washington Group on Disability Statistics, Rio de Janeiro, Brazil.

Mete, Cem, and Stefania R. Cnobloch. 2006. "Socioeconomic Status and Health Outcomes. A Relationship in Disguise?" Manuscript. World Bank, Washington, DC.

Mete, Cem. 2005. "Predictors of Elderly Mortality: Health Status, Socioeconomic Characteristics and Social Determinants of Health." *Health Economics* 14: 135–48.

Mont, Daniel. 2005. "Disability in Central America." Presentation at the 4th meeting of the Washington Group on Disability Statistics, Rio de Janeiro, Brazil.

PRISM. 2006. "Social-Economic Status of Disabled Persons." Final Report, World Bank, Sarajevo, Bosnia and Herzegovina.

Schultz, T. Paul, and Aysit Tansel. 1997. "Wage and Labor Supply Effects of Illness in Côte d'Ivoire and Ghana: Instrumental Variable Estimates for Days Disabled." *Journal of Development Economics* 53 (2):251–86.

Skoufias, Emmanuel, and Susan W. Parker. Forthcoming. "Job Loss and Family Adjustments in Work and Schooling during the Mexican Peso Crisis." *Journal of Population Economics*.

State Agency for Statistics, Republika Srpska Institute for Statistics, Federation of Bosnia and Herzegovina Institute for Statistics. 2003. *Living Standard Measurement Survey in Bosnia and Herzegovina*. Sarajevo: State Agency for Statistics, Republika Srpska Institute for Statistics, Federation of Bosnia and Herzegovina Institute for Statistics.

Straus, John and Duncan Thomas. 1996. "Human Resources: Empirical Modeling of Household and Family Decisions." in *Handbook of Development Economics*, ed. J. Behrman and T.N. Srinavasan, Amsterdam, the Netherlands.

Tsirunyan, Sasun. 2005. "Disability and Poverty in Bosnia and Herzegovina: Findings Based on Living Standards Measurement Survey." Consultant Report Prepared for the World Bank. Sarajevo, Bosnia and Herzegovina.

Townsend, Robert M. 1994. "Risk and Insurance in Village India." *Econometrica* 62 (3): 539–91.

———. 1995. "Consumption Insurance: An Evaluation of Risk-Bearing Systems in Low-Income Economies." *Journal of Economic Perspectives* 9 (3): 83–102.

United Nations. 2005. "Disability Statistics Data Base." Statistics Division, http://unstats.un.org/unsd/demographic/sconcerns/disability/disab2.asp.

Van Doorslaer, Eddy, and Ulf. G. Gerdtham. 2002. "Does Inequality in Self-Assessed Health Predict Inequality in Survival by Income? Evidence from Swedish Data." *Social Science and Medicine*, 57: 1621–29.

Wagstaff, Adam. 2005. "The Economic Consequences of Health Shocks." Policy Research Working Paper No. 3644, World Bank, Washington, DC.

World Bank. 2005. "Bosnia and Herzegovina Case Study." in *Review of Experiences of Family Medicine in Europe and Central Asia*. Volume III, Report No. 32354-ECA, Human Development Unit, Europe and Central Asia, Washington, DC: World Bank.

———. 2003. "Bosnia and Herzegovina Social Insurance Technical Assistance Project, 2003." Human Development Unit, Europe and Central Asia Region, Washington, D.C.

———. 2003. *Uzbekistan Living Standards Assessment*. Vol. 2, Report No. 25923-UZ, Human Development Sector Unit, Europe and Central Asia Region, Washington, DC: World Bank.

———. 2000. "Memorandum of the President of the International Development Association to the Executive Directors on a Country Assistance Strategy of the World Bank Group for Bosnia and Herzegovina." Report No. 20592 Bosnia and Herzegovina.

World Health Organization. 1980. *International Classification of Impairments, Disabilities, and Handicaps*, Geneva: World Health Organization.

CHAPTER 4

Health Disabilities and Labor Productivity in Russia in 2004

Health Consequences Beyond Premature Death

T. Paul Schultz*

Introduction

Health status can directly influence an individual's capacity to work or the person's labor productivity along three or more dimensions. Health can affect the probability that a person participates in the labor force; health can influence the hours worked per week, month, or year; and health can affect the worker's productivity, which is approximated here by the hourly wage rate. Spillovers of a person's health on the economic output of society can also impact what others can accomplish, although these spillovers are less often evaluated in empirical studies. For example, if the worker is engaged in a production team for which other workers within the firm are less than perfect substitutes for the worker, absenteeism from the job due to health reasons is likely to reduce the productivity of other members of the team, and thereby diminish the employer's profits and reduce what the firm is willing to pay for a worker who may be unpredictably absent from work (Pauly et al. 2002). Another spillover that is widely recognized but rarely assessed arises from the burden of health care borne by other household members, and might be approximated by the caregiver's reduction of work in the market economy, in-home production, and leisure activities. This within-household spillover on time allocation might be assessed from labor force surveys that collect health and labor supply information for all household members, assuming that the arrangement of households can be treated as exogenous (Bartel and Taubman 1979; Thirumurthy et al. 2005). Finally,

* T. Paul Schultz is a Malcolm K. Brachman Professor of Economics at the economics department of Yale University. I acknowledge the comments and suggestions of Cem Mete. The research assistance of Paul McGuire is greatly appreciated. The author's interpretation of the evidence and analysis are his own and not those of any other groups.

health status and disabilities are expected to influence interhousehold decisions determining whether an elderly or ill individual lives with an adult child or other relative or is institutionalized, when the individual is unable to perform his or her own ADL (Dostie and Leger 2005). If information on health status is comprehensive and reliable, assessments of the economic consequences of health status and disabilities should include not only physical disabilities and chronic illnesses, but also mental conditions with a permanent or transitory effect on economic and physical functioning in society (*Science*, January 27, 2006).

A central problem in assessing the consequences of health on an individual's capacity to work or social spillovers involves how to measure health status as a condition that can be confidently treated as exogenous to the productive behavior of the individual, their household, and extended family members. As Bound (1991) states, there are two problems in performing such an assessment of health consequences that should be acknowledged from the outset. Health status as self-reported by a respondent in a survey is likely to be influenced by the individual's preferences to work and other behavioral conditioning or cultural factors. This could account for why self reports of poor health status tend to rationalize an individual's own reduced labor supply decisions and related social arrangements of households, most likely contributing to an *overestimate* of the causal effect of health on capacity to work, or on the costs of social spillovers.

This "endogeneity bias" associated with self-reported health status may be corrected if an instrumental variable technique is employed and the specified instrument predicts the self-reported health status, yet is not associated with the individual's current preferences for work or preconceptions of what differentiates between good and poor health. The instrumental variable estimation techniques should also correct attenuation bias caused by classical forms of measurement error in health, which is typically substantial in survey-based health indicators. But finding such an instrument is not straightforward. Using more "objective" health conditions, or preconditions in the past as a(n) indicator (measurement for) of current disability or health status, does not entirely solve the problem, although it may reduce it empirically (Stern 1998). Using lagged health status variables or fixed effects for the individual in the analysis of panel data over time is also not a complete answer to the problem, if dynamic changes in health are subject to accumulating measurement error (Griliches and Hausman 1986).

A second problem with drawing policy inferences in this context is that relatively "objective" measures of health status, such as those that may be clinically observed by a health professional, will not necessarily perfectly capture the health conditions that influence work capacity or the many related consequences of health. A body mass index (BMI) that is considered obese, or a risk factor such as high blood pressure, may significantly predict whether an elderly individual will work in the labor force or how productive he or she will be, but these more objective indicators of health will embody substantial classical measurement error. In addition, they will probably not reflect all health conditions relevant to a specific behavioral outcome. Both noisy measures of health status and an imperfect match between the health indicator and the behavioral outcome are likely to lead to an *underestimate* of the causal impact of changes in imprecise measures of health status on productive outcomes. Instrumental variable estimates of self-reported health effects on work capacity are likely to yield different estimated effects of health, depending on which measures of health are considered and which instruments are specified to be influencing the behavior of subpopulations—which could have heterogeneous responses to health—as hypothesized in the literature estimating local average treatment effects (LATE) (Imbens and Angrist 1994; Heckman 1997). For similar reasons, different, more objective or externally validated measures of health will tend to involve less measurement error, and hence result in less downward bias, when used to assess the consequences of poor health and disability on any particular aspect of labor productivity or capacity to work.

Bound (1991) postulates that the effects of self-reported health status on labor force attachment are upward biased, while more "objective" health indicators yield downward biased estimates, and together they might help to establish reasonable measures for true health effects. Because it remains an empirical question whether one source of bias is greater than the other, it is useful to consider a variety of health status indicators and instrumental variable strategies to assess the probable impacts of health disabilities on individuals' economic performance.

Institutional Change and Uncertainties of the Transition: Mental Disabilities

With the breakup of the former Soviet Union, adult mortality increased, especially among middle-aged Russian men, although the lack of improvement in male life expectancy after the 1960s in Eastern European countries may have signaled growing health problems that preceded the restructuring of the Soviet Union after 1989 (Guo 1993). These extraordinary declines in life expectancy among males can be decomposed into a sharp rise in deaths due to cardiovascular disease, but also a disproportionate increase in deaths attributed to trauma, i.e., accidents, homicide, suicide, and alcohol poisoning. Some have inferred that this mortality crisis is caused by the tensions and challenges posed by the transition of the economy from centrally planned to decentralized market oriented, with a lack of accountability in governance; social disorder and dislocations; growing unemployment and unpredictability of life; and the large decline in income levels, at least as measured by Russian national income accounts. The assembled evidence of social and economic causes for the increased mortality is convincing, but it is circumstantial by modern economic statistical standards (Brainerd and Cutler 2004). With hindsight, one is tempted to conclude that women are less vulnerable than men to the social-psychological adjustments required by the Russian transition, or that the traditional Russian habits of drinking and smoking exposed men—more than women—to the health risks associated with these behaviors while coping with these social and economic transitions.

Many studies have sought to identify the causes of death that led to the unprecedented decline in life expectancy among Russian adults. These increases in mortality occurred primarily from heart disease and strokes, lung diseases, alcohol consumption, and violence related to crime and accidents, while death rates due to cancer and childhood infections remained stable or declined gradually. From Russian time series on death rates, which are thought to be reasonably accurate, mortality increased sharply from 1992 to 1994, when the Soviet Union broke apart and the Russian economy began to evidence decline. Death rates then decreased from 1995 to 1998, only to increase again after the devaluation crisis, when the Russian economy contracted further and economic inequality increased. Death rates for women age 30 to 55 followed the same pattern as for men, but with less amplitude. Similar, although less pronounced, increases in adult mortality occurred at the start of the transition in neighboring states, such as Belarus and Ukraine, but not in Eastern Europe or the Caucasus (Nolte et al. 2004). Gorbachev's policies to raise the price and reduce access to alcohol in Russia (1985–87) may have contributed to the initial decline in mortality during the mid-1980s, but was not sustained (World Bank 2005). The recent rise in oil prices has fueled the current economic expansion in Russia, although life expectancy for males may not have yet regained the levels achieved in the 1970s or 1980s, or begun to catch up to that in the European Union (EU). These studies of the causes of mortality, however, do not assess morbidity or other aspects of health, nor do they link these indicators of health and disability to their potential consequences on economic activity of surviving individuals or the performance of the aggregate economy. An objective of this paper is to begin to explore the linkages between aspects of health and disability (as can be measured in a household representative survey) to various dimensions of economic productivity at the individual level.

There is little evidence that widespread malnutrition or deterioration in diet was responsible for the rise in mortality. And the continued gradual decline in mortality among children under age 15, and the stability in mortality among the elderly, suggests the deterioration of the Russian medical and public health system was not the primary cause for the rise in male adult mortality. Environmental pollution may have been a contributory factor, but not one which could reasonably cause an upsurge in mortality among only men aged 15 to 65 (Nolte et al. 2004). One is left with nonquantified social-psychological risk factors that resulted in stress, which may have been expressed in excessive alcohol consumption and risky behavior (Brainerd and Cutler 2004; Suhrcke et al. 2005). Mental illness and disabilities could play a major role in the rise in mortality, and it might also affect morbidity and productivity, though this is more difficult to document, especially in Russia, where institutionalizing the mentally ill is common, and commitment to medical and psychiatric institutions may have also served political objectives. This paper describes how health status is related to disability within the noninstitutionalized population, where disability is defined as being unable to participate in the market economy and work for wages. It also considers how health status affects hours worked and the after-tax hourly wage rate.

Why is it Hard to Measure the Consequences of Disabilities?

Many studies confirm the divergence between self-assessed and more objective indicators of health status, unless problems of endogeneity and measurement are recognized and corrected in any analysis of the consequences of health status. Mete and Cnobloch (2006) show that mothers' self-assessed reports of their children's health status in Uzbekistan are not closely related to objective indicators of health, such as the child's stunting (i.e., short for age and sex), wasting (i.e., low weight for height), anemia, and hypertension. Lokshin and Ravallion (2005) also find that self-assessed health status in Russia is not associated with income, whereas objective indicators of good health status often are positively associated with permanent consumption in the Russian Longitudinal Monitoring Survey (RLMS). They caution researchers against relying directly on self-assessed health status, and their findings suggest that instrumenting for self-assessed health status with more objective indicators can identify more reliable components of health status, as concluded by Schultz and Tansel (1997).

The assessment of the economic burden due to disabling diseases requires the estimation of how the condition *independently* affects the individual's welfare, as well as his or her family and community. This assessment task is complicated by puzzles which probably stem from measurement difficulties. These are even more extreme in the case of health indicators derived from representative surveys (Strauss and Thomas 1995, 1998). Individuals of the same age and sex in high-income countries report disability more often than individuals in low-income countries. This positive association between self reporting a disability and increased longevity, and diminished clinically confirmed morbidity, illustrates the potential for subjective standards of what people call "good" health to rise with economic development faster than (actual) health conditions (Johansson 1991).

Relatively little is known about the costs and effects of introducing preventive measures to reduce the prevalence of disabling mental or behavioral illness, such as may have occurred in Russia. The instrumental variable specified by the researcher to predict the occurrence of illness should replicate to the extent possible the pathway by which private and public resources could be employed to reduce these forms of illness and disability and thereby improve health. Evaluating policy options to prevent and ameliorate the economic outcomes associated with disabilities requires monitoring, as well as preventive and curative health interventions where their administrative and opportunity costs are fully documented. This is not feasible in this study.

The objective of this paper is more modest. A rudimentary framework is proposed to represent how health is produced and health-related behavior is determined, within which the economic consequences of adult disabilities are assessed. Based on the 13th round of the RLMS, conducted in 2004, relationships are estimated that can be interpreted within this framework.[1] First, descriptive ordinary least squares (OLS) regressions are reported between adult health and productivity in Russia. Then, instrumental variable (IV) estimates are contrasted of these same productivity-health relationships. These are designed to mitigate specific sources of bias in the estimation process due to error in measuring health status and the joint determination of health-related behavior, self-reported health status, and work behavior. Unobserved factors such as household endowments, preferences, and community infrastructure and prices may also be responsible for causing the relationships between health and productivity.[2]

Figure 1 illustrates that 42 percent of Russian females and 49 percent of Russian males age 15 to 24 are students. Only about 1 percent of those age 25 to 34 are students. Consequently, this study focuses on adults over the age of 25 to avoid dealing with the allocation of time between school and work, although both should probably be regarded as approximately of the same value in equilibrium, because the allocation of time to school or work is more or less voluntary. For Russian males, 72 percent of those between the ages of 25 and 64 report that they have worked in the last 30 days. This compares to 64 percent of Russian females. Because an objective is to assess the consequences of health on productivity, labor force participation, hours worked, and wage rates, the distinction must also be drawn for those who report themselves working in the last 30 days, but do not provide sufficient information about their jobs to calculate an hourly wage and the number of hours worked. This "not reporting" category could occur for a variety of reasons.[3] Whatever the cause for not reporting, it is an issue for a substantial segment of the population in the RLMS for 2004, and the information is lacking for nearly 15 percent of the males and close to 10 percent of the females (figure 1).

The subsequent analysis of the consequences of poor health and disability on labor productivity focuses on four component outcomes: (1) overall rate of participation in the labor force (extensive margin of labor supply), (2) with participation in the "reporting" labor force, [and the logarithm of monthly earnings of the reporting group, which is the sum of] (3) the log of the hourly wage (productivity), and (4) the log of hours worked per month (intensive margin of labor supply) for persons with positive wages and hours.

Descriptive Statistics of the Russian Survey Population

The nationally representative RLMS for 2004 samples about 4,000 households including 2,953 men and 3,632 women between the ages of 25 and 64 for which the basic variables are defined as tabulated in tables 1, 2, and 3.[4] Table 1 reports the descriptive statistics on aspects of labor productivity as inferred from this RLMS, in which columns 2 and 3 are the means for the total sample, and the last six columns report the means for those in the reporting labor force (defined as those who report earnings and hours on their primary or secondary jobs).[5] Labor force participation for men declines after ages 25 to 34, whereas it peaks later for women, at

FIGURE 1

Economic Activity of Russian Population, 2004

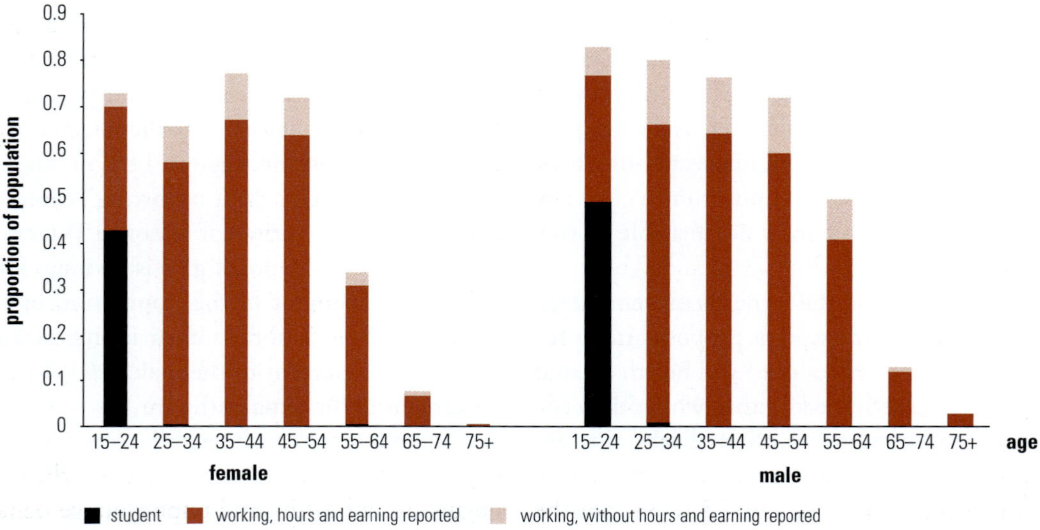

Source: Authors' calculations from the 2004 RLMS.

TABLE 1

Russian Longitudinal Monitoring Survey for 2004: Labor Market Participation, Hours and Wages by Age and Sex

Sample, sex and age	Total sample size [1]	Proportion working in 30 days [2]	Proportion report hours and earnings [3]	Hours per month [4]	Hourly wage rate [5]	Monthly earnings [6]	Log hours [7]	Log wage rate [8]	Log earnings [9]
Males, ages:									
15–24	495	.66	.54	190	35.7	6,261	5.20	3.27	8.47
25–34	969	.80	.66	187	45.3	7,537	5.18	3.49	8.67
35–44	814	.76	.64	189	45.2	7,511	5.18	3.43	8.61
45–54	736	.72	.60	187	39.4	6,827	5.19	3.30	8.49
55–64	434	.49	.41	166	43.2	5,890	5.04	3.37	8.41
65–74	391	.13	.12	164	24.0	4,061	5.08	2.96	8.04
75 or more	140	.029	.029	154	20.0	2800	5.00	2.88	7.88
Total 25–64	2,953	.72	.60	186	43.6	7,190	5.17	3.41	8.58
Females, ages:									
15–24	618	.52	.47	164	27.7	3,994	5.02	2.99	8.01
25–34	1,071	.65	.58	162	31.0	4,567	5.03	3.09	8.12
35–44	903	.77	.67	166	30.3	4,734	5.06	3.08	8.15
45–54	1,021	.72	.63	164	36.6	4,741	5.02	3.14	8.16
55–64	637	.33	.31	163	27.0	4,202	5.03	3.04	8.07
65–74	783	.074	.066	141	24.6	3,272	4.87	2.89	7.76
75 or more	470	.002	.002	168	4.17	700	5.12	1.43	6.55
Total 25–64	3,632	.64	.57	164	32.3	4,636	5.04	3.10	8.14

Source: Authors' calculations from the RLMS 2004.

Note: Variables defined and their sources in the survey questionnaire provided in appendix table A-1. The currency units are 2004 Rubles. The disability classification variable is defined in table A-1 and described in the text and in a footnote and is a recoding of the original variable which could not be directly employed.

ages 35 to 44, when it marginally exceeds that for men, at 77 percent compared to 76 percent, respectively. The decline in participation after age 45 to 54 is substantial, dropping by a third for men and by a half for women ages 55 to 64. Russian women are eligible for pensions at age 55 and men at 60 (figure 2).

Hours worked by those in the paid labor force decrease for men [among paid workers] by 11 percent from ages 25 to 34 to ages 55 to 64, and is essentially stable for women (table 1). Hourly wage rates for men also peak at ages 25 to 34, whereas they peak 20 years later for women. Thus, earnings for women in the paid labor force increase until ages 45 to 54, while earnings for men fall steadily after ages 25 to 34. For both sexes, earnings are lower for those ages 55 to 64 than for those ages 25 to 34, but the decline is 22 percent for men, and only 9 percent for women.

The product of the participation rate in the labor force (table 1, column 2) and the earnings of this group (column 6) may be interpreted as an approximation of the average of the productive value of the time of a birth cohort supplied to the labor force, if one assumes that those in the labor force but not reporting earnings or hours are equally well compensated and work as many hours as those who do report earnings and hours. This type of synthetic cohort aggregation of productivity also assumes that the time of people spent outside of the labor force is not (economically) productive—an exaggeration to be sure—but one that is implicit in national income accounts. According to this heuristic calculation, the expected value of the monthly earnings of a male Russian ages 25 to 34 is 6,030 rubles (i.e., .80* 7,537), and is 4,915 at ages 45 to 54, and then drops with the onset of retirement to 2,886 at ages 55 to 64.[6] This decline in labor market productivity could be due in part to a deterioration of health and vigor, or conversely, this decline in earnings could contribute to depression, which in turn induces them to engage in unhealthy and unproductive behaviors, such as working less, binge drinking, and engaging in risky activities associated with mortality. Or declining productivity could be caused by other factors changing across birth cohorts, such as improvements among younger Russians in the quality and productivity of education.

For Russian women, the life cycle decline in productivity occurs much later, after age 55, when the labor force participation rate for

FIGURE 2

Proportion of Russian Population with a Pension, 2004

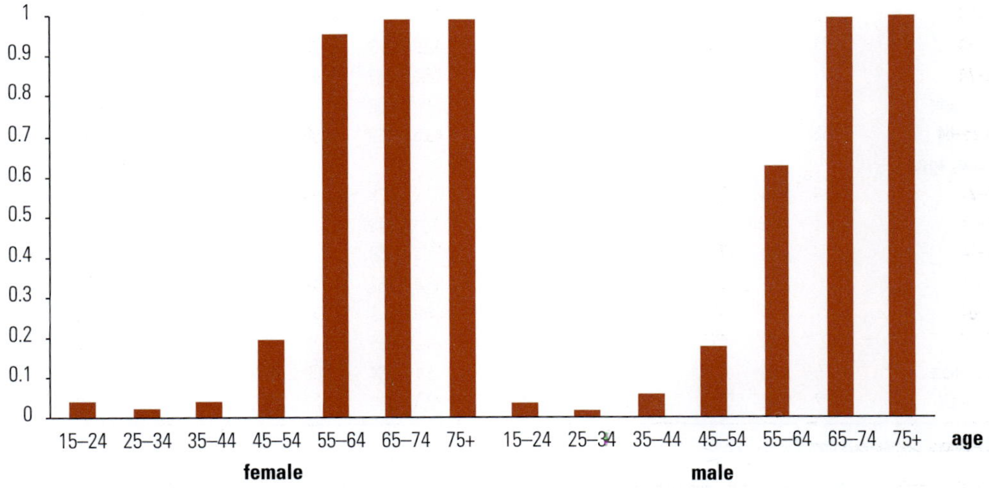

Source: Authors' calculations from the 2004 RLMS.

women also drops sharply and they increasingly rely on pensions (figure 2). Thus, for women, expected earnings increase 15 percent, from 2,969 rubles per month in 2004 for those age 25 to 34, to 3,414 rubles for those age 45 to 54, and then falls to 1,387 at age 55 to 64, when two-thirds of these older women leave the labor force and rely largely on pensions.[7] The focus here is on the determinants of labor force participation, working in a job for which earnings and hours in the last 30 days are reported (i.e., a wage job), and then the log of hours and log of the hourly wage rate among this final group in the "reporting" labor force.[8] Hours are also expressed in logs to facilitate a parallel treatment to wages, which then allows an additive decomposition of the log earnings into effects on proportionate variation in labor productivity and labor supply. [9]

Table 2 reports the sample averages for a variety of measures of current and lagged chronic health conditions, cross-tabulated by age and sex. In the basic sample studied here, of persons between the ages of 25 and 64, the likelihood that an individual reports any health problem in the last 30 days doubles from 22 percent for men in the youngest ages to 44 percent for men in the oldest ages. Health problems are reported more often for women than men, increasing from 31 percent among the youngest group to 61 percent in the oldest group (table 2, column 2). Self-assessed health status (from 0=very good, to 2=average, to 4=very bad) increases for men over this same age range from 1.5 to 2.1, while for women it is slightly worse, increasing from 1.6 to 2.2 (column 1).

Nonetheless, the gender gap in life expectancy has widened in Russia, with recent age-specific mortality estimates indicating that on average, women lived 12 years longer than men by 2000—perhaps the largest [recorded]

TABLE 2

Indicators of Poor Health, Classified Disabilities, Chronic Health Conditions, by Age and Sex

Sample, sex and age	Health status (0–4, 0 = very good) [1]	Health problem (0–1 in 30 days) [2]	Days missed due to illness [3]	Disability classification [4]	Chronic disease condition (M20.6) Heart [5]	Lung [6]	Liver [7]
Males, ages:							
15–24	1.36	.202	.465	.044	.040	.034	.040
25–34	1.48	.224	.531	.048	.035	.037	.040
35–44	1.64	.272	.554	.095	.053	.043	.047
45–54	1.81	.294	.408	.222	.099	.053	.046
55–64	2.07	.441	.404	.373	.205	.092	.071
65–74	2.24	.550	.271	.413	.319	.141	.090
75 or more	2.55	.750	.157	1.059	.421	.158	.129
Total 25–64	1.70	.286	.488	.152	.081	.051	.048
Females, ages:							
15–24	1.50	.295	.427	.039	.044	.023	.029
25–34	1.61	.313	.540	.043	.034	.029	.057
35–44	1.83	.352	.566	.068	.082	.042	.081
45–54	2.01	.504	.555	.153	.156	.066	.134
55–64	2.17	.612	.400	.268	.311	.078	.190
65–74	2.49	.753	.126	.515	.481	.093	.235
75 or more	2.79	.816	.021	.564	.519	.068	.241
Total 25–64	1.87	.429	.526	.120	.129	.051	.108

Source: Authors' calculations from the RLMS 2004.

Note: Variables defined and their sources in the survey questionnaire provided in appendix table A-1. M20.6 refers to the source of the variable in the adult questionnaire of the RLMS that asks about chronic illnesses.`` The disability classification is explained in table A-1 and text and footnote 11. It does not refer to percentage.

discrepancy in death rates by gender that has been noted in the world. Mortality of males from 25 to 64 is fourfold higher than in the EU, apparently due to cardiovascular illness, cancer, violence, and accidental death associated particularly with alcohol consumption. For Russian women, mortality is roughly twice the EU level (Suhrcke et al. 2005; Nolte et al. 2004). After the Soviet Union separated, mortality in the Russian Federation increased slowly and then abruptly for adult men from 1992 to 1994, whereas the increase was more moderate and transitory for women. Meanwhile, mortality among infants, children under 15, and elderly over age 65 was stable or continued to decline gradually (World Bank 2005). The number of days ill and unable to work in *usual* activities (not only labor force activity) in the last month averages about a half day for men and women, and this absenteeism level is not strongly related to age among those between the ages of 25 and 64 (table 2), or among those who are in the paid labor force in these ages (not reported).[10] The administrative/medical classification of disability assigned to an individual distinguishes among three disability groups (1 to 3, where 0 is not disabled), with the average numerical disability classification (0 to 3) increasing for men age 25–34 to 55–64 from .03 to .30, and increasing for women from .03 to .22, across the same age groups.[11]

Specific chronic health conditions are reported more frequently among older individuals, and are more often reported by women than by men, even for chronic lung diseases, despite the tendency for males to smoke four to five times the number of cigarettes per day as Russian women (table 3). A serious nervous disorder or depression in the year before the survey is self-reported by 14 percent of the men and 24 percent of the women between the ages of 25 and 64, increasing sharply to age 35 to 44,

Chronic disease condition (M20.6)				Depression in last 12 months	High blood pressure	Diagnosed with diabetes
Kidney [8]	Stomach [9]	Spinal [10]	Other [11]	[12]	[13]	[14]
.051	.083	.071	.131	.131	.100	.006
.030	.090	.070	.093	.116	.184	.006
.037	.122	.121	.108	.146	.269	.012
.046	.184	.176	.172	.147	.354	.016
.071	.154	.199	.242	.145	.424	.044
.118	.203	.214	.290	.160	.545	.064
.080	.259	.207	.496	.175	.584	.058
.042	.132	.129	.139	.136	.285	.016
.081	.141	.062	.109	.219	.103	.006
.094	.120	.065	.157	.200	.191	.008
.100	.158	.143	.219	.243	.330	.017
.119	.192	.233	.280	.254	.532	.038
.186	.287	.270	.342	.269	.691	.110
.184	.305	.299	.381	.289	.752	.139
.137	.267	.274	.473	.240	.767	.145
.119	.179	.169	.240	.238	.409	.037

and thereafter increasing only gradually for both genders. High blood pressure is more common with advancing age and higher for women than men, at 41 and 29 percent, respectively, in the ages 25 to 64. It should be noted that all of these health conditions, along with chronic health problems, may be more likely to be diagnosed if the person consults medical professionals and has regular contact with the health care system. The frequency of chronic illnesses and medically diagnosed diseases reported in a survey may therefore vary from actual prevalence rates.

The positive self-selection of individuals into the health care system may be greater for those who assign a higher value to their health and are more willing to make investments in their cumulated stock of good health human capital, many of which will not be observed by the researcher. A negative self-selection might occur if individuals with latent health problems who are in worse objective health are more likely to see doctors for a medical diagnosis of their problem in any specified retrospective period, such as the last three months in the RLMS. In addition, there is likely to be a subjective interpretation by the respondent as to whether his or her health condition constitutes a serious enough ailment to seek a medical checkup, or to report in the RLMS as a chronic health condition. It would seem likely that individual heterogeneity in reporting health and engaging in related behaviors would interject bias when estimating with single equation statistical methods (such as OLS) the causal effects among health behaviors, health outcomes, and labor productivity (e.g., Rosenzweig and Schultz 1983).

TABLE 3

Health-Related Characteristics and Behaviors, by Age and Sex

Sample, sex and age	Years of schooling [1]	Cigarettes per day [2]	Alcohol grams per day [3]	Medical checkup 3 months [4]	Exercise frequency [5]	Body mass index [6]	Waist-to-hip ratio [7]	Height in cm [8]	Cohabiting and married [9]
Males, ages:									
15–24	11.8	10.4	88.9	.168	.584	22.8	0.850	176.7	.337
25–34	12.4	12.0	107.2	.160	.496	24.7	0.881	176.4	.764
35–44	12.3	12.6	114.3	.125	.361	25.6	0.898	175.0	.854
45–54	12.2	11.9	104.5	.136	.333	26.1	0.914	173.2	.874
55–64	11.8	11.1	85.3	.118	.252	26.4	0.927	170.8	.885
65–74	9.46	6.48	62.2	.123	.487	26.5	0.938	168.4	.831
75 or more	9.52	2.67	36.20	.171	.360	26.5	0.938	167.6	.629
Total 25–64	12.2	12.01	105.2	.140	.382	25.6	0.900	174.4	.834
Females, ages:									
15–24	12.8	3.04	38.30	.251	.434	22.4	0.774	164.0	.523
25–34	13.1	3.17	42.20	.229	.371	24.6	0.784	164.0	.763
35–44	12.7	2.89	43.20	.207	.342	27.0	0.803	162.7	.729
45–54	12.5	1.78	31.30	.211	.314	29.5	0.827	160.7	.689
55–64	12.1	1.08	23.30	.152	.446	30.0	0.844	159.7	.560
65–74	9.44	0.240	12.00	.105	.345	29.9	0.867	157.1	.377
75 or more	7.34	0.122	5.00	.070	.284	28.4	0.881	154.6	.143
Total 25–64	12.7	2.33	35.90	.205	.357	27.6	0.811	162.0	.701

Source: Authors' calculations from the RLMS 2004. Variables defined and their sources in the survey questionnaire provided in appendix table A-1.

Note: The variable is described in footnote 14 and is not included in table A-1 because it was not used in the final model estimated, in part because it was unrelated to all outcomes. Medical consultation in the last three months is the question and married is having a civil marriage, cohabiting is opposite sexes living together but not married to each other.

Economic Determinants of Individual Labor Supply and Wages

Participation in the labor force and the number of hours worked are generally assumed to be determined by the after-tax hourly wage opportunities available to individuals, and by other sources of income they have that are independent of their labor supply behavior and add to their consumption opportunities. Transfer income, such as pensions and unemployment benefits, are sources of other income which are affected by prior and current work behavior, and possibly also by health status. Therefore, receipt of these forms of transfer income is not strictly exogenous to the labor productivity outcomes examined here. Other income may, however, be generally associated with life cycle savings and health. Controls are included for a smoothed quadratic function in age plus a dummy variable that take the value of 1 when the individual reaches the pension-eligible age of 55 to 64 for women and 60 to 64 for men, and is otherwise 0.

Nonearned income may represent income from savings and physical wealth, and also may arise from intra- and interhousehold private transfers, as well as differential access to public services and subsidies, such as community-provided housing and social services. It is generally expected that age eligibility for a pension or unearned income will decrease current labor supply, although some part of unearned income could be a choice, at least in terms of when an individual dissaves from their assets to boost current income and consumption.

Wage opportunities to work are expected to increase labor force participation because at the moment of entry into the labor force, this wage effect does not exert an offsetting income or wealth effect. However, in the determination of hours worked conditional on participation, the wage effect may be initially positive for part-time workers and possibly become negative among workers whose income effect of the wage dominates the substitution effect (Killingsworth 1983). Because the wage offered to individuals is not observed for those who do not decide to participate in the labor force and find employment, the researcher can replace the wage with productive characteristics of individuals which are generally positively correlated with their wage offers, other things being equal, such as their years of schooling, years of potential experience after schooling, height, and weight for height (i.e., BMI). These productive characteristics perform the function of "instrumental variables" for the potential wage offer, and therefore are expected to increase labor force participation of the individual, but are not necessarily expected to be associated with increasing the number of hours worked, conditional on the individual participating.

For example, education is often associated with increased labor productivity and wage rates, and is also positively associated with participation but not always with hours worked among participants. Education is also closely linked to many indicators of health status and good health outcomes, such as diminishing consumption of cigarettes and alcohol. Consumption of alcohol by Russians is thought to be high by international standards, and is often implicated in the frequency of deaths due to cardiovascular disease, stroke, accidents, homicides, and suicides, but alcohol consumption has not been treated as a factor in Russian labor productivity (Shkolnikov and Nemtsov 1997; Leon et al. 1997, Ryan 1995).[12] Illegal production of alcohol is common, especially in rural areas, and thus self-reported alcohol consumption in surveys, such as the RLMS, may be understated, but nonetheless approximate consumption magnitudes.

The safety net of social programs in Russia is not precisely targeted to the least productive, disabled, or poor, and may therefore not exert a differential or salient effect on who works and how much they work.[13] The actual receipt of pensions and other transfers are contingent on an individual's application and qualification, which may therefore depend on health and productivity, and also might be related to individual preferences for leisure and subjective attitudes toward health and work (Bound 1991). Thus, the actual receipt of public transfers or pensions is viewed here as endogenous and not used to explain health and productivity outcomes.

Unearned income is not directly reported, but is constructed by subtracting from total individual income (adult questionnaire, J60) the earnings of the worker on their primary (J10) and secondary (J40) jobs, other earnings (J57), and transfer income in the form of pensions (J76) and unemployment benefits (J89). This measure of unearned income is 418 rubles per month for the average woman age 25 to 64, or 11 percent of their total monthly income, and 438 rubles for men in these ages, which represents 7 percent of their total income (appendix table A-1). As an exogenous constraint on choice, "nonearned" income would decrease labor force participation and possibly hours worked among participants, and increase the demand for normal goods, including preventive health care services, other things being equal.

Three health-related inputs are analyzed as determinants of Russian labor productivity: having a medical checkup in the last three months, consumption of grams of ethanol alcohol per day, and number of cigarettes smoked per day.[14] What is more distinctive about this analysis is that these inputs are treated as potentially endogenous and correlated with the errors in the health outcome and productivity equations. Thus, they are estimated using two stage least squares (2SLS), which are identified on the basis of exclusion restrictions. An indicator of access to or use of medical care in the RLMS is whether the respondent has seen a doctor in the last three months. About one in five women and one in eight men indicate having had such a medical consultation, although it is unclear from the RLMS whether the visit is for a preventive checkup, or due to an illness and the need for diagnosis and curative care.

As a form of preventive health care, this measure of utilization might be positively related to a person's good health status. Its correlation with health and productivity is likely to overstate the benefits of the care allocated randomly in the population because those using the observed form of preventive care are likely to use other unobserved health services and the estimated relation would attribute the effect of the omitted variables to the observed variable. On the other hand, if the visit to the doctor was for curative health care, it is likely that the correlation between the visit and health outcomes and productivity would be biased in a negative direction, or downward (Rosenzweig and Schultz 1983). In these cases, a community questionnaire measure of the price of a doctor consultation visit or the time costs required of the patient to gain access to doctors and medical care should be used to predict who does and who does not visit a doctor. As a result,these community instrumental variables would not be correlated with an individual's desire for preventive care, or the likelihood that the person is sick and in need of curative care. To determine medical care usage, the community questionnaire of the RLMS provides the time required to reach a hospital and a private doctor for each of the 159 survey sample clusters. It also considers whether the community has a social welfare office, and whether the office provides medical services (table A-1).

Alcohol consumption is assessed in the survey in five different forms and is converted here into total grams of ethanol equivalent consumed per day in the last 30 days. Alcohol consumption tends to peak for men and women during the ages of 35 to 44, when men, on average, consume 114 grams per day, while women consume about a third as much, or 43 grams.[15] It is believed that moderate alcohol consumption provides a protective effect against some cardiovascular diseases and related mortality, whereas higher levels of consumption are harmful. Binge drinking, defined in some cases as five or more drinks (or 80 grams ethanol) on one occasion, causes health problems, especially when the alcohol is consumed in the form of spirits that are absorbed more rapidly (Kauhanen et al. 1997). However, the composition or frequency of "binge" drinking, which may contribute to health problems and violence, is not reported in the RLMS, and thus only the quantity consumed on average for the last 30 days is included.

The nonlinearity of the effect on health and productivity is approximated by estimating the effect of a linear and squared consumption term, for which significance levels must be evaluated jointly. Empirical evidence of this nonlinear effect of alcohol on health outcomes is widely documented in the health literature, but alcohol consumption is generally assumed to be exogenous, even though it is widely recognized that unobserved individual factors may affect both alcohol consumption and other welfare outcomes, including health and labor productivity. Mullahy and Sindelar (1991) relate alcohol consumption to labor force participation and income in the United States, and show that the relationship of alcohol consumption to participation among middle-aged women and men is negative and larger for women, whereas the link between alcohol and household income is weaker, especially for women. Tekin (2002) shows an inverse U-shaped effect of alcohol consumption on employment (but not wages) in the RLMS for males, and a positive effect for females, though these patterns are weakened when fixed effects for the individual are included to correct for unobserved persistent individual heterogeneity. Baltagi and Gekshecker (2006) use a panel of observations from the RLMS to model the effect of changes in the price of alcohol on the levels of consumption and lagged consumption, and identify negative consumption responses to prices. In this study, I allow for a flexible quadratic effect of alcohol consumption on health and productivity outcomes, assuming the local prices of low-quality vodka identify the endogenous consumption level of alcohol.

Although there is less evidence of nonmonotonic effects of tobacco consumption on health or productivity than alcohol, the same specification is used to treat cigarette consumption as endogenous and identify it with the community price of low-quality cigarettes. Of the 159 sample cluster sites in the working sample, information on the price of low-cost vodka (the dominant source of alcohol) and low-cost cigarettes is reported in 137 and 135 community questionnaires, respectively. In the sample sites not reporting their own prices for vodka and cigarettes, the prices in the closest neighboring sample sites are used in this analysis.

Other characteristics possibly related to health status and productivity are reported in table 3 and appendix table A-1. Schooling has been relatively constant at 12 years for Russians born after the Second World War, increasing slowly among younger adults, with women receiving slightly more years of schooling than men, but occupying less well-paid professions and specializations, which could help to explain why women's wages are about one-third lower than those of men (column 8, table 1. See also Glinskaya and Mroz 2000).[16] I distinguish among years of regular schooling through grade 12, vocational school, technical post-secondary school, and university and post-graduate education, as defined in appendix table A-1.

Adult height is one characteristics of individuals which is significantly associated with lower risks of mortality within age and sex groups, and also associated with increased labor productivity (Waaler 1984; Fogel 2004; Schultz 2005). Adult height is relatively stable for an individual from age 25 to 50, and then declines only gradually as vertebra become more compressed with later age. Adult height reflects genetic potential to be tall, but is also responsive to developing in a more healthy uterine environment and early child development, including reduced exposure to childhood infections (Barker 1994; Manton 1986; Bengtsson et al. 2004). According to the RLMS, height has increased markedly among younger Russian men (table 3, column 8) age 25 to 34 who are 176.4 centimeters tall, whereas those who have survived and are over age 75 are only 167.6 centimeters.[17] Of this increase in height of 8.8 centimeters in those Russians men born in about 1975 compared to those born 50 years earlier in about 1925, it appears that early childhoold nutritional and health conditions have improved substantially. Among Russian women in 2004 their height among those age 25 to 34 is 9.4 centimeters larger than among women over the age of 75, and within the age span represented in my sample women born in 1975 are about 4.3 centimeters taller than those born in about 1925. A monotonic relationship between height and relative risks of mortality is reported in Norway in the 1970s and mortality risks appears to decline at an approximately linear rate with increased height for both men and women. Therefore, in this analysis height is treated as a linear determinant of health as well as labor productivity in Russia for both men and women, and when a quadratic term in height is included in the subsequent regressions it was not statistically significantly different from zero (Waaler 1984; Fogel 1994).

BMI, or weight in kilograms divided by height in meters squared, is considered "overweight" following conventions established by the WHO if BMI exceeds 27 (table 3). According to this indicator, Russian women are more often overweight than men, with the proportion rising to 70 percent of Russian women age 55 to 64, and 39 percent of men in this age group. BMI as a factor determining health and labor productivity is represented in the form of the inverted U-shaped profile (Costa 1996) following Waaler (1984) and Fogel (2004), who fit relative mortality risks to BMI in a U-shaped relationship. Here a quadratic function in BMI is estimated, allowing the Russian data to suggest at what level increased BMI reduces individual health and productivity. Another anthropometric indicator that is predictive of cardiovascular health problems is the waist-to-hip ratio, for which Russian males exceed females (table 3).

Marital status is often correlated with labor supply behavior and even wages. Assuming marital status is exogenous to health and productivity, dummy variables are included for whether the person is currently married, cohabiting but unmarried, and divorced, where being single or widowed is the excluded category. Table 3 reports how the percentage of married plus cohabiting varies by age and sex within the sample. Finally, residents in rural areas represent about 24 percent of the RLMS sample, and an additional 6 percent reside in what are called secret cities (*posyolok gorodskogo tipa*, or PGT), which were omitted from standard maps until 1995, and might have special attributes such as pollution or a restrictive labor market with military facilities or defense industries. The 70 percent of survey respondents residing in the remaining urban areas are the excluded category in this case. Ten regions of the country are also included as controls, where the city of Moscow is the excluded category (see table A-1).

A Conceptual Framework to Guide the Econometric Analysis

Five classes of variables will be analyzed from the 2004 RLMS. The first set will be referred to as **P**, for the market productivity of the adult population between the ages of 25 and 64, which includes: (1) participation in the labor force in the last 30 days; (2) whether the individual reports both earnings in this job and hours worked in the job (or is in the "reporting" labor force); (3) the natural logarithm of the hourly wage in current rubles; and (4) the logarithm of the hours worked in the last 30 days. The last two variables are analyzed only for the sample with positive hours and wages, or in the "reporting" labor force (table 1).

The second and third sets of variables indicate health status, and are divided into those that are measured contemporaneously and subjectively, and those representing lagged stocks of health human capital. The current health status, **HC**, includes: (1) a self evaluation of current health status from 1 to 5, with 1 being very good and 5 being very bad; (2) whether the individual has had a health problem in the last 30 days; and (3) the disability classification of the individual (0–3), which is an official, medically confirmed designation, with a higher value indicating someone is more severely disabled. The third set of lagged health status indicators, **HL**, may be measured with less subjective error than the current indicators of health status because they refer to chronic illnesses, diseases, or conditions that are thought to have a persisting effect on health, including: (1–7) chronic health conditions or diseases; (8) nervous breakdown or depression in the last year; and (9) high blood pressure, as summarized in table 2.[18] A critical assumption made in this investigation is that **HC** may be treated as endogenous or measured with error, whereas **HL** may be treated as exogenous to the current health state, **HC**, or economic productivity, **P**.

The fourth set of variables refer to health-related inputs or behaviors, **I**, which include: (1) whether the individual had seen a doctor in the last three months; (2) the number of cigarettes consumed per day: and (3) the grams of pure alcohol equivalent consumed per day in the last 30 days (table 3).[19]

The fifth set of variables refers to three classes of controls, **C**. The first set of control variables relates to the individual, **Ci**, such as: (1) age, approximated by a quadratic function; (2) dummy variables for the ages when regular pensions are available for women and men in Russia;[20] (3) education, approximated by a spline in different levels and types of schooling (years of grade school, vocational, technical, or university training); (4) unearned income (i.e., total income minus earned and transfer income); (5) height in centimeters; (6) BMI (i.e., weight in kilograms compared to height in meters squared), and its square; (7) waist-to-hip ratio; (8–10) marital status (married, cohabiting, divorced, with the excluded category being single), (11) resident of a rural or urban-type settlement; or (12) in a secret city (i.e., PGT).[21] The second set of control variables represents constraints due to the community, as measured at the level of the sample cluster, **Cc**, of which there are 161 sites distinguished here, and the community questionnaire provides control variables for the: (1) distance to the nearest hospital; (2) distance to the nearest private doctor in the administrative area; (3–4) whether there is no response to these questions in the community site questionnaire, and the community (low-quality) price for (5) vodka and (6) cigarettes.[22] The third set of control variables, **Cr**, refers to the 10 regions of the Russian Federation for which fixed effects are included, thereby estimating regional deviations from the omitted region, which is the city of Moscow. All variables are defined in terms of the coded variables in the RLMS in appendix table A-1.

Reduced-form linear relationships could be estimated among the four productivity variables and all of the control variables and the lagged chronic health conditions:

$$P = P\,(Ci\ ,Cc\ ,\ Cr\ ,\ HL,\ e1), \qquad (1)$$

where e's represent errors that embody the effect of omitted variables, errors in functional form, measurement error, and other forms of presumably random variation. The allocation of inputs to increase health and productivity of the individual may respond to the individual's heterogeneity in preferences for health, differences in the unobserved quality of health care, or unobserved latent health endowments of the individual. This individual heterogeneity is likely to contribute to a correlation between **HC** and **I** and the residual error **e1**. Consequently, estimating directly in equation (1) the relationship between productivity due to current health status, **HC**, or health inputs and behavior, **I**, would not yield estimates of the causal effects of these health conditions or health inputs for an average individual, as discussed below (Rosenzweig and Schultz 1983). However, reduced-form equations can also be estimated for current health input demands and current health status indicators using OLS:

$$I = I\,(Ci, Cc, Cr, HL, e2), \qquad (2)$$

$$HC = HC\,(Ci, Cc, Cr, HL, e3). \qquad (3)$$

To assess how current health inputs and current health status affects productivity, structural assumptions are required. It is assumed that community health care facilities and local prices, **Cc**, as well as lagged chronic health conditions, **HL**, influence productive outcomes only through their impact on a single current health status indicator for the individual:

$$P = P\,(Ci, Cr, HC^*(Cc, HL), e4), \qquad (4)$$

where **HC*(Cc, HL)** denotes that the effect of one of the **HC** variables on labor productivity may be estimated by two-stage least squares (2SLS), relying on the exclusion restriction of **Cc** and **HL** not directly entering the productivity function. These health production and productivity functions (4) are first estimated by OLS under the assumption that the current measures of health, **HC**, are exogenous. Because these closely related dimensions of health are highly correlated, only one of these three health indicators is considered at a time. These OLS estimates are reported to estimate likely endogenous risk factors affecting health and productivity. The second set of estimates relies on 2SLS, which treat current health measures as endogenous or correlated with classical measurement error in **e4**, and identify these estimates by including **Cc** and **HL** as determinants of **HC**, but excluding them from directly entering equation (4).

These OLS and 2SLS estimates of the coefficients of **HC** are reported in the first row of tables 4A and 4B for males and females where the "self-evaluation of current health status" is treated as the indicator of **HC**, excluding the potentially endogenous three health inputs: medical care, alcohol, and cigarettes. The F test of weak instruments from the first-stage estimates of the determinants of **HC** is reported in appendix table A-2, indicating the joint statistical significance of the identifying variables. The Durbin-Wu-Hausman specification test is then interpreted as a test of the exogeneity of **HC** in the health production process, and reported in appendix table A-3. The first two rows of the male and female productivity estimates in table 5 report the estimates of equation (4) based on the other potentially endogenous current health status variables, "having a health problem in the last 30 days," and "being assigned an ordered disability classification," without health inputs as shown in tables 4A and 4B. To save space, only the coefficients estimated for these alternative current health **HC** indicators are reported in table 5, because the other coefficients on the exogenous variables in tables 4A and 4B controlling for the self-evaluation of health status tend to closely parallel those for the other current health indicators.

The productivity equations are then reestimated, including as determinants the three health-related input variables:

$$P = P\,(Ci, Cr, HC^*(Cc, HL), I^*(Cc, HL), e5), \qquad (5)$$

where the marginal effects in individual productivity due to the use of health inputs is first estimated by OLS subject to the strong assumption that the health inputs are exogenously allocated across individuals, and then by 2SLS, where estimates are identified by the exclusion restrictions embodied in **Cc** and **HL.** The first-stage predictive power of the instruments is reported in table A-2, and the Durbin-Wu-Hausman test of the exogeneity of the inputs is reported in table A-3.[23]

Empirical Findings

Familiar empirical regularities emerge in tables 4A and 4B, some of which are analogous to those found either in studies of labor supply—in terms of participation probabilities and hours worked (Killingsworth 1983), or in the litera-

TABLE 4A

Labor Force Productivity Determinants, Including Current Self-Evaluated Health Status: Males

(Beneath coefficient is absolute value of t ratio in parentheses)

	Working in 30 days		Reporting hours and wage		ln hours in 30 days		ln wage rate	
Dependent variable	OLS	2SLS	OLS	2SLS	OLS	2SLS	OLS	2SLS
estimation method	1	2	3	4	5	6	7	8
Variables:								
Self-evaluation of	−0.0888	−0.146	−0.0766	−0.125	0.0119	−0.0684	−0.132	−0.0245
Health (0-4)	(6.93)	(5.33)	(5.47)	(4.17)	(0.73)	(1.69)	(3.91)	(0.29)
Age (x10-1)	0.0149	0.0189	0.0728	0.0761	0.121	0.142	0.0798	0.0516
	(0.20)	(0.25)	(0.87)	(0.91)	(1.39)	(1.61)	(0.44)	(0.28)
Age squared	−0.0063	−0.0055	−0.0134	−0.0127	−0.0168	−0.180	−0.0172	−0.0157
(x10-2)	(0.68)	−0.59	(1.32)	(1.25)	(1.58)	(1.67)	(0.78)	(0.71)
Pension age	−0.298	−0.298	−0.200	−0.200	−0.166	−0.157	0.0237	0.0124
	(5.78)	−5.76	(3.55)	(3.54)	(2.22)	(2.09)	(0.15)	(0.08)
Schooling years								
Grade school	0.0141	0.0136	0.0156	0.0152	0.0035	0.0032	0.0232	0.0236
	(2.06)	(1.97)	(2.08)	(2.02)	(0.39)	(0.36)	(1.27)	(1.29)
Vocational	0.0122	0.0124	0.0100	0.0102	−0.0080	−0.0074	0.0291	0.0236
	(1.69)	(1.72)	(1.27)	(1.29)	(0.96)	(0.87)	(1.67)	(1.29)
Technical	0.023	0.0227	0.0168	0.0164	−0.0097	−0.0097	0.046	0.0459
	(3.84)	(3.75)	(2.54)	(2.48)	(1.45)	(1.43)	(3.30)	(3.28)
University	0.0136	0.0131	0.0116	0.0112	0.0012	0.0007	0.0560	0.0565
	(3.58)	(3.75)	(2.80)	(2.68)	(0.28)	(0.18)	(6.62)	(6.66)
Unearned income	−0.0629	−0.0595	−0.114	−0.111	0.0144	0.0241	−0.0190	−0.0320
(x10-4)	(2.82)	(2.65)	(4.69)	(4.55)	(0.29)	(0.47)	(0.18)	(0.30)
Height (cm)	0.0020	0.0018	0.0025	0.0024	0.0010	0.0010	0.0051	0.0052
	(1.63)	(1.50)	(1.92)	(1.82)	(0.76)	(0.72)	(1.80)	(1.82)
Married	0.153	0.152	(0.166)	0.166	0.0195	0.0216	0.158	0.156
	(5.43)	(5.39)	(4.69)	(5.38)	(0.55)	(0.61)	(2.16)	(2.12)
Cohabiting	0.132	0.133	0.126	0.127	0.0017	0.0047	0.077	0.0730
	(3.90)	(3.92)	(3.42)	(3.44)	(0.04)	(0.11)	(0.90)	(0.85)
Divorced	−0.026	−0.021	−0.034	−0.0298	−0.065	−0.065	−0.034	−0.035
	(0.67)	(0.53)	(0.79)	(0.69)	(1.27)	(1.25)	(0.32)	(0.32)
Body Mass Index	0.0502	0.0397	0.0486	0.0397	−0.024	0.0091	0.354	0.0484
(x10-1)	(3.16)	(2.40)	(2.80)	(2.20)	(0.69)	(0.47)	(0.90)	(1.19)
BMI squared	−0.0796	−0.0615	−0.731	−0.0579	−0.136	−0.0059	0.0532	−0.0769
(x10-2)	(2.78)	(2.07)	(2.34)	(1.79)	(0.87)	(0.17)	(0.75)	(1.05)
Waist-hip ratio	−0.309	−0.275	−0.362	−0.332	−0.136	−0.107	−0.0476	−0.0854
	(2.39)	(2.09)	(2.56)	(2.33)	(0.87)	(0.68)	(0.15)	(0.26)
Rural resident	−0.110	−0.116	−0.199	−0.204	−0.134	−0.0164	0.571	−0.568
	(5.49)	(5.71)	(9.06)	(9.19)	(0.56)	(0.66)	(11.1)	(10.9)
Secret city (PGT)	−0.151	−0.153	−0.254	−0.257	0.0455	0.0427	−0.333	−0.329
	(4.25)	(4.31)	(6.54)	(6.58)	(0.95)	(0.88)	(3.33)	(3.28)
Intercept	−0.0954	0.11	−0.337	−0.164	4.50	4.66	2.30	2.08
	(0.27)	(0.31)	(0.88)	(0.42)	(10.8)	(10.9)	(2.65)	(2.35)
R squared	0.181	n.a.	0.175	n.a	0.033	n.a	0.265	n.a.
F	21.9	.21.1	21.00	20.5	2.10	2.15	22.4	21.7
p-value	(0.0001)	(0.0001)	(0.0001)	(0.0001)	(0.0008)	(0.0006)	(0.0001)	(0.0001)

Note: All regressions include regional dummies as defined in table A-1.

TABLE 4B

Labor Force Productivity Determinants, Including Current Self-Evaluated Health Status: Females

(Beneath coefficient is absolute value of t ratio in parentheses)

Dependent variable	Working in 30 days		Reporting hours and wage		In hours in 30 days		In wage rate	
estimation method	OLS	2SLS	OLS	2SLS	OLS	2SLS	OLS	2SLS
	1	2	3	4	5	6	7	8
Variables:								
Self-evaluation of	−0.0487	−0.0585	−0.0563	−0.0782	−0.0046	−0.0378	−0.0501	−0.0123
Health (0-4)	(3.70)	(1.89)	(4.12)	(2.43)	(0.26)	(0.86)	(1.65)	(0.16)
Age (x10-1)	0.826	0.828	0.749	0.753	0.167	0.180	0.388	0.374
	(10.9)	(10.9)	(9.54)	(9.57)	(1.55)	(1.64)	(2.06)	(1.96)
Age squared	−0.101	−0.101	−0.0914	−0.0913	−0.0205	−0.0214	−0.0456	−0.0446
(x10-2)	(10.7)	(2.50)	(9.34)	(9.34)	(1.51)	(1.57)	(1.92)	(1.88)
Pension age	−0.0976	−0.0980	−0.0746	−0.0755	0.0457	0.0444	−0.0959	−0.0945
	(2.49)	(2.50)	(1.83)	(1.86)	(0.88)	(0.85)	(1.06)	(1.04)
Schooling years								
Grade school	0.0188	0.0186	0.0215	0.0211	−0.0117	−0.0120	0.0599	0.0602
	(2.85)	(2.82)	(3.15)	(3.08)	(1.16)	(1.19)	(3.40)	(3.41)
Vocational	0.0163	0.0166	0.0194	0.0199	0.0095	0.0104	0.0240	0.0230
	(2.01)	(2.03)	(2.30)	(2.35)	(0.90)	(0.98)	(1.31)	(1.25)
Technical	0.0275	0.0275	0.0323	0.0322	−0.0013	−0.0011	0.0566	0.0566
	(5.33)	(5.32)	(6.03)	(6.00)	(0.17)	(0.17)	(4.98)	(4.97)
University	0.0235	0.0235	0.0243	0.0241	−0.0097	−0.0098	0.0879	0.0880
	(6.60)	(6.57)	(6.55)	(6.49)	(2.36)	(2.38)	(12.3)	(12.3)
Unearned income	−0.140	−0.140	−0.261	−0.262	−0.0470	−0.0466	0.162	0.162
(x10-4)	(3.83)	(3.83)	(6.91)	(6.91)	(0.85)	(0.84)	(1.68)	(1.67)
Height (cm)	0.0024	0.0024	0.0026	0.0026	0.0032	0.0031	0.0054	0.0055
	(1.97)	(1.95)	(2.06)	(2.01)	(2.05)	(2.00)	(2.02)	(2.04)
Married	−0.0635	−0.0644	−0.0613	−0.0632	−0.064	−0.0656	−0.0032	−0.0015
	(3.03)	(3.05)	(2.81)	(2.88)	(2.46)	(2.51)	(0.07)	(0.03)
Cohabiting	−0.121	−0.122	−0.102	−0.102	−0.0253	−0.0258	0.0088	0.0093
	(4.13)	(4.14)	(3.33)	(3.35)	(0.69)	(0.70)	(0.14)	(0.15)
Divorced	0.0236	0.0228	0.0152	0.0134	0.0026	−0.0001	−0.0180	−0.0149
	(0.87)	(0.83)	(0.54)	(0.47)	(0.08)	0.00	(0.32)	(0.26)
Body Mass Index	0.0281	0.0276	0.0295	0.0283	−0.0017	−0.0033	0.0381	0.0400
(x10-1)	(2.91)	(2.82)	(2.94)	(2.79)	(0.13)	(0.25)	(1.69)	(1.75)
BMI squared	−0.0400	−0.0387	−0.0422	−0.0400	0.0022	0.0053	−0.0545	−0.0581
(x10-2)	(2.51)	(2.41)	(2.57)	(2.40)	(0.10)	(0.24)	(1.46)	(1.53)
Waist-hip ratio	0.417	−0.417	−0.449	−0.444	−0.023	−0.025	−0.309	−0.306
	(3.52)	(3.51)	(3.16)	(3.60)	(0.15)	(0.16)	(1.15)	(1.14)
Rural resident	−0.0576	−0.0580	−0.119	−0.120	0.134	−0.135	−0.311	−0.311
	(2.94)	(2.95)	(5.83)	(5.86)	(5.30)	(5.30)	(7.04)	(7.03)
Secret city (PGT)	−0.101	−0.102	−0.149	−0.151	−0.054	−0.0570	−0.256	−0.253
	(3.02)	(3.04)	(4.31)	(4.35)	(1.17)	(1.23)	(3.19)	(3.14)
Intercept	−0.153	1.52	1.47	−1.43	4.41	4.46	0.948	0.886
	(5.25)	(5.07)	(4.86)	(4.59)	(11.1)	(11.1)	(1.37)	(1.27)
R squared	0.199	n.a.	0.178	n.a.	0.034	n.a	0.271	n.a.
F	29.5	29.1	27.2	26.8	2.56	2.58	27.1	27.0
p-value	(0.0001)	(0.0001)	(0.0001)	(0.0001)	(0.0001)	(0.0001)	(0.0001)	(0.0001)

Note: All regressions include regional dummies as defined in table A-1.

ture that estimates the covariates of log of wage rates (Mincer 1974). Schooling is generally associated with higher wages, and consequently with greater labor force participation. One interpretation of these empirical regularities is that they are consistent with individual labor supply being upwardly sloped with respect to an individual's wage opportunities, and investments in schooling are associated in most studies with increased wages and labor force participation, at least where there is a safety net for the disabled, sick, unskilled, and unemployed (Welch 1997).

The private wage returns of individuals who have invested their time in schooling as students appear in columns 7 and 8 to be moderate in Russia, increasing from about 2 percent per year in school grade completed for men, and 6 percent for women. For university training, the increase is 5 percent for men and 9 percent for women. The smaller groups with vocational and technical schooling receive lower wage returns and little impact on their labor force participation or hours. However, the partial relationships between schooling and standard measures of labor supply and earnings would be positive and larger if the self-evaluation of health status, as well as the physical stature of the individual proxied by height and BMI, were excluded from the reported wage equations, as in standard earnings functions that include only schooling and post-schooling experience (Mincer 1974). Each additional year of schooling for men and women is associated a 1 to 2 percent increased likelihood of working in the labor force. As noted in table 1, without controls, male wages do not vary with age after controlling for these health indicators, whereas female wages rise and then fall over the life cycle, reaching their maximum value when women are in their early 40s. Participation in the labor force is 10 percentage points lower for women age 55 to 64, when they are eligible for a pension, controlling for the quadratic age life-cycle pattern, and about 30 percentage points lower for men age 60 to 64, who are age eligible for general pensions. Men at the age that is eligible for a pension also tend to work 16 log points fewer hours. An individual who receives 1,000 rubles more in unearned income per month is likely to participate less often in the labor force. These nonearned income effects are larger for women, 1.4 percentage points in the labor force and 2.6 percentage points in the wage labor force, than they are for men, respectively. These gender differences in nonearned income effects on labor supply by gender are also estimated in the United States and other high-income countries (Killingsworth 1983).

As in some other populations, adult height is associated with higher wages, participation, and hours, although this pattern is weakened in this framework by the inclusion of many other long-term indicators of health that are inversely correlated with height (Schultz 2005). An increment of 1 centimeter in height is related to a half percent increase in wages of men and women. Fitting a quadratic function to BMI reveals the expected inverted U-shaped pattern, which is jointly significant in these regressions for participation and log wages, but suggests the maximum likelihood of labor force participation occurs when an individual's BMI is between 32 to 35 for men and women. This level of BMI is conventionally regarded as being overweight and subject to elevated risk of mortality after age 45 (Waaler 1984; Fogel 1994; Costa 1996). Waist-to-hip ratio is also a sign of cardiovascular disease risk and is significantly associated in Russia with reduced probabilities of labor force participation.[24] Being currently married or cohabiting is associated with men and women receiving 15 and 7 percent higher wages, respectively, and there is greater labor force participation for women than men who are currently single or divorced. Among Russian women who are currently married or cohabiting versus single or divorced, wages are not significantly different, although the women with partners participate less frequently in the labor force and in wage employment by about 6 and 12 percentage points, respectively. Residents in rural areas report receiving much lower wage rates, –.57 log points for men and –.31 for women, with the secret cities (PGT) log wages –.33 for men and –.25 for men and women, respectively, compared to the urban residents. Given the much lower rural wages, labor force participation rates are also lower in these areas, at 11 percentage points for men and 6 percentage points for women. All of these coefficients estimated for the covariates of labor productivity are not greatly affected by shifting from OLS to 2SLS estimates for the self-assessed health evaluation variable in tables 4A and 4B. Because the alternative indicators of current health status, namely, health problems and disability classification indicator, also yield similar estimated effects of the other exogenous variables on current health status regardless of whether OLS or 2SLS estimates are reported, they are not included in the summary table 5 to save space.

The critical estimates for this paper are the productivity effects of the health status variables, which are reported in the first row of tables 4A and 4B, and in table 5. When the self-assessed evaluation of an individual's health is larger and health status worsens one unit, say from good to average health, the OLS estimated association is for participation in the labor force to decrease by 9 percent for men and 5 percent for women. When this health

TABLE 5

Labor Force Productivity Determinants of Health Status, with and without Inputs

Dependent variable	Working		Reporting		ln hours		ln wage	
estimation method	OLS 1	2SLS 2	OLS 3	2SLS 4	OLS 5	2SLS 6	OLS 7	2SLS 8
Sex specification:								
Male:								
Without input:								
1 Health problems in last 30 days	−0.0844 (4.76)	−0.249 (5.48)	−0.0667 (3.45)	−0.195 −3.95	−0.0372 (1.81)	−0.0933 (1.68)	0.0188 (0.57)	−0.0891 (0.77)
2 Disability classification	−0.240 (13.0)	−0.404 (7.16)	−0.215 (10.5)	−0.337 (5.47)	−0.0218 (0.42)	−0.648 (2.87)	−0.320 (2.95)	−0.329 (0.73)
With inputs:								
3 Self-evaluation	−0.0912 (7.12)	−0.193 (2.89)	−0.0784 (5.60)	−0.141 (2.40)	0.0109 (0.67)	−0.0715 (1.20)	−0.128 (3.79)	−0.0192 (0.13)
4 Health problems	−0.0883 (4.99)	−0.256 (2.76)	−0.0703 (3.64)	−0.148 (1.75)	−0.0383 (1.86)	−0.0945 (1.24)	−0.0400 (0.93)	−0.0271 (0.15)
5 Disability classification	−0.255 (13.70)	−0.425 (3.59)	−0.226 (11.00)	−0.384 (3.42)	−0.0182 (0.35)	−0.666 (2.12)	−0.326 (3.01)	0.415 (0.51)
Females:								
Without inputs:								
1 Health problems in the last 30 days	−0.0457 (2.95)	−0.0933 (2.33)	0.0414 (2.57)	−0.105 (2.53)	−0.0197 (1.05)	0.024 (0.48)	−0.039 (0.91)	0.0035 (0.04)
2 Disability classification	−0.191 (10.5)	−0.217 (2.93)	−0.176 (9.30)	−0.183 (2.37)	−0.117 (2.71)	−0.125 (0.46)	−0.0508 (0.68)	0.0805 (0.17)
With inputs:								
3 Self-evaluation	−0.0528 (4.06)	−0.0614 (1.24)	−0.0597 (4.42)	−0.0729 (1.34)	−0.0067 (0.38)	−0.0882 (1.39)	−0.0457 (1.51)	0.0304 (0.26)
4 Health problems	−0.0469 (3.07)	0.107 (1.60)	−0.0423 (2.66)	−0.108 (1.44)	−0.0214 (1.13)	−0.0579 (0.76)	0.0121 (0.37)	0.0325 (0.22)
5 Disability classification	−0.194 (10.8)	−0.327 (2.27)	−0.167 (8.89)	−0.238 (1.80)	−0.118 (2.75)	−0.345 (0.88)	−0.0423 (0.57)	−0.487 (0.66)

evaluation is treated as endogenous and reestimated using 2SLS, this decline is estimated to reduce male participation by 15 percent and female participation by 6 percent, with slightly larger effects on working in a wage job (columns 4-3). The OLS estimates suggest 13 percent lower wages for men who report their health status as poorer, and an insignificant 5 percent lower for women. In this case the 2SLS estimates are insignificant for wages as well as for hours for both men and women. In table 5, row 1, reporting a health problem in the last 30 days, without controlling for health-related inputs, is associated (OLS) with men working 8 percentage points less often, but when treated as endogenous and estimated by 2SLS, the impact increases to a 25 percentage point reduction. Hours also decline, according to OLS estimates, by 4 percentage points for men, and when estimated by 2SLS, the decline is 9 percentage points, although the latter estimate is not significant. For women, having one more health problem is associated with a 5 percentage point decrease in participation (OLS), and this becomes a 9 percentage point decrease according to 2SLS. No effects of women's health problems are apparent on their wage rate or on their hours of work.

The government-assigned disability classification is rare and intended to designate those who are unable to work or can only work with difficulty and with assistance. A one-unit increase in this variable, indicating worse health, is associated (OLS) with men working 24 percentage points less and women working 19 percentage points less. But when estimated by 2SLS, which should correct for classical measurement errors and endogeneity, the impact is to reduce working by 40 percentage points for men and 22 percentage points for women. Disability classification also reduces the work hours for males with a wage job, according to the 2SLS estimates, but not for women, and does not appear to affect wages for those few individuals classified as disabled and still working and reporting wages. All three measures of current health status are estimated to exert larger impacts on labor productivity, especially on participation in the labor force, when treated as endogenous, measured with error, and identified by chronic health problems and local access to medical services. Should these 2SLS estimates that are substantially larger than conventional OLS estimates be viewed as reliable and reasonably precise? These results are consistent with the labor supply literature drawn mostly from the United States, in which labor supply responds to economic constraints measured by education and health mostly through variation in participation. Estimates of the responsiveness of hours worked among those already in the wage labor force are poorly defined, especially for males in their prime (Killingsworth 1983).

Estimated Effects of Health-Related Inputs: Medical Care, Alcohol, and Cigarettes

Having a medical checkup in the last three months is associated by OLS with a 9 percentage point increase in men participating in the labor force, and a 17 percentage point increase for women in tables 6A and 6B. Seeing a doctor more frequently is directly associated with increased participation, although it is not evidently related to higher wages or hours of work for men, and is even associated with lower wages rates for women (OLS). However, when estimated by 2SLS, the identified predicted frequency of medical checkups is unrelated to working, hours, or wages, for either men or women. Specification tests in the case of medical checkups indicate that the local infrastructure and prices provide satisfactory levels of explanatory power for the full population sample, at better than 1 percent for men and women, but less power for the wage sample of persons reporting hours and earnings (table A-2). The Durbin-Wu-Hausman tests also confirm the medical checkup coefficients estimated by OLS and 2SLS differ significantly for participation and reporting hours and earnings

($p<.0001$), but only for women's hours and men's wages (table A-3). More frequent visits to a doctor do not appear to be causally increasing participation in the labor force or productivity. The direct association (OLS) between medical checkups and labor force participation may be due to individual heterogeneity, where those who prefer to see doctors more often are also engaged in other behaviors designed to improve their health. Working may facilitate periodic checkups if the medical care is encouraged by employers or even provided at the place of employment. Medical consultations and checkups may increasingly require the provision of bribes in the Russian market–oriented economy, and if linked to an employer these side payments may be moderated.

It is often hypothesized that moderate levels of alcohol consumption may be physically protective from some risks of cardiovascular disease and stroke, and may facilitate the formation of social relationships and networks that could improve work productivity. But excessive alcohol consumption can lead to accidents, violence, disease, and health problems (Russell 1987; Roman 1988; Mullahy and Sindelar 1991; French and Zavkin 1995; Tekin 2002; and Baltagi and Gekshecker 2006). Thus, a quadratic form for alcohol consumption may help to estimate nonmonotonic health consequences of alcohol consumption, and a quadratic-form specification is also adopted for cigarette consumption to assess nonlinearity (table 6).

The power of the identifying instruments in the first-stage equation explaining alcohol consumption are jointly significant for both men and women in the whole sample, and in the sample of individuals reporting positive hours and earnings (table A-2). The Durbin-Wu-Hausman test rejects the joint exogeneity of the alcohol and alcohol-squared inputs for women's participation in the labor force equation, and men's and women's wage participation (table A-3). Higher alcohol consumption is initially associated in the preferred 2SLS estimates with greater participation, and the turning point of the quadratic is after the individual consumes 122 grams of alcohol per day for men, well above the sample mean for men of 105 grams (table A-1). The maximum participation for women occurs at 124 grams per day, almost two standard deviations above their sample mean of 36 grams. By United States standards, these detrimental effects of alcohol are estimated for men and women who are consuming on an average day alcohol levels which would qualify as binge drinking.

Cigarette smoking is associated in the preferred 2SLS estimates in an inverted U-shaped relationship with labor force participation for men, where the positive initial effects of smoking on participation changes sign after smoking more than 12 cigarettes per day, roughly the sample average. Among women, the negative effects of cigarettes on participation and working for wages are more significant for the OLS estimates in table 6b than the 2SLS, but women also smoke fewer cigarettes per day than men, averaging 2.3.

Including the three health-related inputs in the second-stage productivity equations (5) results in minor changes in the estimated effects of the current health variables when they are significant, as reported in tables 4A, 4B, and rows 3 to 5 in table 5. The reversal in sign of the benefits of medical care from the OLS to the 2SLS estimates are consistent with the hypothesis that unobserved preferences for health lead some individuals to invest selectively in more healthy patterns of consumption and behavior, which are associated with improved productivity, especially for women. This individual heterogeneity in preferences contributes to the positive OLS estimates in tables 6A and 6B. But the variation in demand for health care predicted by the access to local health care infrastructure and doctors does not indicate that the associated variation in periodic checkups with these instruments contributes to improved productivity of men or women (Rosenzweig and Schultz 1983).[25]

TABLE 6A

Labor Force Productivity Determinants, Including Medical Care, Smoking, and Alcohol: Males

Dependent variable	Working in 30 days		Reporting hours and wage		ln hours in 30 days		ln wage rate	
estimation method	OLS 1	2SLS 2	OLS 3	2SLS 4	OLS 5	2SLS 6	OLS 7	2SLS 8
Medical checkup in 3 months	0.0913	−0.318	0.0685	−0.242	−0.0005	0.25	−0.0163	1.03
	(4.05)	(1.05)	(2.79)	(0.89)	(0.02)	(0.87)	(0.33)	(1.47)
Cigarettes per day	−0.0017	0.0555	−0.0039	0.0445	0.0012	0.0251	−0.0130	0.0909
	(1.86)	(2.01)	(2.05)	(1.81)	(0.64)	(1.42)	(3.32)	(2.13)
Cigarettes squared (x10^-2)	0.0094	−0.178	0.0125	−0.182	0.0026	−0.0548	0.0293	−0.246
	(1.82)	(1.89)	(2.21)	(2.18)	(0.46)	(1.19)	(2.54)	(2.21)
Alcohol per day squared (x10^-2)	0.0104	0.203	0.0220	0.163	0.0267	0.0423	0.0078	0.755
	(0.89)	(1.20)	(1.73)	(1.08)	(1.44)	(0.24)	(0.20)	(1.80)
Alcohol squared (x10^-4)	0.0035	−0.0833	−0.0073	−0.0456	0.0068	−0.0635	0.0021	−0.197
	(1.77)	(2.65)	(3.44)	(1.63)	(1.52)	(1.38)	(0.22)	(1.77)
Joint significance of cigarettes	(0.16)	(0.13)	(.086)*	(.079)*	(.072)*	(0.36)	(.0029)*	(.080)*
Joint significance of alcohol	(0.14)	(0.003)*	(.0006)*	−0.213	(0.31)	(.017)*	(0.69)	(0.19)
R squared	0.165	n.a.	0.174	n.a.	0.037	n.a.	0.264	n.a.
F	18.2	7.36	18.2	10.5	2.06	1.47	19.3	9.7
p-value	(0.0001)	(0.0001)	(0.0001)	(0.0001)	(0.0005)	(0.0464)	(0.0001)	(0.0001)

* Statistically significant jointly at the 10 percent level.

TABLE 6B

Labor Force Productivity Determinants, Including Medical Care, Smoking, and Alcohol: Females

Dependent variable	Working in 30 days		Reporting hours and wage		ln hours in 30 days		ln wage rate	
estimation method	OLS 1	2SLS 2	OLS 3	2SLS 4	OLS 5	2SLS 6	OLS 7	2SLS 8
Medical checkup in 3 months	0.165	−0.235	0.163	−0.327	0.0191	−0.0176	−0.146	−0.544
	(9.04)	(1.08)	(8.57)	(1.35)	(0.92)	(0.09)	(4.09)	(1.44)
Cigarettes per day	−0.0018	0.0246	−0.0036	−0.0731	0.0032	0.0562	−0.0030	−0.0171
	(1.86)	(2.01)	(2.05)	(1.81)	(0.74)	(1.47)	(0.79)	(0.71)
Cigarettes squared (x10^-2)	−0.0136	0.195	−0.0067	0.251	−0.0043	−0.3430	0.0285	0.265
	(0.86)	(0.75)	(0.40)	(0.87)	(0.21)	(1.73)	(0.79)	(0.71)
Alcohol per day squared (x10^-2)	0.0807	0.563	0.107	0.936	−0.0081	−0.170	0.0821	0.979
	(3.26)	(1.79)	(4.17)	(2.80)	(0.22)	(0.64)	(1.30)	(1.93)
Alcohol squared (x10^-4)	−0.0243	−0.303	−0.0350	−0.399	0.0040	0.066	0.0110	−0.136
	(2.76)	(2.12)	(3.83)	(2.50)	(0.25)	(0.44)	(0.40)	(0.48)
Joint significance of cigarettes	(0048)*	(0.66)	(0.0041)*	(0.158)	(0.41)	(0.22)	(0.55)	(0.56)
Joint significance of alcohol	(.0050)*	(0.105)	(.0001)*	(.019)*	(0.97)	(0.80)	(.0041)*	(.021)*
R squared	0.211	n.a.	0.198	n.a.	0.035	n.a	0.281	n.a.
F	29.3	17.3	27.0	13.9	2.31	2.03	24.8	17.5
p-value	(0.0001)	(0.0001)	(0.0001)	(0.0001)	(0.0001)	(0.0007)	(0.0001)	(0.0001)

* Statististically significant jointly at the 10 percent level.

Conclusions

Physical or mental inability to function normally in society can be viewed as a disability. The conditions that contribute to a person being thus unable to work or function in his or her regular activities are specific to individuals, as well as the household and social support network within which they function, and the threshold that qualifies a person to be called disabled is shaped by culture, norms, and institutions. This complex health-economy-culture process determining who is reported to be disabled may explain why low-income countries generally report lower levels of disability than do high-income countries, even though mortality and medically documented morbidity is higher in poor countries than in rich ones. This paper proposes to resolve this problem of objectively measuring disability by employing chronic and lagged health conditions of the individual to predict (as instrumental variables) current health status indicators, which may otherwise be more subjective and heterogeneous than the individual's specific chronic diagnosed health preconditions. The study outlines a replicable methodology for assessing the economic and social consequences of health and disabilities on individual productivity in the labor market, and the resulting estimation strategy may also prove replicable across different socioeconomic strata within a country, and possibly even across cultures and countries in the world, when self-reported health indicators are not causally related to productivity. It is also important to control for other demographic and human capital characteristics that are not subject to choice by adults over their mature working years in the economy.

This study describes quantitatively the determinants of economic activity and productivity in terms of observable health conditions and human capital of the individual, and in terms of his or her location and current access to medical care and health-related inputs, as well as past health problems. However, because health-related inputs and behavior are in turn selected by individuals, based in part on their preferences and their health status (which the statistician generally does not observe) it is necessary to model the determinants of these basic health production processes by policies that can be widely implemented and scaled up, and which are not subject to choice by the individual. Only when these policy and price variables can be appropriately viewed as exogenous to the health and economic system can the researcher treat these variables conditioning health outcomes as instrumental variables to identify exogenous variation in current health status. Therefore, a goal is to explain the underlying demands for these inputs and behaviors that contribute to better health to assess without statistical bias how these inputs improve health and enhance the productive capacity of a population. This investigation has made progress in understanding the forms of health-related behavior that affect health and labor productivity in post-transition Russia, such as high levels of smoking and drinking. Perhaps by reorienting the analysis to focus more on variation over time in prices of these commodities and productive medical services and regionally distinct policies toward alcohol consumption, and the use of preventive medical care and health education programs that encourage healthier behaviors, it might be possible to identify more clearly the pathways from policy instruments to survey measures of health status, and to the size and productivity of the Russian labor force.

Self-assessed health status questions from a representative survey should be recognized as measured with error and subject to individual choice and interpretation. This requires that the researcher attempt to explain these health status responses accordingly as endogenous choices subject to measurement error. This requires the employment of at least an implicit structural framework as outlined in this paper. In this analysis, it was assumed that chronic health conditions could be treated as exogenous instruments to predict the more subjective current responses to health status questions, and the empirical results confirmed that this approach yielded reasonable patterns that were statistically different from those obtained by conventional single-equation methods, i.e. OLS or logit. In the case of participation in the labor force, these 2SLS estimates of the effects of health on productivity were much larger than conventional OLS estimates. Intervening with early health education, changing health-related behaviors, and inducing the population to use effectively medical care to avoid the development of chronic degenerative diseases has the potential to reduce what in the future will be the past health problems and improve people's stock of current health human capital. According to the estimates reported in this paper, such an improvement in current health status would result in large increases in labor force participation, work in wage jobs for which they report hours and earnings, and, to some extent, increase hours and wage rates among those who already are in the wage labor force.

Age-specific mortality among Russian males age 25 to 64 was four times the levels recorded in Western Europe at the end of the 1990s, whereas Russian females' mortality was twice West European levels. Half of this East-West mortality differential among prime aged adults emerged in the 1990s, during the first decade of the Russian transition from a centralized communist state to a partly decentralized market oriented economy (Guo 1993; Nolte et al. 2004; World Bank 2005). The 2004 RLMS survey data examined here did not explicitly link mortality to morbidity and health status of the sampled population. The RLMS samples addresses and does not follow household members who move or link their identities to death registration. By exploiting the household panel feature of the RLMS, it might be possible to trace the connections between actual adult mortality between rounds of the survey, and the predicted prior health status and disabilities of that individual in earlier rounds of the survey. This study instead analyzed a representative sample of all middle-aged men and women to see whether their widely reported health behaviors and indicators of their current health status are individually associated with chronic health problems. Then these prior health conditions and current local community conditions as employed to predict current health status and disabilities, and assess how this predicted variation in health impacts labor productivity, as measured by variation in labor force participation, hours worked, and wage rates.

Appendix

TABLE A1

Definitions and Sources of Variables and Sample Statistics from Russian Longitudinal Monitoring Survey, 2004[a]

Class of variable\ Variable definition	Alternative samples — age 25 to 64			
	All persons		Reporting positive hours and wages in last 30 days	
(Questionnaire source adult and community modules)	Females [1]	Males [2]	Females [3]	Males [4]
Working sample size	3,429	2,708	1,999	1,699
(Variables reported)				
Productivity (P)				
1. Working in last 30 days (J.7 & 30)	0.645	0.729	1.00	1.00
2. Reporting earnings and hours (8 &10 or 38 & 40)	0.583	0.627	1.00	1.00
3. Ln hours in 30 days (8 & 38)	n.a[b]	n.a	5.04 [0.408]	5.17 [0.366]
4. Ln wage rate in 30 days (10/8 or 40/38)	n.a	n.a	3.10 [0.819]	3.41 [0.873]
Health Status Current (HC)				
1. Self-evaluation (0–4, Excellent to Poor; M3)	1.87 [0.615]	1.69 [0.656]	1.81 [0.553]	1.61 [0.574
2. Any health problems in last 30 days (L5)	0.428 [0.495]	0.283 [0.451]	0.393 [0.488]	0.251 [0.434]
3. Assigned disability classification (0–3; M 20.8)	0.0916 [0.410]	0.104 [0.427]	0.0275 [0.212]	0.023 [0.172]
Health Lagged (HL)				
1. Chronic heart disease (M20.6.1)	0.130	0.081	0.099	0.060
2. Chronic lung disease (M20.6.2)	0.052	0.051	0.047	0.040
3. Chronic liver disease (M20.6.3)	0.108	0.046	0.091	0.038
4. Chronic kidney disease (M20.6.4)	0.116	0.042	0.104	0.031
5. Chronic stomach disease (M20.6.5)	0.179	0.129	0.172	0.128
6. Chronic spinal disease (M20.6.6)	0.170	0.129	0.166	0.126
7. Other chronic disease (M20.6.7)	0.240	0.138	0.233	0.117
8. Had serious nervous disorder or depression in the last 12 months (M131)	0.235	0.137	0.215	0.112
9. Doctor diagnosed high blood pressure (M58.1)	0.412	0.288	0.372	0.277
Health Related Inputs/Behaviors (I)				
1. Medical checkup in last 3 months (L26)	0.206	0.143	0.267	0.166

Class of variable\ Variable definition	Alternative samples — age 25 to 64: All persons		Reporting positive hours and wages in last 30 days	
	Females [1]	Males [2]	Females [3]	Males [4]
2. Alcohol consumption per	0.359	1.05	0.391	1.02
day in last 30 days in gr.	[0.546]	[1.17]	[0.526]	[1.02]
ethanol (x 10^{-2}).[c]				
3.Cigarettes consumed per day[d]	2.33	12.0	2.28	11.9
	[5.59]	[10.4]	[5.41]	[10.6]
Control - Independent Variables [C]				
Individual Variables [C_i]				
1. Age in years (x 10^{-1})	4.29	4.15	4.13	4.01
	[1.11]	[1.09]	[0.97]	[1.00]
2. Age in years squared	19.6	18.4	18.0	17.1
(x 10^{-2})	[9.69]	[9.36]	[8.11]	[6.25]
3. Pension-eligible age	0.181	0.058	0.096	0.024
(women: 55–64; men: 60–64)				
4. Education years completed				
(a) Grade school (0–12)	9.57	9.43	9.68	9.52
(J70.1)	[1.18]	[1.23]	[0.983]	[1.10]
(b) Vocational (0–6)	0.563	0.893	0.565	0.903
(J7 2.2 +72.3)	[1.04]	[1.24]	[1.04]	[1.25]
(c) Technical (0–9)	1.15	0.735	1.28	0.830
(J72.4)	[1.58]	[1.41]	[1.61]	[1.47]
(d) University & graduate (0–13)	1.40	1.17	1.67	1.39
(J72.5 & J72.6)	[2.35]	[2.28]	[2.51]	[2.44]
5. Unearned income in last 30	0.0438	0.0418	0.0276	0.0208
days (x 10^{-4})	[0.204]	[0.351]	[0.164]	[0.175]
(J60 - J10 – J40 - J76 - J89)				
6. Height in cm. (R3)	162.0	174.0	162.0	175.0
	[6.37]	[6.91]	[6.22]	[6.89]
7. Currently married	0.587	0.703	0.586	0.748
(J72.17)				
8. Cohabiting currently	0.111	0.132	0.104	0.132
(J72.17)				
9. Divorced currently	0.137	0.072	0.154	0.052
(J72.17)				
10. BMI (weight in	27.6	25.6	27.3	25.8
kg/height in MT squared)	[5.87]	[4.14]	[5.69]	[4.08]
(R4 & R3)				
11. BMI squared	7.94	6.71	7.78	6.80
(x10^{-2})	[3.53]	[2.28]	[3.38]	[2.25]
12. Waist/hip ratio	0.812	0.899	0.804	0.897
(R5 & R6)	[0.072]	[0.070]	[0.069]	[0.067]
13. Rural resident	0.230	0.260	0.178	0.188
(SETT_TYP)				
14. PGT_secret city	0.062	0.061	0.046	0.042
(SETT_TYP)				
Community Variables (C_c)				
1. Low price of vodka liter	110.0	110.0	110.0	110.0
(10^{-2} rubles: A1.90)	[22.2]	[22.1]	[21.1]	[20.8]
2. Low price of cigarettes pkg.	5.37	5.48	5.41	5.62
(rubles: A1.82)	[4.41]	[4.71]	[4.36]	[4.57]

TABLE A1 (*continued*)

Definitions and Sources of Variables and Sample Statistics from Russian Longitudinal Monitoring Survey, 2004[a]

Class of variable\ Variable definition	Alternative samples — age 25 to 64: All persons		Reporting positive hours and wages in last 30 days	
	Females [1]	Males [2]	Females [3]	Males [4]
3. No community questionnaire available	0.109	0.107	0.120	0.133
4. Hospital in area (Q46)	0.744	0.733	0.765	0.754
5. Time to reach hospital in hours (Q48)	5.15 [15.2]	5.81 [16.5]	3.57 [11.2]	3.62 [12.3]
6. Private doctor in area (Q46)	0.640	0.623	0.682	0.676
7. Time to reach private doctor (Q48)	25.0 [70.0]	26.3 [70.9]	21.6 [66.0]	18.4 [58.4]
8. No doctor time reported	0.032	0.037	0.017	0.017
9. Social welfare office in area (Q79A)	0.700	0.691	0.733	0.739
10. Does social welfare office provide medial services (Q80)	0.668	0.656	0.697	0.692
Regional Variables (C_R)-Omitted Region Moscow City				
1. St. Petersburg	0.044	0.038	0.049	0.046
2. Moscow Oblast	0.043	0.038	0.041	0.038
3. North and North West	0.063	0.064	0.070	0.067
4. Central and Black Earth	0.131	0.130	0.141	0.141
5. Volga-Vaytski	0.175	0.181	0.168	0.171
6. North Cauzasian	0.131	0.137	0.105	0.110
7. Urals	0.136	0.137	0.151	0.149
8. West Siberia	0.094	0.093	0.093	0.082
9. East Siberia and Far East	0.094	0.093	0.087	0.086

Note:

a. The standard deviations of binary variables are not reported because standard deviations are equal to (m(m-1)exp. 0.5.

b. n.a. not available or defined.

c. Ethanol consumption is based on the following weighted function:

0.05 beer + 0.11 table wine or champagne + 0.19 fortified wine + 0.40 vodka + 0.45 home-made liquor (samogen) + 0.20 other alcohol (Q80.1 - 80.6).

No information is reported on "binge" drinking, often measured as having five or more drinks on one occasion, or 80g. ethanol or more. These binges may be more harmful to health than more moderate, uniform consumption, but this aspect cannot be assessed with these data. Alcohol consumption in grams of ethanol per day is divided by 100, and alcohol consumption squared is divided by 10,000 in the regressions, i.e., 100 squared.

d. Tobacco consumption is summarized by the number of regular cigarettes consumed per day. Paperosi may be stronger tobacco, but are shorter or contain less tobacco per cigarette than normal ones measured here. Cigarettes per day is divided by 10 in the regressions.

TABLE A2

Joint F-Test of Significance of Identifying Instruments in First-Stage Regressions

(p-values in parentheses)

Dependent variable	All persons age 25–64		Reporting hours and wage	
	Males	Females	Males	Females
Self-evaluation	39.59	39.31	16.88	19.38
	(0.0001)	(0.0001)	(0.0001)	(0.0001)
Health problems	26.07	31.32	14.01	16.56
	(0.0001)	(0.0001)	(0.0001)	(0.0001)
Disability classification	17.50	11.41	5.29	2.66
	(0.0001)	(0.0001)	(0.0001)	(0.0001)
Medical checkup	2.78	2.22	1.17	1.52
	(0.0001)	(0.0017)	(0.28)	(0.0687)
Cigarette consumption	3.05	3.35	1.79	1.46
	(0.0001)	(0.0001)	(0.0193)	(0.0902)
Cigarette squared	2.11	2.20	2.19	1.16
	(0.0034)	(0.0020)	(0.0022)	(0.28)
Alcohol consumption	4.37	3.58	2.84	2.38
	(0.0001)	(0.0001)	(0.0001)	(0.0007)
Alcohol squared	2.78	1.75	2.58	1.30
	(0.0001)	(0.0229)	(0.0002)	(0.17)

TABLE A3

Hausman Specification Tests (t or F) of the Exogeneity of Dependent Variables*

	Working in 30 days		Reporting hours & wage		ln hours per month		ln wage per hour	
Dependent variable	Males	Females	Males	Females	Males	Females	Males	Females
Self-evaluation	(0.0001)	(0.0014)	(0.0001)	(0.0006)	(0.121)	(0.93)	(0.0001)	(0.084)
Health problems	(0.0054)	(0.0263)	(0.0416)	(0.0842)	(0.204)	(0.35)	(0.50)	(0.55)
Disability classification	(0.0001)	(0.0001)	(0.0001)	(0.0001)	(0.684)	(0.0073)	(0.0037)	(0.53)
Medical checkups*	(0.0001)	(0.0001)	(0.0009)	(0.0001)	(0.95)	(0.37)	(0.96)	(0.0001)
Cigarettes and cigarettes squared*	(0.0596)	(0.0065)	(0.0253)	(0.0072)	(0.073)	(0.39)	(0.0005)	(0.62)
Alcohol and alcohol squared*	(0.34)	(0.0059)	(0.0008)	(0.0003)	(0.30)	(0.99)	(0.82)	(0.0133)

Note: * Estimated jointly with other health-related inputs.

Notes

1. This exploratory analysis does not identify policy priorities that would be most cost-effective means to reduce the prevalence of adult disabilities or mitigate the economic consequences of these disabilities emerging during the transition health crisis. Nor does this study distinguish between mental and physical disabilities.
2. The private and social costs of changing the instrumental variables constraining an individual's environment that are associated with the frequency of observed disabilities in Russia could be a (the) focus of future study, based on more detailed local administrative health care delivery data from Russia. Perhaps the repeated rounds of the RLMS during which health infrastructure, insurance, employment conditions, economic shocks, and disability pensions may have changed over time and across regions of Russia would allow a researcher the opportunity to estimate the health consequences of macro and micro economic changes (Currie and Madrian 1999).
3. The person "not reporting" could work for an employer who is in arrears on his payments to his workforce. If they completed the subsequent questions in the survey, they are attributed the actual payment received for actual hours worked, but some may have failed to respond to both questions. Alternatively, the individual may be self-employed and cannot distinguish his or her wages from returns to his or her capital and reward for taking risks. The worker may also be paid in periods other than months, or does not know or want to divulge his earnings or hours last month for fear he may owe taxes, perhaps because his work in the "black market" economy is unregulated, i.e., untaxed.
4. The survey questionnaires and sampling methodology are described and the data was downloaded from the Web site: http://www.cpc.unc.edu/projects/rlms. The sample statistics for the final estimation samples are reported in appendix table A-1, which includes 2,708 men and 3,429 women for whom all of the control variables and instruments are defined or identified by missing variable dummies.
5. A few percent are included in the "paid labor force" who do not report earnings and hours in their primary job, but do in their secondary job. Hours are then set to the sum of those hours reported, and the hourly wage is taken from the second job and assumed to apply to the primary job as well. This group for whom the secondary job is relied on constitutes less than 2 percent of the paid labor force.
6. In 2004, US$1 equals about 29 rubles. For additional information on Russian social security programs, consult: www.ssa.gov/policy/docs/progdesc/ssptw/2004-2005/europe/russia.
7. If one assumed that those who report no earnings or no hours, but nonetheless indicate they worked in the last 30 days, received less compensation per hour and worked fewer hours than did those reporting their earnings and hours, the expected levels of cohort productivity for men and women would be lower than the above calculations suggest, but the magnitude of this sample selection bias in reporting work, hours, and earnings has not to my knowledge been assessed in Russia.
8. The distribution of wage rates tends to be skewed to right. When the wage is expressed in logarithms, it is distributed more nearly to normal. If errors in the wage function are normally distributed, OLS regression and maximum likelihood methods are more attractive, and the earnings function as conceptualized in the human capital literature by Mincer (1974) is more readily interpreted.
9. There is also the convenience of being able to decompose the marginal effects of explanatory variables on log earnings into a linear model where the coefficients are the sum of those coefficients in the analogous linear model for log wages and log hours.
10. Although days missed or absenteeism has been emphasized in studies of Russia as being unusually high, I did not find it particularly large, nor was it responsive to control variables, or strongly associated with any of the indicators of labor supply and productivity examined here, with the possible exception of hours of work in the OLS estimates. For another perspective, see the analysis by Suhrcke et al. 2005.
11. For example, among men age 55 to 64, 83 percent have no disability (disability classification variable = 0), 5 percent have first-degree disability (=1)—of whom about half work, 10 percent have second-degree (=2), and 2 percent have the most severe, third-degree disability (=3) and very few work. Note that survey code 1 refers to third-degree disability, and survey code 3 refers to first-degree disability (adult questionnaire 20.7 and 20.8), which required a recoding of the disability classification variable analyzed here.

12. However, Bobak and Marmot (1999) remind one that the causal evidence for the connection between alcohol consumption and cardiovascular mortality is ambiguous, and the officially reported levels of alcohol consumption in Russia are relatively moderate by European standards, though probably underestimated given the extent of illegal production of spirits (Samogan) in Russia (i.e., Trelm 1982).
13. The total budget for social expenditures of the federal government in Russia is estimated to be 13 percent of GDP, and 48 percent of this budget is allocated to general pensions (Tesliuc and Zotova 2004: table 6). There are also special pensions for the disabled, as well as for maternity and sick leaves, all of which are funded by the centralized Social Insurance Fund, which is independent of contributions from employers or employees. Unemployment benefits are very small, representing only 0.1 percent of the budget for social expenditures in 2003, perhaps because they have not always been adjusted for inflation (Foley 1997). Child allowances are widespread because they are not selectively granted to those with low incomes, but they have declined in real value from 1998 to 2003 as a share of minimum subsistence levels (Tesliuc and Zotova 2004: figure 9). As noted above, the age of eligibility for pensions is included in this analysis as an exogenous conditioning variable, holding constant also for a quadratic function in age to approximate broader biological and behavioral variation over the life cycle.
14. The amount of physical exercise an individual engages in is rated by the respondent, but it does not clearly vary by gender or age (table 3), or any of the three health status indicators or four productivity measures, and is therefore not included in the final specification of the model.
15. The grams consumed per day of various types of alcoholic beverages are reported in the survey and are converted by the author into ethanol alcohol equivalents following the example of Baltagi and Gekshecher (2006), who adopted the conversion rates of Mullahy and Sindelar (1991). I have used those mentioned in the survey: 5 percent beer, 10 percent wine, 19 percent fortified wine, 40 percent vodka, 45 percent other home-produced spirits. The large supplies of private illegal distilled spirits produced in Russia have been estimated to increase when state prices of vodka are raised (Treml 1982), and did so during Gorbachev's brief 1985–88 campaign to reduce Russian consumption of alcohol, which was then associated with declines in adult mortality (Carcone 1994; Shkolnikov et al. 1997; Leon et al. 1997). I have calculated my own variable of total ethanol consumption from the five categories of consumption reported, rather than use the derived variable in the survey file, which I could not duplicate or otherwise explain its origins.
16. Men age 25 to 64 have received more years of vocational education than women, at .88 years compared to .56, whereas women have received more years of technical and university education, 1.15 compared to .74 for technical school, and 1.41 compared to 1.18 for university education.
17. Older age groups probably overstate the secular gains across birth cohorts in childhood health and nutrition, although selective survival favoring the tall could operate in the opposite direction to understate these height improvements inferred from differences between young and elderly age groups in a cross-sectional survey such as the RLMS.
18. Diabetes was not significantly associated with health status indicators or productivity of labor, perhaps because of its infrequency (last column table 2) , and is not included in the reported estimates. Nor is tuberculosis, which is reported to be much rarer.
19. A question regarding individuals' self-reported exercise was not significantly related to health status outcomes or productivity, and was not included in the final model.
20. In Russia, pensions for the elderly are routinely available for women after age 54 and for men after age 59, although in contrast to some countries, receipt of the pension does not preclude working unless prepension incomes are very high. Some pensions are awarded on "merit" because of disabilities, sickness, maternity leave, unemployment, etc.
21. It might be argued that some of the controls are endogenous to health and productivity of the individual, such as marital status, for one might imagine that healthy and productive individuals would be more likely to be married. Remaining in a rural area and not migrating to the city where wages and living conditions might be economically better could be explained by an individual having a stronger than average preference for a rural lifestyle, which could also have a bearing on his or her productivity or healthiness in either location. The existence of the PGT cities was acknowledged only after 1995, and these

hidden cities may have special industrial and environmental problems for their population's health. Regular urban areas are the omitted category, and health in the PGT cities appears somewhat better than rural areas, but not as good as urban areas.

22. In a few clusters, the community consumption questionnaire did not provide a price, in which case the average for the primary sampling unit, of which there are 38 in the RLMS, is extrapolated from an adjacent sample cluster to the site for which no price data were reported.
23. The problem described in Bound (1991) is that errors in measuring HC would bias the OLS estimate of HC's effect on P toward 0 in estimating (4) by OLS, whereas the endogenous effects of preferences for leisure might be expected to lead to an overstatement of negative effect of disabilities on labor supply and productivity indicators. The RLMS information on health input behavior is quite limited, and variables reported by all respondents are unlikely to measure community access to and prices of health care, on which the endogenous demand for health-related inputs or behaviors might reasonably be determined and identified with satisfactory precision. The community program, policy, and price variations are, therefore, likely to be "weak instruments" on which to base the otherwise desirable 2SLS estimates of the effects of community and household variables on adult health status and labor productivity. Such a case of weak instruments is expected to yield estimates that are biased toward the OLS estimates.
24. As this final indicator of stature is not (to my knowledge) included in previous multivariate studies of labor productivity or health, I also excluded the waist-hip ratio from the model and noted the estimated fit of BMI in the participation and wage functions as otherwise specified in tables 4A and 4B implied that maximum productivity was associated with BMI values of 30 and 32 for men and women, respectively, which are more in accord with the standard literature.
25. A sign reversal in the estimated effect of medical care is analogous to seeing a doctor earlier in a woman's pregnancy, which was associated (OLS) with a lower birthweight outcome, but when the timing of her first prenatal visit was estimated by 2SLS and identified by local access to medical facilities, prices of medical care, and household resources, earlier prenatal care was beneficial for the child's birthweight (Rosenzweig and Schultz 1983).

References

Baltagi, Badi H., and I. Gekshecker. 2006. "Rational Alcohol Addiction: Evidence from the Russian Longitudinal Monitoring Survey." Discussion Paper No. 2134, IZA, Bonn, Germany.

Barker, D.J.P. 1994. *Mothers, Babies, and Disease in Later Life*. London: BMJ Publishing Group.

Bartel, A., and P. Taubman. 1979. "Health and Labor Market Success: The Role of Various Diseases." *Review of Economics and Statistics* 61 (10): 1–8.

Bengtsson, Tommy, et al. 2004. *Life under Pressure: Mortality and Living Standards in Europe and Asia, 1700–1950*. Cambridge, MA: MIT Press.

Bobak, Martin, and M. Marmot. 1999. "Alcohol and Mortality in Russia: Is it Different than Elsewhere?" *Annals of Epidemiology* 9 (6): 335–38.

Bound, John. 1991. "Self-Reported versus Objective Measures of Health in Retirement Models." *Journal of Human Resources* 26 (1): 106–38.

Brainerd, Elizabeth, and D.M. Cutler. 2004. "Autopsy on an Empire: Understanding Mortality in Russia and the Former Soviet Union." Working Paper 10868, National Bureau of Economic Research, Cambridge, MA.

Carcone, J.A. 1994. "Alcohol-Related Problems as an Obstacle to the Development of Human Capital." Technical Paper No. 219, World Bank, Washington, DC.

Costa, D. 1996. "Health and Labor Force Participation of Older Men, 1900–1991." *Journal of Economic History* 56: 62–89.

Currie, Janet, and B. Madrian. 1999. "Health, Health Insurance, and the Labor Market." In *Handbook of Labor Economics*, ed. O. Ashenfelter and D. Card, 3309–3415. Amsterdam, the Netherlands: Elsevier Science BV.

Dostie, Benoit, and P.T. Leger. 2005. "The Living Arrangement Dynamics of Sick, Elderly Individuals." *Journal of Human Resources* 40 (4): 989–1014.

Fogel, R.W. 1994. "Economic Growth, Population Theory, and Physiology." *American Economic Review* 84 (3): 369–95.

Fogel, R.W. 2004. *The Escape from Hunger and Premature Death: Europe, America, and the Third World, 1700–2100*. New York: Cambridge University Press.

Foley, Mark C. 1997. "Labor Market Dynamics, Unemployment Duration, and Multiple Job Holding in Russia during Economic Transition." Unpublished PhD dissertation, Yale University, New Haven, CT.

French, Michael, and G.A. Zavkin. 1995. "Is Moderate Alcohol Use Related to Wages?" *Journal of Health Economics* 14: 319–44.

Glinskaya, Elena, and T. Mroz. 2000. "The Gender Gap in Wages in Russia from 1992 to 1995." *Journal of Population Economics* 13 (2): 353–86.

Griliches, Z., and J. Hausman. 1986. "Errors in Variables in Panel Data." *Journal of Econometrics* 31 (1): 93–118.

Guo, Guang. 1993. "Mortality Trends and Causes of Death: A Comparison between Eastern and Western Europe, 1960s-1980s." *European Journal of Population* 9: 287–312.

Heckman, J.J. 1997. "Instrumental Variables: A Study of Implicit Behavioral Assumptions in One Widely Used Estimator." *Journal of Human Resources* 32 (3): 441–62.

Imbens, G.W., and J.D. Angrist. 1994. "Identification and Estimation of Local Average Treatment Effects." *Econometrica*, 62: 467–76.

Johansson, S.R. 1991. "The Health Transaction: The Cultural Inflation of Morbidity during the Decline in Mortality." *Health Transition Review* 1 (1): 39–68.

Kauhanen, J., G.A. Kaplan, D.E. Goldberg, and J.T. Salonen. 1997. "Beer Binging and Mortality: Results from the Kuopio Ischaemic Heart Risk Factors Study, a Prospective Population-Based Study." *British Medical Journal* 315: 846–51.

Killingsworth, Mark R. 1983. *Labor Supply*, Cambridge, MA: Cambridge University Press.

Leon, D.A., L. Chenet, V. Shkolnikov, S. Zakharov, J. Shapiro, and G. Rakhmanova. 1997. "Huge Variation in Russian Morality Rates 1984–94: Artefact, Alcohol or What?" *Lancet*, 350, 383–388.

Lokshin, Michael, and M. Ravallion. 2005. "Searching for the Economic Gradient in Self Assessed Health." Development Research Group, World Bank, Washington, DC.

Manton, K.G. 1986. "Past and Future Life Expectancy Increases in Later Ages: Their Implications for the Linkage of Chronic Morbidity, Disability, and Mortality." *Journal of Gerontology* 41: 672–81.

Mete, Cem, and S.R. Cnobloch. 2006. "Socioeconomic Status and Health Outcomes: A Relationship in Disguise." Processed paper. World Bank, Washington, DC.

Michell J., and R. Burkhauser. 1990. "Disentangling the Effects of Arthritis on Earnings: A Simultaneous Estimate of Wage Rates and Hours Worked." *Applied Economic Letters* 22: 1291–1310.

Mincer, J. 1974. *Schooling, Experience, and Earnings.* New York: Columbia University Press.

Mullahy, J., and J.L. Sindelar. 1991. "Gender Differences in Labor Market Effects of Alcoholism." *American Economic Review* 81: 161–65.

Nolte, Ellen, M. McKee, and A. Gilmore. 2004. "Mortality, Morbidity in Transition Countries in the European Context." Background paper for European Population Forum 2004, London School of Hygiene and Tropical Medicine.

Pauly, Mark V., et al. 2002. "A General Model of the Impact of Absenteeism on Employer and Employee." *Health Economics* 11: 221–31.

Pelkowski, J.M., and M.C. Berger. 2004. "The Impact of Health on Employment, Wages, and Hours Worked over the Life Cycle." *Quarterly Review of Economics and Finance* 44: 102–21.

Rosenzweig, Mark R., and T.P. Schultz. 1983. "Estimating a Household Production Function: Heterogeneity and the Demand for Health Inputs and the Effects on Birthweight." *Journal of Political Economy* 91 (5): 723–46.

Roman, P.M. 1988. "Biological Features of Women's Alcohol Use." *Public Health Reports*, 103: 628–37.

Ryan, M. 1995. "Alcoholism and Rising Mortality in the Russian Federation." *British Medical Journal* 310: 646–48.

Schultz, T.P. 2005. "Productive Benefits of Health: Evidence from Low-Income Countries." In *Health and Economic Growth: Findings and Policy Implications*, ed. G. Lopez-Casasnovas, B. Rivera, and L. Currais, pp. 257–285 Cambridge, MA: MIT Press.

Schultz, T. Paul, and A. Tansel. 1997. "Wages and Labor Supply Effects of Illness in Côte d'Ivoire and Ghana: Instrumental Variable Estimates for Days Disabled." *Journal of Development Economics* 53 (2): 251–86.

Science. 2006. "Mental Health Disabilities in the World." January 27: 459.

Shkolnikov, V.M., and A. Nemtsov. 1997. "The Anti-Alcohol Campaign and Variation in Russian Mortality." In *Premature Death in the New Independent States*, ed. J.L. Bobadilla, C.A. Castello, and F. Michell, Washington, DC: National Academy Press.

Stern, Steven. 1989 "Measuring the Effect of Disability on Labor Force Participation." *Journal of Human Resources* 24 (3): 361–95.

Strauss, John, and D. Thomas. 1995. "Human Resources: Empirical Modeling of Household and Family Decisions." In Vol. 3A of *Handbook of Development Economics*, ed. J. Behrman, and

T.N. Srinivasan, pp. 1883–2023 Amsterdam, the Netherlands: Elsevier.

Suhrcke, Marc, L. Rocco, D. Urban, M. McKee, S. Mazzuco, and A. Steinherr. 2005. "Economic Consequences of Noncommunicable Diseases and Injuries in the Russian Federation." European Office for Investment for Health and Development, World Health Organization, Venice, Italy.

Tekin, E. 2002. "Employment, Wages, and Alcohol Consumption in Russia." Working Paper No. 432, IZA, Bonn, Germany.

Tesliuc, Emil D., and E. Zotova. 2004. "A Social Safety Net for the Poor." Paper prepared for conference on targeting social program in Russia, World Bank, Washington, DC.

Thirumurthy, Harsha, J. G. Zivin, and M. Goldstein. 2005. "The Economic Impact of AIDS Treatment: Labor Supply in Western Kenya." Working Paper 11871, National Bureau of Economic Research, Cambridge, MA.

Treml, Vladimir G. 1982. *Alcohol in the USSR: A Statistical Study.* Durham, NC: Duke Press Policy Studies.

Waaler, H.T. 1984. "Height, Weight, and Mortality: The Norwegian experience," *Acta Medica Scandinava* 77, suppl. no. 679.

Welch, Finis. 1997. "Wages and Participation." *Journal of Labor Economics* 15 (1) pt. 2: S77–S106.

World Bank. 2005. *Dying Too Young.* Washington, DC: World Bank.

World Health Organization. 1992. *World Health Report 1991.* Geneva, Switzerland: World Health Organization.

Yemtsov, Ruslan G., S. R. Cnobloch, and C. Mete. 2006. *Evolution of the Predictors of Earnings during Transition.* Washington, DC: World Bank.

CHAPTER 5

The Implications of Poor Health Status on Employment in Romania

Cem Mete and Shirley H. Liu*

Introduction

The economic collapse and emergence of widespread poverty in the transition countries during the early 1990s was followed by respectable economic growth rates and significant reductions in poverty starting from the late 1990s. During this recovery period, a key policy question is the extent to which health inequalities in these countries will be an obstacle against equitable (and sustainable) economic growth and poverty reduction. Yet little is known about the strength of the relationship between poor health status and employment in this context. Furthermore, it is not clear if the observed health inequalities are driven primarily by factors that cannot be influenced by policy makers in the short term (such as schooling attainment and household wealth), or by other factors such as the accessibility and quality of health care.

The linkage between the health status and socioeconomic characteristics of adults is found to be strong in transition economies (Gilmore, McKee, and Rose 2002; Kopp, Skrabski, and Szedmak 2000; Bobak et al. 1998; Bobak et al. 2000; Leinsalu 2002; Wroblewska 2002; Thompson, Miller, and Witter 2003). But this literature might be overstating the impact of socioeconomic characteristics on health because the estimated relationships are subject to omitted-variables bias: none of the papers listed above consider household health environment (e.g., humidity, cold, noise, polluted air, poor water quality, etc.) or availability of health facilities in the community as determinants of healthiness.[1]

This approach is inconsistent with the theoretical formulations of the determinants of

* Cem Mete is a senior economist at the Europe and Central Asia region of the World Bank. Shirley Liu is an assistant professor at the economics department of the University of Miami.

health status, which acknowledge the possible role of local environmental factors (Strauss and Thomas 1998). Ignoring local environmental conditions and public health infrastructure could be acceptable for studies focusing on industrialized countries—where basic health infrastructure is universally available and most individuals are able to shield themselves from adverse environmental conditions.[2] This is not necessarily the case for transition countries, where poverty is widespread and there are growing concerns about deteriorating public health, central heating, and water services (Lampietti and Meyer 2002; World Bank 2003a). Indeed, BEEPS interviews with firms in 21 transition countries reveal serious concerns about the quality of water and public health services, especially in poorer countries (figures 1 and 2).[3] Thus, there is a possibility that the existing studies end up interpreting circumstances such as "a poor household cannot afford heating and safe water on a regular basis, and there is no hospital nearby (which might symbolize quality and availability of treatment), and the members of the household are in poor health status" simply as a black-box relationship between poverty (or low levels of schooling) and health outcomes, or as supportive evidence for social determinants of health theory—as elaborated by Wilkinson and Marmot (1999) to explain variation in health outcomes across industrialized countries—which states that an individual's relative social standing has a direct influence on his or her health status.

The studies that use household survey data from transition countries also tend to overlook the economic implications of poor health. While both cross-country growth regression setup (Bloom, Canning, and Sevilla 2003) and micro-level evidence from other developing

FIGURE 1

Quality of Water and Public Health Services in 21 Transition Countries

Reported percentages are obtained by the summation of "slightly bad," "bad," and "very bad" responses

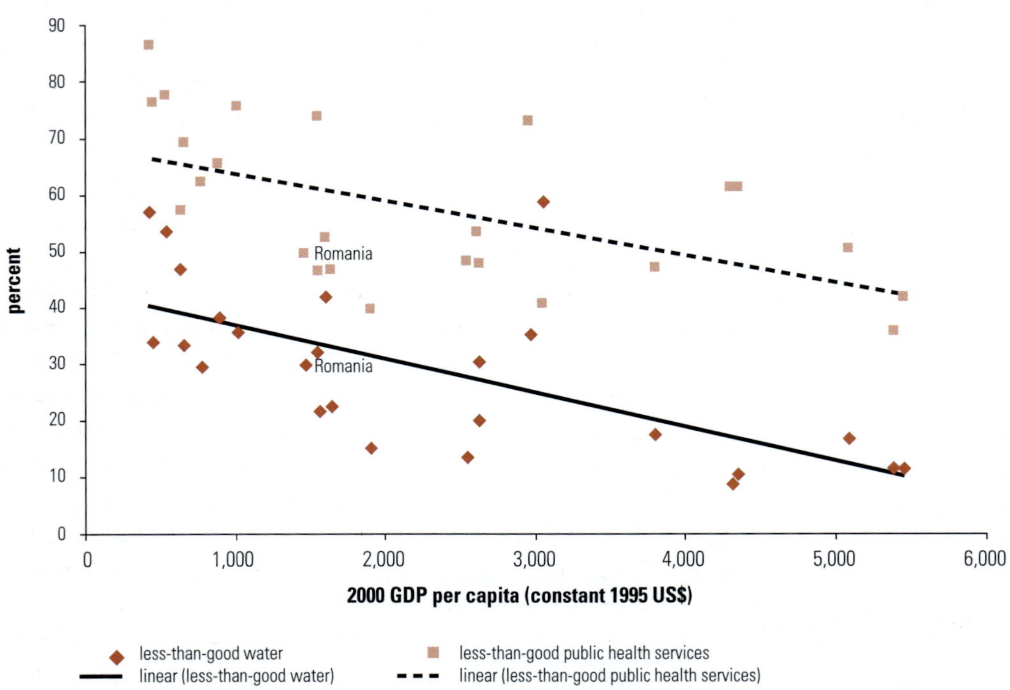

Source: 1999–2000 BEEPS survey interviews of 3,878 firms.

FIGURE 2

Quality of Water and Public Health Services in 21 Transition Countries

Reported percentages are obtained by the summation "bad" and "very bad" responses

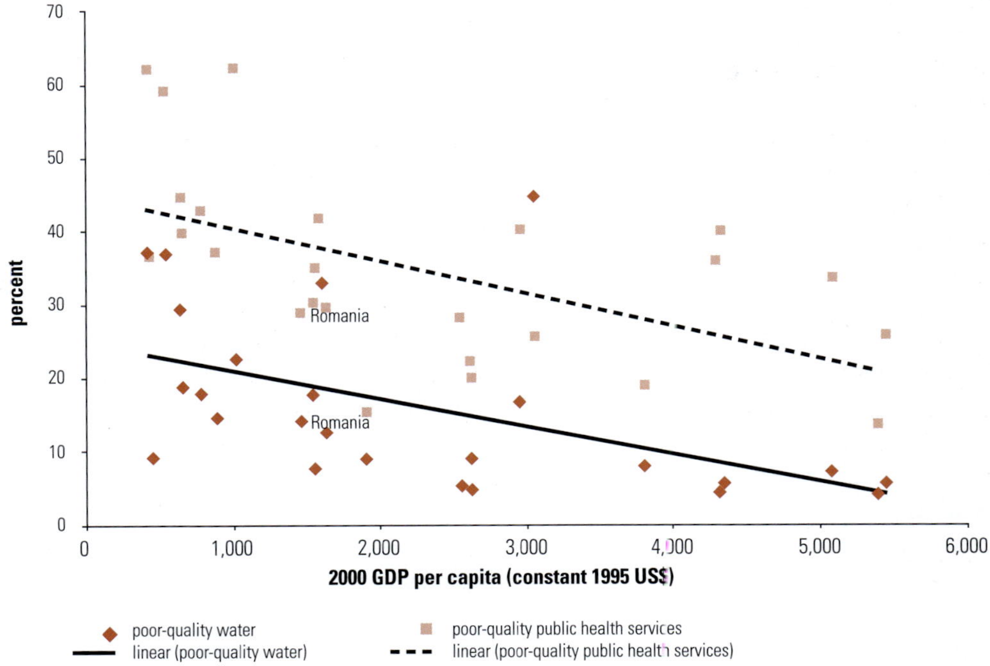

Source: 1999–2000 BEEPS survey interviews of 3,878 firms.

countries (Schultz 2002) testify to the importance of the population's health on the economy, this relationship remains understudied in the transition economy context.

The shortcomings in the literature arise not because these issues are considered to be unimportant, but rather due to data limitations. This research relies on two sets of data from Romania—the nationally representative 2000 Living Conditions Survey, with a sample size of 25,395 individuals, matched with community-level information from locality records of 1995.[4] On the positive side, the variables that allow the formulation of a better-specified health function are also those that can be used as instrumental variables to sort out the causal impact of health on employment. But there is certainly room for further improvement, either by using a richer set of instrumental variables that capture the childhood environment experienced by the interviewed adults (see, for example, Mete and Schultz 2007), or by using panel data that would give one more options to tackle causality issues (Hurd, McFadden, and Merrill 2001; Attanasio and Emmerson 2001; Mete 2004).

The Context: Romania in Transition

The significant output collapse that Romania experienced in the early years of transition came to an end in 2000, with a real GDP growth rate of 2 percent for that year, followed by yearly GDP growth rates over 4 percent until 2003.[5] The labor force participation rates declined in the early 1990s, similar to the experience of other transition countries. If one focuses on individuals aged 15 to 64, the share of employed individuals declined from 72 percent in 1996 to 68.5 percent in 2001 (which is slightly below the EU average of 69.2 percent).[6] The health implications of economic collapse were visible, leading to increases in mortality rates in the early and mid-1990s. But compared to the Russian experience, one- or two-year declines in life expectancy at birth can be considered to be moderate (for comprehensive reviews and country-specific statistics, see Cornia and Paniccia 2000; Bobadilla, Costello, and Mitchell 1997).

A health insurance fund was established in 1997, and mandatory health insurance was introduced in 1999. The 2000 Living Conditions Survey shows that about 75 percent of individuals surveyed had enrolled in the health insurance program. The Roma were less likely to be enrolled (with a 34 percent enrollment rate), as well as the households headed by those with no schooling (with a 57 percent enrollment rate).[7] The 2003 Public/Private Transfers and Social Capital Survey data reveal that 7.5 percent of households have some household members not registered with a family physician (10.4 percent in rural areas, 5.7 percent in urban areas). The same survey reveals that the main reasons that make it difficult to get to a family physician is the distance to a medical facility (27.3 percent of responses), followed by the long waiting time during consultation (16.7 percent), and services being too expensive (15.8 percent).

Data and Descriptive Trends

The Romania Living Conditions Surveys (RLCS) are nationally representative household surveys that have been implemented annually by the Romanian National Institute of Statistics since 2000. The survey sample consisted of 10,521 households (25,395 individuals) in 2000. To incorporate information on public hospital and public health center/policlinic availability, these data are linked to locality data files that contain information on 365 localities in Romania. The final data set contains information on individual-level (self-evaluated) health outcomes and characteristics, household environment (including exposure to cold, etc.), and community.

Table 1 presents means and standard deviations of the variables included in the empirical analysis, separately for younger individuals (defined as ages 25 to 39 here) and older individuals (ages 40 to 59). About 16 percent of younger individuals reported their health status to be less than good, and about 71 percent of those who said their health was less than good worked. As expected, older individuals were more likely to report "less-than-good" health status (41 percent), and a smaller percentage worked (62 percent). As for residing in dwellings with potentially undesirable health implications: exposure to excessive noise is most prevalent (31 percent), followed by polluted air/smells (17 percent), dwelling water not proper to drink/bad color or taste (12 percent), cold (8 percent), and excessive humidity (6 percent).

As mentioned previously, the health impact of socioeconomic status variables might be overstated if socioeconomic status indicators are correlated with health care facility availability and environmental condition indicators, and if these latter set of variables is excluded from the empirical model. While the next section evaluates the validity of this hypothesis using multivariate analysis, it is useful to display the variation of these variables by household wealth, as proxied by a household possessions index.[8] From this point forward, the term "wealthiest" refers to the wealthiest 25 percent of the population and the term "poorest" refers to the poorest 25 percent of the population.

Highlights from table 2 are as follows: in rural areas, wealthier individuals are much more likely to have a hospital or a health center/policlinic available in their locality (availability is 11.3 percent for the wealthiest, as opposed to 6.9 percent for the poorest). The urban residents have significantly better access to health facilities (with around 97 percent having a health facility in their locality), regardless of wealth status.

Humid and cold environmental conditions are reported more often by the poor in general, but especially by the urban poor. About 14 per-

TABLE 1

Means and Standard Deviations of the Variables Examined in the Models of Health and Employment Status

	Ages 25 to 39		Ages 40 to 59	
	Mean	Std dev.	Mean	Std dev.
Health status (1 if reported health status as less than good)	.159	.366	.412	.492
Health status (1 if reported chronic illness)	.101	.30	.277	.447
Employment status (1 if working)	.707	.455	.622	.485
Age	31.8	4.23	48.9	5.53
Gender (1 if male)	.489	.499	.484	.499
Marital status (1 married)	.715	.451	.829	.376
No schooling	.010	.101	.011	.105
Primary	.019	.138	.110	.313
Gymnasium (5–8)	.119	.324	.264	.441
Vocational	.230	.421	.237	.425
High school	.486	.439	.215	.411
Post-high school or foreman	.039	.192	.074	.261
College and higher	.095	.293	.090	.286
Romanian	.892	.310	.903	.295
Hungarian	.068	.252	.068	.252
Roma	.030	.172	.018	.134
Other	.009	.094	.010	.099
Household possessions index	.396	.162	.408	.166
Urban residence	.538	.499	.531	.499
Never smoked in his/her life	.554	497	.617	.486
Availability of public hospital in locality	.526	.499	.531	.499
Availability of public health center or polyclinic in locality	.535	.499	.530	.499
Environment				
Humidity	.067	.250	.055	.228
Cold	.082	.274	.071	.256
Noise (traffic, commercial activity, industrial, etc.)	.313	.464	.316	.465
Polluted air, smells	.174	.379	.163	.369
Dwelling water not proper to drink/bad color or taste	.123	.328	.119	.325
Number of observations	4,628		7,216	

cent of urban poor report humidity in their dwellings, and 15 percent report cold, compared to 4.5 percent of wealthiest individuals reporting humidity, and 6 percent reporting cold. However, when considering noise and air pollution, this trend is reversed: wealthier individuals report more complaints. Separate tabulations for urban and rural areas show significantly high noise and polluted air complaints in urban areas overall. An odd finding in this table is that "dwelling water undrinkable, bad color/taste" rates are most common among the wealthiest urban residents. This may be due to variations in acceptable standards of water quality by socioeconomic status. In fact, such reporting bias is likely to influence some other indicators as well. For example, it may be that the wealthy-poor gap would be even more pronounced if objective indicators of "exposure to cold weather" were available.

Results

Predictors of (Less-than-Good) Health Status

This section first provides a brief description of findings from our preferred specification that includes household health environment variables and health facility availability indicators.

TABLE 2

Health Environment Variables by Household Wealth

Reported numbers are percentages[a]

Wealth grouping	Hospital and health center/policlinic (HCP) availability in the locality			Humidity	Cold	Noise	Polluted air	Dwelling water undrinkable, bad color/taste
	Either	Hospital	HCP					
Total	51.3	48.1	48.6	5.8	7.1	29.7	15.5	11.4
Poorest 25 percent	27.0	23.9	24.4	7.1	6.8	20.7	10.7	8.2
Middle 50 percent	57.9	54.5	55.1	5.6	7.7	31.0	17.0	11.7
Wealthiest 25 percent	70.0	67.5	67.5	4.0	4.4	42.9	18.1	16.7
Urban	97.1	95.9	94.4	7.7	10.1	42.5	23.3	16.3
Poorest 25 percent	94.5	92.8	92.0	13.7	14.8	36.9	22.4	14.4
Middle 50 percent	97.4	96.0	94.7	7.4	10.3	42.0	23.5	15.6
Wealthiest 25 percent	97.8	97.6	95.2	4.5	6.0	48.9	23.2	20.7
Rural	8.6	3.6	5.9	4.0	4.2	17.8	8.2	6.8
Poorest 25 percent	6.9	3.4	4.2	5.1	4.4	15.9	7.2	6.3
Middle 50 percent	9.6	3.7	6.7	3.4	4.5	17.4	9.0	7.0
Wealthiest 25 percent	11.3	4.1	9.3	2.9	1.2	30.5	7.2	8.4

a. The proxy for wealth is the household possessions index. The data for hospital and health center/policlinic availability come from administrative records. Other "health environment" information comes from the household survey questionnaire (as revealed by the household head).

Next, we discuss the differences with a specification that excludes these variables. All these models are estimated separately for individuals between the ages of 25 to 39, and those between the ages of 40 to 59. Finally, we turn to insights from various alternative specifications that relax some of the assumptions associated with the basic model (estimating separate coefficients for males and females, for urban and rural residents, allowing interaction terms between household wealth and health facility availability, etc).

Basic (preferred) specification. The coefficient estimates for the basic/preferred specification are reported in table 3. The dependent variable takes the value 1 if an individual reports his or her health status as less than good. It takes the value 0 otherwise. The explanatory variables are age (and age-squared/100); gender; marital status; schooling; ethnicity; household possessions index; urban/rural residence; an indicator for having never smoked; availability of a public hospital in the locality; availability of public health center/policlinic in the locality; and exposure to undesirable environmental factors, such as humidity, cold, noise, polluted air/smells, poor dwelling water (not proper to drink/bad color or taste).

The signs of the estimated coefficients for the "standard" variables are as typically found in the literature, namely: (i) males are less likely to report less-than-good health; (ii) being married is associated with reduced likelihood of reporting less-than-good health; (iii) those with a primary education or less are most likely to report less-than-good health—the health impact of increased schooling is mixed for the age group 25 to 39, while a more steady trend exists for those aged 40 to 59; (iv) the Roma—who are almost three times more likely to be poor compared to others in Romania (see World Bank 2003b)—are less likely to report less-than-good health (one explanation for this counterintuitive finding is cultural differences in interpreting what conditions qualify as less-than-good health); (v) those who are wealthier are less likely to report less-than-good health; (vi) urban residence increases the likelihood of reporting less-than-good health, although the estimated coefficient is not statistically significant for the 25 to 39 age group.

The estimates for other variables are as follows. If a person has never smoked, the likelihood of reporting less-than-good health declines by 2.1 percentage points for younger individuals, and by 3.3 percentage points for older individuals. The estimated coefficients are statistically significant at 10 and 5 percent levels for younger and older individuals, respectively. The larger smoking impact on health for older individuals might be in part because having never smoked is more indicative of an older individual's permanent, long-term health investment behavior. It could also be because younger and older individuals differ when it comes to the duration of, and exposure to, smoking; the average age for first-time smokers; and the likelihood (as well as timing) of quitting smoking.

Availability of a public hospital or a public health center/policlinic in the locality is not a statistically significant predictor of health status of younger individuals. Accessibility of health care facilities may be a more important factor in determining the health status of the older population, because the elderly are more likely to be in poorer health status and have higher utilization of health care facilities if in poor health. Indeed, for those who are between the ages of 40 to 59, presence of a public hospital in the locality is associated with a 10.7 percentage point reduction in the probability of reporting less-than-good health. (This finding is driven by the females in the sample, as discussed later.)

The signs of the coefficients on "humidity," "cold," "noise," "polluted air/smells," and "bad dwelling water" are all in the expected direction. The only household health-environment variable that is not a statistically significant predictor of health status (at the 10 percent level or better) is exposure to humidity. As for the remaining variables, the estimated coefficients are larger for the older individuals. Exposure to cold increases the probability of reporting less-than-good health by 6.1 and 18.0 percentage points for younger and older individuals, respectively. Similarly, if the dwelling water is reported to be "not proper to drink/bad color or taste," the probability of reporting less-than-good health is 6.9 percentage points higher for the younger individuals and 9 percentage points higher for the older individuals. The estimated coefficients for "noise" and "polluted-air/smells" are smaller.

How different are the coefficient estimates in an underspecified model? The estimated relationship between socioeconomic status and health may be biased if variations in health care availability and household environmental factors are not taken into account. In table 3, the figures in brackets are the coefficient estimates and |t|-statistics for a model that includes all variables in the preferred specification except individual health behavior variables and health environment factors: never smoked; availability of public hospital in the locality; availability of public health center/policlinic in the locality; and presence of humidity, cold, noise, polluted-air/smells, and bad dwelling water. As discussed previously, this is more or less the typical specification in the literature. How do the results compare for the variables that appear in both models?

Interestingly, the underspecified model produces similar estimates for all variables in the model. The only difference to note is that in the fully specified model, urban residence does not have a statistically significant impact on health status of younger individuals, but in the underspecified model, the urban-residence effect is statistically significant at the 1 percent level. Thus, to the extent that the Romanian findings can be generalized, it seems the shortcoming of previous studies is not so much wrong estimates for the variables that are included in the models (with the usual caveats about causality issues that are often not tackled by studies that use cross-sectional data sets), but rather the inability to provide insights about the role of health behavior, household health environment (cold, humidity, etc.), and health facility availability on the health status of individuals.

Alternative specifications. Further insights emerge from adopting more flexible specifications that: (i) consider the predictors of male and female health status separately; (ii) consider urban and rural areas separately; (iii) allow for interaction terms between health facility availability indicators and household possessions index used as a proxy for household wealth; and (iv) use reported chronic illness instead of self-evaluation of health status. The main findings are as follows.

Appendix tables A1 and A2 illustrate the estimation results separately for males and females. Rather than getting into a lengthy discussion about commonly observed gender differences in self-reported health status, we will point out a few interesting trends here. The variable "public hospital availability" has a statistically significant impact on health status only for females aged 40 to 59. Older females who live in a locality that has a public hospital are 14.9 percentage points less likely to report less-than-good health. As for the two key household-environment variables with the largest impact on health status, exposure to cold and poor dwelling water, the gender differences are also visible. The impact of exposure to cold on health status is considerably larger for males—8.3 and 20.2 percentage points for younger and older males, respectively, compared to 4.3 and 15.8 percentage points for younger and older females, respectively—while the health implications of bad dwelling water are larger for females—6.4 and 6.7 percentage points for younger and older males, respectively, compared to 7.4 and 11.2 percentage points for younger and older females.

When the basic model is estimated separately for rural and urban areas (not reported), the following key findings emerge. For younger individuals, poor-quality water has a negative impact on health in both urban and in rural areas, though the effect is larger in rural areas (a 9 percentage point versus 6 percentage point increase in the likelihood of reporting less-than-good health). Humidity and air pollution in urban areas are statistically significantly related to poor health. In contrast, in rural areas, cold and noise variables have statistically significant coefficient estimates. For older individuals, the impact of the household possessions index is more pronounced in urban areas. In urban areas, cold, noise, and bad water are linked to less-than-good health reporting, while in rural areas, all household-environment variables except air pollution have statistically significant impacts on health status in the expected direction.

When interactions between the household possession index and health facility availability indicators are introduced (not reported), we find that hospital availability in a locality decreases the probability of less-than-good health more for the wealthy. The interaction term between the household possessions index and health center/policlinic availability indicator does not have a statistically significant coefficient estimate. These findings are valid for both age groups considered by this study. The reason why the wealthy benefit more from hospital availability may have to do with health insurance enrollment patterns, which reveal the disadvantaged situation of those with little or no schooling, as discussed previously in section 2. In this context, the practice of informal payments and the importance of "private connections" to solve health problems in Romania deserve further attention. Tabulations from the 2003 World Bank Public/Private Transfers and Social Capital Survey show that about 45 percent of households that faced a health problem in the last year reported offering "gifts" as part of the consultation process (the probability of offering gifts increased from 39 percent for the poorest quintile of households to 51 percent for the wealthiest quintile of households). The same survey reveals larger disparities when it comes to "knowing someone who can help solve a health problem:" 34 percent of the poorest and 75 percent of the wealthiest quintiles of households replied positively to this question.

Finally, when the dependent variable takes the value 1 if the individual has a chronic illness (0 otherwise), we find that for younger individuals, smoking behavior does not have a statistically significant coefficient estimate. Also for younger individuals, the only statistically significant health-environment coefficient estimate is for "bad water." Availability of a health center/policlinic becomes statistically significant in the expected direction. For older individuals, everything looks similar except in this specification: Among the household environment variables, only exposure to cold and noise have statistically significant coefficients.

The Impact of Less-than-Good Health on Probability of Being Employed

To single out the causal impact of (less-than-good) health status on employment, a two-stage conditional maximum likelihood (2SCML) model is estimated, as proposed by Rivers and Vuong (1998). The basic/preferred specification reported in the previous section serves as the first-stage equation. The inclusion of first-stage equation residuals in the second-stage specification allows for a specification test for the null hypothesis that the health status variables are exogenous: the reported t-statistics show that this null hypothesis is rejected at the 1 percent level for the overall sample and for the female sample, while it is rejected at the 5 percent level for the male sample. The set of instruments (the variables that are in the first-stage health equation but not in the second-stage employment equation) include: never smoked; availability of public hospital in the locality; availability of public health center/policlinic in the locality; and exposure to humidity, cold, noise, polluted air/smells, bad dwelling water. The household possessions index is also excluded from this reduced-form employment model because the direction of causality between employment and household wealth is unclear. Table 4 presents the predictors of employment status, where the dependent variable takes the value 1 if the individual works, and the value 0 otherwise. Estimates are reported separately for the two age groups (25 to 39 and 40 to 59). The estimates in brackets are from an alternative specification that (in the first-stage equation) considers the reporting of chronic illnesses as one of the determinants of self-reported health status.

For brevity, here we discuss only the impact of less-than-good health on employment. For the younger individuals, the less-than-good health coefficient is not statistically significant, at the 10 percent level. But for those who are 40 to 59 years old, the causal impact of less-than-good health on employment is extremely large, reducing probability of employment by somewhere between 41.2 percentage points and 56.7 percentage points, depending on the empirical specification that is used. This finding—i.e., a stronger linkage between health status and employment for older individuals—is consistent with the literature (see the review by Currie and Madrian 1999). When these models are estimated separately for males and females (appendix tables A3 and A4), we find that the estimated coefficient for less-than-good health is statistically significant at the 10 percent level for young males (but not for young females), reducing probability of employment by 41.4 percentage points. For those between the ages of 40 and 59, the impact of less-than-good health on employment is larger for females, leading to a 58 percentage point decline in the probability of employment (as opposed to 54.3 percentage points for males).

Putting the magnitude of the relationship between health status and employment into context is more difficult, though. Costa (1996) finds that the labor force participation of men was more responsive to BMI in the 1900s compared to the present time. Because in many transition countries a large share of jobs are in the industrial and agricultural sectors (as opposed to the service sector), and because physical fitness is arguably more important for industrial and agricultural sector jobs, one can expect a larger health effect on employment in transition countries. On the other hand, a large public sector presence might weaken the relationship between health status and employment. If one reviews the comprehensive list of studies and summary results documented by Currie and Madrian, a

TABLE 3

Predictors of Less-than-Good Health Status

The dependent variable takes the value 1 if self-reported health status is less than good. It takes the value 0 otherwise. Marginal effects from the probit model and |t|-ratios are reported below. The numbers in brackets [] are those from an alternative specification that does not include the health facility, health behavior, and health environment variables in bold.

	Ages 25 to 39		Ages 40 to 59	
	Marginal eff.	|t|-value	Marginal eff.	|t|-value
Age	.013	0.68	.071***	3.47
	[.013]	[0.63]	[.065***]	[3.15]
Age squared / 100	−.004	0.13	−.052**	2.51
	[−.002]	[0.06]	[−.046**]	[2.24]
Gender (1 if male)	−.053***	4.58	−.123***	8.68
	[−.046***]	[4.23]	[−.108***]	[8.65]
Marital status (1 married)	−.031**	2.41	−.042**	2.55
	[−.031**]	[2.36]	[−.045***]	[2.78]
No schooling[a]	—	—	—	—
Primary	−.128***	4.08	−.161***	2.84
	[−.131***]	[4.15]	[−.160***]	[2.83]
Gymnasium (5–8)	−.166***	5.95	−.177***	3.09
	[−.171***]	[6.08]	[−.171***]	[3.00]
Vocational	−.209***	6.42	−.169***	2.92
	[−.213***]	[6.50]	[−.163***]	[2.82]
High school	−.320***	6.89	−.218***	3.82
	[−.326***]	[6.98]	[−.214***]	[3.75]
Post-high school or foreman	−.151***	6.00	−.235***	4.16
	[−.154***]	[6.06]	[−.222***]	[3.91]
College and higher	−.181***	7.68	−.288***	5.33
	[−.184***]	[7.71]	[−.283***]	[5.22]
Romanian[a]	—	—	—	—
Hungarian	−.052**	2.51	−.027	1.15
	[−.056***]	[2.70]	[−.034]	[1.45]
Roma	−.070**	2.41	−.075	1.64
	[−.071**]	[2.41]	[−.054]	[1.20]
Other	−.056	1.02	−.114*	1.86
	[−.062]	[1.13]	[−.111*]	[1.83]
Household possessions index	−.076*	1.89	−.289***	6.13
	[−.076*]	[1.90]	[−.289***]	[6.20]
Urban residence	.045	1.58	.138***	3.93
	[.047***]	[4.14]	[.100***]	[7.42]
Never smoked in his/her life	−.021*	1.78	−.033**	2.25
Availability of public hospital in locality	−.026	0.86	−.107***	3.03
Availability of public health center or a policlinic in locality	.004	0.15	.029	0.99
Environment				
Humidity	.032	1.42	.023	0.80
Cold	.061***	2.81	.180***	6.91
Noise (traffic, commercial activity, industrial, etc.)	.022*	1.82	.045***	3.26
Polluted air, smells	.025*	1.71	.029*	1.67
Dwelling water not proper to drink/bad color or taste	.069***	4.02	.090***	4.72
F-test (p-value): Joint significance of the identifier variables (bold above)	0.0000		0.0000	
Overall significance (p-value)	0.0000		0.0000	
Number of observations	4,628		7,216	

a. Significance levels: * — 10%; ** — 5%; *** — 1%.

TABLE 4

Predictors of Employment

The dependent variable takes the value 1 if the individual is employed. It takes the value 0 otherwise. Marginal effects from the probit model and |t|-ratios are reported below. The estimates in brackets [] are from an alternative specification that (in the first-stage equation) considers the reporting of chronic illnesses as a determinant of self-reported health status.

	Ages 25 to 39		Ages 40 to 59	
	Marginal eff.	|t|-value	Marginal eff.	|t|-value
Estimated less-than-good health	−.247	1.40	−.567***	6.59
	[−.217]	[6.81]	[−.412***]	[19.2]
Residual from first-stage regression	−.087***	4.75	−.190***	15.3
	[−.025]	[1.11]	[−.091***]	[6.01]
Age	.103***	3.96	.090***	4.23
	[.103]	[3.97]	[.084***]	[4.03]
Age squared / 100	−.137***	3.35	−.104***	4.92
	[−.138]	[3.39]	[−.102***]	[4.82]
Gender (1 if male)	.185***	11.5	.178***	12.0
	[.188]	[13.2]	[.196***]	[15.4]
Marital status (1 married)	.064***	3.67	−.021	1.24
	[.064]	[3.93]	[−.012]	[0.74]
No schooling[a]	—	—	—	—
Primary	.193**	2.50	.081	1.40
	[.201]	[3.21]	[.111**]	[1.98]
Gymnasium (5–8)	.170*	1.89	.031	0.53
	[.183]	[2.82]	[.065]	[1.14]
Vocational	.264***	2.96	.085	1.44
	[.277]	[4.39]	[.121**]	[2.13]
High school	.329***	3.01	.158***	2.68
	[.349]	[4.60]	[.200***]	[3.68]
Post-high school or foreman	.269***	4.14	.173***	2.91
	[.272]	[5.94]	[.211***]	[3.95]
College and higher	.309***	4.56	.275***	4.94
	[.314]	[7.06]	[.311***]	[6.59]
Romanian[a]	—	—	—	—
Hungarian	.056**	2.00	−.089***	3.61
	[.058]	[2.20]	[−.083***]	[3.39]
Roma	−.108**	2.31	−.083*	1.76
	[−.104]	[2.36]	[−.080*]	[1.69]
Other	−.232***	3.02	−.103	1.62
	[−.231]	[3.02]	[−.087]	[1.39]
Urban residence	.099***	5.97	−.044***	2.87
	[.097]	[6.72]	[−.058***]	[4.24]
Overall significance (p-value)	0.0000		0.0000	
Number of observations	4,628		7,216	

a. Significance levels: * — 10%; ** — 5%; *** — 1%.

41.2 to 56.7 percentage point reduction in the probability of work due to less-than-good health status is a large effect (although some studies report effects that come close to that. See for example Bound et al. 1996) and thus the findings seem to support the first possibility.[9]

Conclusions

This paper argues that a recent wave of studies aiming to display correlates of self-reported poor health status in transition countries have been too quick to dismiss the role of environmental factors and health facility availability on health status. In the context of transition economies, the identification of those who are most vulnerable to adverse environmental conditions and those with limited access to health facilities—jointly with the extent to which these disadvantages are associated with poor health outcomes—provide indispensable information for the design of health sector reforms that build on comprehensive but often unsustainable pre-transition health service delivery systems.

This study shows that while schooling attainment and household wealth are associated with reduced likelihood of reporting less-than-good health status, it is also true that the members of households that report exposure to cold weather and poor dwelling water are much more likely to report less-than-good health (even after taking into account a variety of individual, household, and community characteristics). If one subscribes to the view that "socioeconomic characteristics are all that matter, an individual's social standing in the society is critical for his or health," then the implication is that unless socioeconomic differences are eliminated, health inequalities are here to stay. But there are other things that matter for transition economies, and they should not be ignored. While it may be difficult, unrealistic, and even undesirable to change the distribution of a population's socioeconomic characteristics in the short term, one can certainly aim for policies that improve the infrastructure for delivering adequate heat and clean water to the general population.

The findings regarding the correlation between health facility availability and self-reported health status are less clear cut. A relationship between availability of a hospital in the locality and health outcomes is found for older females. But for males, there is no statistically significant relationship. Availability of a health center/policlinic in the locality is not correlated with health status of males or females. Furthermore, in rural areas, the distribution of health facilities favors the wealthy. As can be expected, urban-area residents have similar access to health facilities, regardless of differences in socioeconomic characteristics. Also, the wealthier individuals' health status is more responsive to having a hospital in the locality. These findings—when combined with survey statistics that reveal the prevalence of informal payments in the health sector and the importance of "having contacts to solve health problems"—suggest that a poor household's geographical proximity to a public health facility, by itself, does not necessarily mean this household has access to adequate public health services.

Many transition countries, including Romania, have experienced respectable economic growth rates starting from the late 1990s. But rising health inequalities in these countries could well be the main obstacle for equitable (and sustainable) economic growth and poverty reduction because the relationship between health status and employment is extremely strong: for those individuals who are between the ages of 40 and 59, we find that poor health status leads to somewhere between a 41.2 and 56.7 percentage point decline in the probability of employment. Reflecting on the past, the population's deteriorating health status during transition might have contributed significantly to the decline in employment rates. For example, the employment rate in Romania in 2000 was 59 percent, which is considerably lower than the EU average of 65 percent. As for the upcoming challenges in the near future, the population's poor health status emerges as a serious obstacle to achieving higher employment rates, and by extension, a more equal distribution of income.

Appendix

TABLE A1

Predictors of Less-than-Good Health Status of Males

The dependent variable takes the value 1 if self-reported health status is less than good. It takes the value 0 otherwise. Marginal effects from the probit model and |t|-ratios are reported below.

	Ages 25 to 39		Ages 40 to 59	
	Marginal eff.	|t|-value	Marginal eff.	|t|-value
Age	.004	0.14	.062**	2.17
Age squared / 100	.008	0.19	−.045	1.53
Marital status (1 married)	−.036**	2.15	−.060**	2.39
No schooling[a]	—	—	—	—
Primary	−.128***	4.41	−.251***	3.24
Gymnasium (5–8)	−.157***	5.16	−.251***	3.05
Vocational	−.259***	5.79	−.257***	2.92
High school	−.341***	5.90	−.278***	3.44
Post-high school or foreman	−.136***	4.72	−.280***	3.68
College and higher	−.165***	6.24	−.313***	4.27
Romanian[a]	—	—	—	—
Hungarian	−.055**	2.00	−.017	0.51
Roma	−.040	1.01	−.048	0.77
Other	−.029	0.39	−.092	1.17
Household possessions index	−.022	0.41	−.312***	4.66
Urban residence	.014	0.39	.127***	2.67
Never smoked in his life	−.018	1.24	−.039**	2.23
Availability of public hospital in locality	−.009	0.22	−.064	1.35
Availability of public health center/policlinic in locality	−.001	0.02	.009	0.24
Environment				
Humidity	−.004	0.15	−.011	0.29
Cold	.083***	2.68	.202***	5.53
Noise (traffic, commercial activity, industrial, etc.)	.023	1.38	.052***	2.71
Polluted air, smells	.027	1.36	.017	0.71
Dwelling water not proper to drink/bad color or taste	.064***	2.75	.067**	2.52
F-test (p-value): Joint significance of the identifier variables (bold above)	0.0019		0.0000	
Overall significance (p-value)	0.0000		0.0000	
Number of observations	2,262		3,493	

a. Significance levels: * — 10%; ** — 5%; *** — 1%.

TABLE A2

Predictors of Less-than-Good Health Status of Females

The dependent variable takes the value 1 if self-reported health status is less than good. It takes the value 0 otherwise. Marginal effects from the probit model and |t|-ratios are reported below.

	Ages 25 to 39		Ages 40 to 59	
	Marginal eff.	|t|-value	Marginal eff.	|t|-value
Age	.027	0.89	.075**	2.56
Age squared / 100	−.021	0.45	−.054*	1.83
Marital status (1 married)	−.021	1.01	−.028	1.27
No schooling[a]	—	—	—	—
Primary	−.090	1.37	−.082	1.06
Gymnasium (5–8)	−.162***	3.14	−.113	1.47
Vocational	−.168***	3.13	−.110	1.39
High school	−.280***	3.70	−.161**	2.07
Post-high school or foreman	−.169***	3.95	−.188**	2.32
College and higher	−.190***	4.37	−.262***	3.38
Romanian[a]	—	—	—	—
Hungarian	−.050	1.60	−.038	1.13
Roma	−.097**	2.21	−.089	1.36
Other	−.081	1.00	−.144	1.53
Household possessions index	−.145**	2.39	−.258***	3.91
Urban residence	.078*	1.82	.149***	2.92
Never smoked in her life	−.032*	1.75	−.022	0.89
Availability of public hospital in locality	−.048	1.04	−.149***	2.89
Availability of public health center/policlinic in locality	.006	0.17	.049	1.15
Environment				
Humidity	.070**	2.01	.058	1.39
Cold	.043	1.39	.158***	4.32
Noise (traffic, commercial activity, industrial, etc.)	.022	1.26	.038*	1.94
Polluted air, smells	.020	0.92	.042*	1.74
Dwelling water not proper to drink/bad color or taste	.074***	2.98	.112***	4.18
F-test (p-value): Joint significance of the identifier variables (bold above)	0.0010		0.0000	
Overall significance (p-value)	0.0000		0.0000	
Number of observations	2,366		3,723	

a. Significance levels: * — 10%; ** — 5%; *** — 1%.

TABLE A3

Predictors of Employment of Males

The dependent variable takes the value 1 if the individual is employed. It takes the value 0 otherwise. Marginal effects from the probit model and |t|-ratios are reported below.

	Ages 25 to 39		Ages 40 to 59	
	Marginal eff.	|t|-value	Marginal eff.	|t|-value
Estimated less-than-good health	−.414*	1.91	−.543***	5.19
Residual from first-stage regression	−.057**	2.38	−.189***	12.3
Age	.048	1.50	.054**	2.04
Age squared / 100	−.054	1.07	−.067**	2.53
Marital status (1 married)	.134***	6.51	.134***	5.69
No schooling[a]	—	—	—	—
Primary	.157**	2.04	.049	0.66
Gymnasium (5–8)	.120	1.17	.017	0.23
Vocational	.185	1.63	−.006	0.07
High school	.213*	1.65	.034	0.42
Post-high school or foreman	.176**	2.15	.023	0.28
College and higher	.192**	2.17	.141*	1.92
Romanian[a]	—	—	—	—
Hungarian	.048	1.40	−.079**	2.52
Roma	−.169***	2.91	−.162***	2.59
Other	−.142	1.52	−.112	1.47
Urban residence	.058***	2.86	−.073***	3.95
Overall significance (p-value)	0.0000		0.0000	
Number of observations	2,262		3,493	

a. Significance levels: * — 10%; ** — 5%; *** — 1%.

TABLE A4

Predictors of Employment of Females

The dependent variable takes the value 1 if the individual is employed. It takes the value 0 otherwise. Marginal effects from the probit model and |t|-ratios are reported below.

	Ages 25 to 39		Ages 40 to 59	
	Marginal eff.	|t|-value	Marginal eff.	|t|-value
Estimated less-than-good health	−.115	0.43	−.580***	4.60
Residual from first-stage regression	−.109***	4.04	−.169***	9.37
Age	.141***	3.57	.133***	4.30
Age squared / 100	−.196***	3.17	−.149***	4.84
Marital status (1 married)	−.033	1.18	−.130***	5.57
No schooling[a]	—	—	—	—
Primary	.193	1.38	.084	1.01
Gymnasium (5–8)	.196	1.32	.019	0.22
Vocational	.310**	2.21	.136	1.60
High school	.385**	2.26	.216**	2.52
Post-high school or foreman	.353***	3.22	.288***	3.34
College and higher	.413***	3.68	.364***	4.27
Romanian[a]	—	—	—	—
Hungarian	.060	1.41	−.091***	2.62
Roma	−.071	0.94	−.039	0.58
Other	−.292**	2.52	−.066	0.68
Urban residence	.129***	5.17	−.020	0.86
Overall significance (p-value)	0.0000		0.0000	
Number of observations	2,366		3,723	

a. Significance levels: * — 10%; ** — 5%; *** — 1%.

Notes

1. One possibility is to employ econometric techniques that account for unobserved heterogeneity at the village level, to take into account health environment in the community (see, for example, Skoufias [1998], who focuses on determinants of child health in Romania relying on the 1994 Integrated Household Survey data). But this empirical strategy does not take into account health environment at the household level, and it is silent about the presence or lack of a relationship between access to health care and health outcomes.
2. Indeed there is empirical evidence revealing the disconnect between access to health care and mortality rates in industrialized countries (see Deaton 1999 for a review).
3. The only country transition that we excluded from the BEEPs data set is Slovenia, which is a major outlier with a 2000 GDP per capita of $11,646 (although it is not an outlier in terms of overall trend, because a small share of firms in Slovenia reported bad-quality water and public health services).
4. We prefer to use lagged community characteristics to model health outcomes, although note that none of the findings change if one uses locality records of 2000.
5. Real GDP had grown by about 4 percent, thanks to an election-year push in 1996, which did not turn out to be sustainable.
6. Data source: Romania Labor Force Surveys (1996 and 2002).
7. For more information, see 2003 Romania Poverty Assessment (The World Bank).
8. The household possessions index varies between 0 and 1, and it takes into account ownership of cooker, stove, refrigerator, freezer, washing machine, sewing machine, vacuum, TV, radio, video, microwave, PC, cell phone, and car.
9. As Currie and Madrian (1999) observe, there is no consensus on the magnitude of effects in the industrialized country literature—modeling and different approaches to measuring health status emerge as main obstacles against making comparisons.

References

Attanasio, O., and C. Emmerson. 2001. "Differential Mortality in the UK." National Bureau of Economic Research Working Paper Series 8241. Cambridge, MA.

Bloom, D., D. Canning, and J. Sevilla. 2004. "The Effect of Health on Economic Growth: A Production Function Approach." *World Development* 32 (1): 1–13.

Bobadilla, J.L., C.A. Costello, and F. Mitchell. 1997. *Premature Death in the New Independent States*. Washington, DC: National Academy Press.

Bobak, M., H. Pikhart, C. Hertzman, R. Rose, and M. Marmot. 1998. "Socioeconomic Factors, Perceived Control, and Self-Reported Health in Russia. A Cross-Sectional Survey." *Social Science & Medicine* 47 (2): 269–79.

Bobak, M., H. Pikhart, R. Rose, C. Hertzman, and M. Marmot. 2000. "Socioeconomic Factors, Material Inequalities, and Perceived Control in Self-Rated Health: Cross-Sectional Data from Seven Post-Communist Countries." *Social Science & Medicine* 51: 1343–50.

Bound, J., M. Schoenbaum, and T. Waismann. 1996. "Race Differences in Labor Force Attachment and Disability Status." *The Gerontologist* 36: 311–21.

Cornia, G A., and R. Paniccia. 2000. *The Mortality Crisis in Transitional Economies*. New York: Oxford University Press.

Currie, J., and B.C. Madrian. 1999. "Health, Health Insurance, and the Labor Market." In *Handbook of Labor Economics Volume 3C*, ed. O.C. Ashenfelter and C. Card, 3309–3407. New York: Elsevier.

Deaton, Angus. 1999. "Inequalities in Income and Inequalities in Health." National Bureau of Economic Research Working Paper Series 7141. Cambridge, MA.

Gilmore, A.B.C., M. McKee, and R. Rose. 2002. "Determinants of and Inequalities in Self-Perceived Health in Ukraine." *Social Science & Medicine* 55: 2177–88.

Hurd, M.D., D. McFadden, and A. Merrill. 2001. "Predictors of Mortality among the Elderly." In *Themes in the Economics of Aging*, ed. D. Wise, 171–97. Chicago: University of Chicago Press.

Kopp, M.S., A. Skrabski, and S. Szedmak. 2000. "Psychosocial Risk Factors, Inequality, and Self-Rated Morbidity in a Changing Society." *Social Science & Medicine* 51: 1351–61.

Lampietti, Julian A., and Anke S. Meyer. 2002. *Coping with the Cold. Heating Strategies for Eastern Europe and Central Asia's Urban Poor*. Washington, DC: World Bank.

Leinsalu, M. 2002. "Social Variation in Self-Rated Health in Estonia: A Cross-Sectional Study." *Social Science & Medicine* 55: 847–61.

Mete, Cem. 2005. "Predictors of Elderly Mortality: Health Status, Socioeconomic Characteristics, and Social Determinants of Health." *Health Economics* 14 (2): 135–48.

Mete, Cem, and T.P. Schultz. 2007. "Health and Labor Force Participation of the Elderly in Taiwan." In *Riding the Age Waves: Allocating Public and Private Resources across Generations*, ed. A.H. Gauthier, C. Chu, and S. Tuljapurkar. New York: Kluwer.

Rivers, D., and Q. Vuong. 1988. "Limited Information Estimators and Exogeneity Tests for Simultaneous Probit Models." *Journal of Econometrics* 39 (3): 347–66.

Schultz, T.P. 2002. "Wage Gains Associated with Height as a Form of Health Human Capital." *American Economic Review* 92 (2): 349–53.

Schultz, T.P., and A. Tansel. 1997. "Wage and Labor Supply Effects of Illness in Côte d'Ivoire and Ghana: Instrumental Variable Estimates for Days Disabled." *Journal of Development Economics* 53 (2): 251–86.

Skoufias, Emmanuel. 1998. "Determinants of Child Health during the Economic Transition in Romania." *World Development* 26 (11): 2045–56.

Strauss, John, and Duncan Thomas. 1998. "Health, Nutrition, and Economic Development." *Journal of Economic Literature* 36 (2), 766–817.

Thompson, R., N. Miller, and S. Witter. 2003. "Health-Seeking Behavior and Rural/Urban Variation in Kazakhstan." *Health Economics* 12: 553–64.

Wilkinson, Richard G., and Michael Marmot. 1999. *Social Determinants of Health*. New York: Oxford University Press.

World Bank. 2003a. *Water Resources Management in South Eastern Europe*. Vols. 1 and 2. Washington, DC: World Bank.

———. 2003b. *Romania Poverty Assessment*. Vols. 1 and 2. Washington, DC: World Bank.

Wroblewska, W. 2002. "Women's Health Status in Poland in the Transition to a Market Economy." *Social Science & Medicine* 54: 707–26.